CAMBRIDGE SCHOOL

Shakespeare

King
Richard III

Edited by Pat Baldwin and Tom Baldwin

Series Editor: Rex Gibson
Director, Shakespeare and Schools Project

CAMBRIDGE
UNIVERSITY PRESS

PUBLISHED BY THE PRESS SYNDICATE OF THE UNIVERSITY OF CAMBRIDGE
The Pitt Building, Trumpington Street, Cambridge, United Kingdom

CAMBRIDGE UNIVERSITY PRESS
The Edinburgh Building, Cambridge CB2 2RU, UK
40 West 20th Street, New York, NY 10011–4211, USA
477 Williamstown Road, Port Melbourne, VIC 3207, Australia
Ruiz de Alarcón 13, 28014 Madrid, Spain
Dock House, The Waterfront, Cape Town 8001, South Africa

http://www.cambridge.org

First published 2000
Fifth printing 2004

Printed in the United Kingdom at the University Press, Cambridge

Typeface Monotype Ehrhardt 11/13pt. *System* QuarkXPress®

A catalogue record for this book is available from the British Library

Library of Congress Cataloguing in Publication data applied for

ISBN 0 521 648459

Prepared for publication by Stenton Associates
Designed by Richard Morris, Stonesfield Design
Picture research by Callie Kendall

Thanks are due to the following for permission to reproduce photographs:
Cover: *The Burial of the Princes in the Tower* by James Northcote, 1789; 26, 67, 94, 136, 147, 176, 196, 212, 218, 237, 238, 241, 249, © Photostage/Donald Cooper; 60, Reg Wilson/photo courtesy Shakespeare Centre Library, Stratford-upon-Avon; 88, Clive Barda/Performing Arts Library; 116, RSC Library/Shakespeare Centre Library, Stratford-upon-Avon; 160 (detail), © Photo RMN/H Lewandowski; 204, Photo: Gisela Brandt, courtesy of Deutsches Theatre, Berlin/photo courtesy Dennis Kennedy; 234*tl*, *tc*, Shakespeare Centre Library, Stratford-upon-Avon; 234*tr*, *br*, Angus McBean/Shakespeare Centre Library, Stratford-upon-Avon; 234*bl*, David Sim/photo courtesy Shakespeare Centre Library, Stratford-upon-Avon; 247 (detail), Board of Trustees of the National Museums and Galleries on Merseyside (Walker Art Gallery, Liverpool); 248, John Bunting; 250, John Vickers Theatre Collection; 251*t*, © Guild, courtesy of Ronald Grant Archive; 251*b*, 20th Century Fox/The Kobal Collection

Contents

Cambridge School Shakespeare

This edition of *King Richard III* is part of the *Cambridge School Shakespeare* series. Like every other play in the series, it has been specially prepared to help all students in schools and colleges.

This *King Richard III* aims to be different from other editions of the play. It invites you to bring the play to life in your classroom, hall or drama studio through enjoyable activities that will increase your understanding. Actors have created their different interpretations of the play over the centuries. Similarly, you are encouraged to make up your own mind about *King Richard III*, rather than having someone else's interpretation handed down to you.

Cambridge School Shakespeare does not offer you a cut-down or simplified version of the play. This is Shakespeare's language, filled with imaginative possibilities. You will find on every left-hand page: a summary of the action, an explanation of unfamiliar words, and a choice of activities on Shakespeare's language, characters and stories.

Between each act and in the pages at the end of the play, you will find notes, illustrations and activities. These will help to increase your understanding of the whole play.

There are a large number of activities to give you the widest choice to suit your own particular needs. Please don't think you have to do every one. Choose the activities that help you most.

This edition will be of value to you whether you are studying for an examination, reading for pleasure, or thinking of putting on the play to entertain others. You can work on the activities on your own or in groups. Many of the activities suggest a particular group size, but don't be afraid to make up smaller or larger groups to suit your own purposes.

Although you are invited to treat *King Richard III* as a play, you don't need special dramatic or theatrical skills to do the activities. By choosing your activities, and by exploring and experimenting, you can make your own interpretations of Shakespeare's language, characters and stories. Whatever you do, remember that Shakespeare wrote his plays to be acted, watched and enjoyed.

Rex Gibson

This edition of *King Richard III* uses the text of the play established by Janis Lull in *The New Cambridge Shakespeare*.

The context of the play

Richard III is the final play in the cycle of eight plays Shakespeare wrote dramatising English history from 1398–1485. The plays are Shakespeare's version of the struggle for the crown of England. The following brief summaries will help you understand how *Richard III* relates to the earlier plays (particularly events in *Henry VI Part 3*).

- *Richard II* tells how Henry Bullingbrook deposes King Richard and is crowned as King Henry IV.

- *Henry IV Parts 1* and *2* tell of Prince Hal's exploits with Falstaff, his victory at Shrewsbury over Hotspur (*Part 1*) and how he finally rejects Falstaff when he becomes king (*Part 2*).

- *Henry V* tells of Henry's victory at Agincourt and his betrothal to Katherine, the French king's daughter.

- *Henry VI Parts 1, 2* and *3* tell how Henry loses the English possessions in France and sees his kingdom racked by civil war (the Wars of the Roses) as a rival family, the house of York, challenges his right to rule. The Yorkists are triumphant, but the actions of the three York brothers have consequences for what happens in *Richard III*:

  The eldest York brother becomes King Edward IV, but his marriage to Elizabeth Woodville infuriates his younger brothers;

  The middle brother, Clarence, perfidiously changes sides in the wars and is distrusted by Richard;

  The youngest brother, Richard, determines to become king. He kills Henry VI and his son Prince Edward, and this makes Margaret, wife and mother of the two murdered men, an implacable enemy of the Yorkists.

- *Richard III* tells how Richard murders his way to the English throne but is finally overthrown by Richmond (a descendant of the house of Lancaster). Richmond becomes King Henry VII, so establishing the Tudor dynasty. He prepares to marry Elizabeth, daughter of King Edward IV, and so unite the white rose of York with the red rose of Lancaster.

The Tudor myth

The new King Henry VII's claims to the throne were insecure. At a time of patriarchy (where males are head of a family), he traced his royal ancestry back to John of Gaunt, Duke of Lancaster, through a female link. His male ancestor was an obscure Welsh squire Owen Tudor (but Tudor had married the widow of King Henry V). With such a questionable claim to the English throne it became essential for Henry to destroy Richard's reputation.

Under Henry VII and his son Henry VIII, successive historians and writers established the now traditional view of Richard as an evil, unpopular king. Chroniclers related events from the Tudor point of view. This perspective emphasised the horrors of civil war, declared the legitimacy of the Tudor dynasty and praised the Tudors as the bringers of peace and prosperity to England.

During the reign of Henry VII writers stressed that Richard was a usurper (a person who wrongfully seizes power) who had murdered Henry VI, the princes in the Tower and his wife Anne. One 'history' claimed that Richard was born with teeth and hair down to his shoulders. 'History books' of the time were more concerned with moral teaching than today's history books.

Two such 'histories' written during the reign of Henry VIII were responsible for the popular image of Richard as the evil hunchback. Sir Thomas More's *History of Richard III* (written 1513-1518) presents Richard as deformed, evil from his birth and plotting to become king. Polydore Vergil's *Historia Anglia* (1534) was written at the request of Henry VIII to legitimise the Tudor dynasty. Vergil's argument expresses what has come to be called 'the Tudor myth'. It claims that Henry IV's illegal seizure of the crown from Richard II broke the God-given order of the universe and resulted in all the disasters that followed: the early death of Henry V, the bloody civil war of the Roses and Richard III's murderous, despotic reign. Vergil claimed that England was rescued by Henry Tudor as God's instrument on earth bringing peace and plenty by uniting the houses of York and Lancaster.

Under Queen Elizabeth, the historians Edward Hall and Raphael Holinshed incorporated the interpretations of More and Vergil so completely into their history books that by the end of the sixteenth century this very negative portrayal of Richard's appearance and actions was almost universally accepted. This version of history was Shakespeare's major resource as he wrote his play.

The world of the play

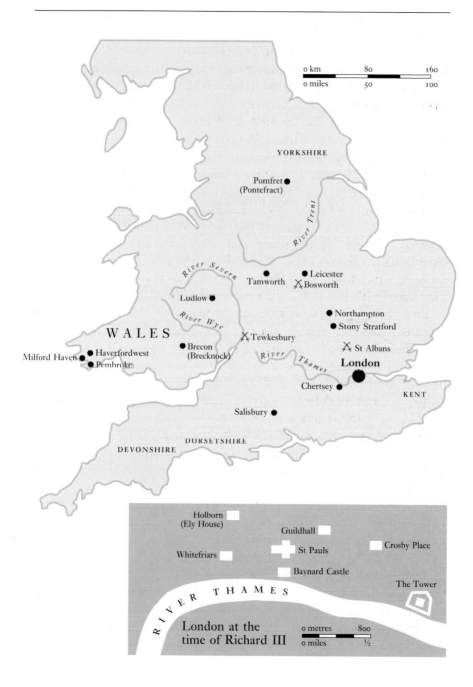

0 km | 80 | 160
0 miles | 50 | 100

YORKSHIRE

Pomfret (Pontefract)

River Trent

River Severn

Tamworth

Leicester

Bosworth

Ludlow

River Wye

Northampton

Stony Stratford

WALES

Brecon (Brecknock)

Tewkesbury

River Thames

St Albans

Milford Haven

Haverfordwest

Pembroke

London

Chertsey

KENT

Salisbury

DORSETSHIRE

DEVONSHIRE

Holborn (Ely House)

Guildhall

Whitefriars

St Pauls

Crosby Place

Baynard Castle

The Tower

RIVER THAMES

London at the time of Richard III

0 metres | 800
0 miles | ½

3

List of characters

The royal family

RICHARD, DUKE OF GLOUCESTER (later King Richard III)

DUCHESS OF YORK his mother

KING EDWARD IV } his brothers
CLARENCE

ANNE his wife (earlier betrothed to Prince Edward, son of King Henry VI)

QUEEN ELIZABETH (wife of King Edward)

PRINCE EDWARD } her sons (the princes in the Tower)
DUKE OF YORK

BOY } Clarence's children
GIRL

QUEEN MARGARET (widow of King Henry VI)

EARL OF RICHMOND (later King Henry VII)

The Woodvilles

MARQUESS OF DORSET } sons of Queen Elizabeth
LORD GREY

LORD RIVERS (brother of Queen Elizabeth)

VAUGHAN

Nobles, church and court

LORD HASTINGS

DUKE OF BUCKINGHAM

LORD STANLEY,
   Earl of Derby

BRAKENBURY

LORD LOVELL

SIR RICHARD RATCLIFFE

SIR WILLIAM CATESBY

JAMES TYRREL

TRESSEL } attendants of
BERKELEY } Lady Anne

BISHOP OF ELY

ARCHBISHOP OF YORK

LORD CARDINAL,
   Archbishop of Canterbury

SIR CHRISTOPHER URSWICK

EARL OF OXFORD

EARL OF SURREY

SIR WALTER HERBERT

SIR JAMES BLUNT

DUKE OF NORFOLK

The people

KEEPER OF THE TOWER	SCRIVENER
LORD MAYOR OF LONDON	SHERIFF
THREE CITIZENS	PURSUIVANT
TWO MURDERERS	PRIEST

Ghosts

(Who appear to Richard and Richmond at Bosworth)

PRINCE EDWARD	VAUGHAN
(son of King Henry VI)	HASTINGS
KING HENRY VI	ANNE
CLARENCE	BUCKINGHAM
RIVERS	THE PRINCES IN THE TOWER
GREY	

Lords, Attendants, Halberds, Messengers, Soldiers, Servants, Citizens, Gentlemen, Page, Guards, two Bishops.

The action of the play takes place in various locations in England.

Richard soliloquises on the end of the civil war and the pleasure of peace. He mocks his brother's sexual games and regrets he cannot enjoy similar pleasures.

1 A dramatic opening (in pairs)

The house of York has seized power and Edward ('this son of York') has been crowned king. In his opening lines 1–41 Richard reflects on how these events affect him.

This opening soliloquy reveals a brilliant and witty mind within a deformed body as Richard begins the plots and deceptions which will fool successive characters. The soliloquy is in three parts:

Lines 1–13: The change from war to peace and the character of the new Yorkist monarch, Edward. Delighting in clever word play, Richard tells how, just as the hardships of war give way to the glories of summer, so the harshness of war has changed to the pleasures of peace. The war over, King Edward enjoys amorous pleasures.

Lines 14–27: Richard's physical deformity prevents him from enjoying sexual exploits ('sportive tricks'). He is imperfectly shaped ('rudely stamped') and lacks the sex appeal that good looks give ('want love's majesty').

Lines 28–41: Because he cannot be a lover, Richard resolves to be a villain and gain power. His first move is to plot the imprisonment of his brother, Clarence.

Take turns to speak the soliloquy then work out how you would stage the lines to greatest dramatic effect. There is more help on page 8 and on page 66. As you work through your presentation, talk together about what you learn of Richard's attitude to the end of the war, his deformity and his future plans.

---

loured scowled, looked threatening
bruisèd arms battered weapons
alarums battle skirmishes
measures dances
front brow

nymph attractive woman
Cheated of feature robbed of
 good looks
descant on comment on, sing
 about

King Richard III

ACT 1 SCENE 1
Outside the Tower of London

Enter RICHARD DUKE OF GLOUCESTER

RICHARD Now is the winter of our discontent
Made glorious summer by this son of York,
And all the clouds that loured upon our house
In the deep bosom of the ocean buried.
Now are our brows bound with victorious wreaths,   5
Our bruisèd arms hung up for monuments,
Our stern alarums changed to merry meetings,
Our dreadful marches to delightful measures.
Grim-visaged war hath smoothed his wrinkled front,
And now, instead of mounting barbèd steeds   10
To fright the souls of fearful adversaries,
He capers nimbly in a lady's chamber
To the lascivious pleasing of a lute.
But I that am not shaped for sportive tricks
Nor made to court an amorous looking-glass,   15
I that am rudely stamped and want love's majesty
To strut before a wanton ambling nymph,
I that am curtailed of this fair proportion,
Cheated of feature by dissembling nature,
Deformed, unfinished, sent before my time   20
Into this breathing world scarce half made up,
And that so lamely and unfashionable
That dogs bark at me as I halt by them,
Why, I in this weak piping time of peace,
Have no delight to pass away the time,   25
Unless to see my shadow in the sun
And descant on mine own deformity.

7

Richard determines he will be evil. He tells the audience that he has arranged for King Edward to find his brother Clarence a threat and imprison him in the Tower. He jokes at Clarence's plight.

1 Richard as villain and actor

In line 30, 'I am determinèd to prove a villain', Richard declares his intention to be evil. Many people think that Shakespeare's portrayal of villainy resembles the character of Vice in medieval morality plays. (see page 246). Vice was a villainous servant of the devil who trapped people into sin by charm, wit and double-dealing. Like Richard, Vice often confided with the audience, encouraging them to delight in his cleverness.

Richard often refers to plays and acting techniques, relishing his skills as an actor throughout the play. For example, 'inductions' (line 32) were the dramatic prologues to plays. In your presentation of the soliloquy, use appropriate gestures and expressions to show how Richard delights in his own cleverness in using such imagery as he invites the audience to share in his plots.

2 Irony

Almost all of what Richard says to Clarence is ironic; he does not want him to have a 'good' day and already knows the answers to the questions he asks. Even his joke about christening is ironic in view of what happens later in the play. Christening uses water as a symbol of re-birth, but Clarence will shortly be drowned in a cask of wine. As you read on, watch for the many other examples of irony. You can find help on page 245.

---

entertain spend, enjoy
inductions preparations
mewed up imprisoned like a hawk
Dive descend
Tend'ring caring for
conduct guard

belike maybe
cross-row alphabet
issue offspring, children
toys fancies
commit imprison

And therefore, since I cannot prove a lover
To entertain these fair well-spoken days,
I am determinèd to prove a villain   30
And hate the idle pleasures of these days.
Plots have I laid, inductions dangerous,
By drunken prophecies, libels, and dreams
To set my brother Clarence and the king
In deadly hate the one against the other.   35
And if King Edward be as true and just
As I am subtle, false, and treacherous,
This day should Clarence closely be mewed up
About a prophecy which says that 'G'
Of Edward's heirs the murderer shall be.   40
Dive, thoughts, down to my soul, here Clarence comes.

Enter CLARENCE *guarded by* BRAKENBURY

Brother, good day. What means this armèd guard
That waits upon your grace?
CLARENCE   His majesty,
Tend'ring my person's safety, hath appointed
This conduct to convey me to the Tower.   45
RICHARD Upon what cause?
CLARENCE   Because my name is George.
RICHARD Alack, my lord, that fault is none of yours.
He should for that commit your godfathers.
Oh, belike his majesty hath some intent
That you should be new christened in the Tower.   50
But what's the matter, Clarence? May I know?
CLARENCE Yea, Richard, when I know, but I protest
As yet I do not. But as I can learn,
He hearkens after prophecies and dreams,
And from the cross-row plucks the letter 'G',   55
And says a wizard told him that by 'G'
His issue disinherited should be.
And for my name of George begins with 'G',
It follows in his thought that I am he.
These, as I learn, and suchlike toys as these   60
Hath moved his highness to commit me now.

Richard claims that Queen Elizabeth has caused King Edward to imprison Clarence, and that she and Jane Shore have become powers behind the throne. Brakenbury's unease is dismissed with innuendo and sexual puns.

1 'Men are ruled by women' (line 62)

In line 64, Richard mockingly refers to Queen Elizabeth as 'My lady Grey' because before her marriage to King Edward in 1464 she was the widow of Sir Thomas Grey. Elizabeth used her position as queen to gain power and influence for her large family, the Woodvilles, and in so doing aroused much jealousy.

Jane Shore's name occurs frequently throughout the play, though she never appears. She is the mistress of both King Edward and Lord Hastings and was believed to be a witch. Clarence hints that Hastings was responsible for keeping her out of prison.

Richard III has often traditionally been regarded as a 'male' play, yet Richard frequently refers to both women as a source of trouble, as if they possessed real power. As you work through the play, try to identify the extent of women's power and influence.

2 Making Brakenbury feel inferior? (in pairs)

Brakenbury greets Richard and Clarence as 'your graces' (line 84) because they are royal dukes, but Richard calls him 'man' (line 90) and makes jokes at Brakenbury's expense by punning on 'nought' and 'naught' meaning 'nothing' and 'to have sex'. Does Richard deliberately use his position to make Brakenbury feel inferior? Take parts as Richard and Brakenbury and act out lines 84–104 showing how Richard might emphasise his social superiority through tone, gesture and actions.

kindred family	**livery** uniform
night-walking heralds	**dubbed** created
secret messengers	**straitly given in charge**
suppliant beggar of favours	strictly ordered
her deity King Edward	**conference** conversation
(or Jane Shore's evil spirits)	**Well struck** advanced

RICHARD   Why, this it is when men are ruled by women.
    'Tis not the king that sends you to the Tower.
    My lady Grey, his wife, Clarence, 'tis she
    That tempts him to this harsh extremity.   65
    Was it not she and that good man of worship,
    Anthony Woodville, her brother there,
    That made him send Lord Hastings to the Tower,
    From whence this present day he is delivered?
    We are not safe, Clarence, we are not safe.   70
CLARENCE   By heaven, I think there is no man secure
    But the queen's kindred, and night-walking heralds
    That trudge betwixt the king and Mistress Shore.
    Heard you not what an humble suppliant
    Lord Hastings was for her delivery?   75
RICHARD   Humbly complaining to her deity
    Got my lord Chamberlain his liberty.
    I'll tell you what, I think it is our way,
    If we will keep in favour with the king,
    To be her men and wear her livery.   80
    The jealous, o'er-worn widow and herself,
    Since that our brother dubbed them gentlewomen,
    Are mighty gossips in our monarchy.
BRAKENBURY   I beseech your graces both to pardon me;
    His majesty hath straitly given in charge   85
    That no man shall have private conference,
    Of what degree soever, with your brother.
RICHARD   Even so. And please your worship, Brakenbury,
    You may partake of any thing we say.
    We speak no treason, man. We say the king   90
    Is wise and virtuous, and his noble queen
    Well struck in years, fair, and not jealous.
    We say that Shore's wife hath a pretty foot,
    A cherry lip, a bonny eye, a passing pleasing tongue,
    And that the queen's kindred are made gentlefolks. 95
    How say you, sir? Can you deny all this?
BRAKENBURY   With this, my lord, myself have nought to do.
RICHARD   Naught to do with Mistress Shore? I tell thee, fellow,
    He that doth naught with her (excepting one)
    Were best to do it secretly alone.   100

Richard promises to do any service he can to ensure Clarence's release. Alone on stage, Richard reveals that he really seeks Clarence's death. Hastings swears vengeance on those who caused his imprisonment.

1 Saying one thing but meaning another (in pairs)

A major feature of Richard's language is that his words frequently have double meanings. Listeners hear one thing but he means something else. Most of what he says to Clarence has meanings which Clarence does not perceive. For example, when Richard says 'Brother, farewell' Clarence probably hears a friendly voice, but Richard may mean 'Goodbye for ever because you'll soon be dead'.

As one person slowly speaks lines 107–16, pausing frequently, the other person says in each pause what Richard probably means.

2 'The new-delivered Hastings' (in pairs)

Lord Hastings is a faithful supporter of the house of York but much opposed to Queen Elizabeth and the rest of the Woodvilles. Hastings' influence weakened during the illness of his patron King Edward and that loss of power may have lead to his imprisonment. As he was the lover of Jane Shore, however, she may have been responsible for Hastings' early release.

Speak lines 123–45 to form a first impression of what Hastings is like and how Richard relates to him.

3 Birds of prey

Throughout the play the imagery of birds and animals is often used to describe Richard. But here 'kites and buzzards' (line 134) refers to the Woodville clan and is ironical because Hastings fails to see that in addressing Richard he is speaking to a much more dangerous bird of prey. When Hastings refers to 'the eagles' (line 133) is it more likely he is referring to himself or Clarence?

---

withal also
Forbear stop
abjects despised outcasts
 (Richard's joking pun on 'subjects')
widow Queen Elizabeth
 (Richard again mocks her)

enfranchise free
 (from prison or from life)
perforce without choice
brooked endured
to give them thanks
 to be revenged on them
mewed imprisoned

BRAKENBURY What one, my lord?

RICHARD Her husband, knave. Wouldst thou betray me?

BRAKENBURY I do beseech your grace to pardon me, and withal
    Forbear your conference with the noble duke.

CLARENCE We know thy charge, Brakenbury, and will obey.   105

RICHARD We are the queen's abjects and must obey.
    Brother, farewell. I will unto the king,
    And whatsoe'er you will employ me in,
    Were it to call King Edward's widow 'sister',
    I will perform it to enfranchise you.   110
    Meantime, this deep disgrace in brotherhood
    Touches me deeper than you can imagine.

CLARENCE I know it pleaseth neither of us well.

RICHARD Well, your imprisonment shall not be long.
    I will deliver you or else lie for you.   115
    Meantime, have patience.

CLARENCE I must perforce. Farewell.

Exeunt Clarence, Brakenbury, and guards

RICHARD Go, tread the path that thou shalt ne'er return.
    Simple, plain Clarence, I do love thee so
    That I will shortly send thy soul to heaven,   120
    If heaven will take the present at our hands.
    But who comes here? The new-delivered Hastings?

Enter LORD HASTINGS

HASTINGS Good time of day unto my gracious lord.

RICHARD As much unto my good lord Chamberlain.
    Well are you welcome to this open air.   125
    How hath your lordship brooked imprisonment?

HASTINGS With patience, noble lord, as prisoners must.
    But I shall live, my lord, to give them thanks
    That were the cause of my imprisonment.

RICHARD No doubt, no doubt, and so shall Clarence too,   130
    For they that were your enemies are his
    And have prevailed as much on him as you.

HASTINGS More pity that the eagles should be mewed
    While kites and buzzards play at liberty.

RICHARD What news abroad?   135

Hastings says Edward is near to death. Richard blames the king's lifestyle. Alone on stage, Richard hopes that Edward will not die until Clarence has been executed. He reveals his plan to marry Anne.

1 What is King Edward like?

On every page so far, there have been clues to King Edward's character. 'An evil diet long' (line 140) suggests that for a long time Edward has lived wildly. Check what Richard, Clarence and Hastings have said about Edward in Scene 1. Jot down six to ten words which sum up your impression of the king. Look back later to see if your forecast is accurate.

2 Shakespeare alters history

Shakespeare was a playwright, not an historian, so throughout *Richard III* he alters history to suit his dramatic purposes. For example, in lines 154–5, Richard plans to marry Anne, daughter of the Earl of Warwick and wife of Prince Edward, both of whom he claims to have killed. But in (historical) fact, Anne was not married to Edward (but engaged), and Richard did not kill Warwick. You will find more examples of how Shakespeare alters history as you read on (see particularly page 246).

3 Bring out the humour (in pairs)

Lines 146–63 are full of revelations of Richard's wickedness. Often actors play the lines with a great deal of humour. In line 153, 'bustle' often gains a laugh as it catches the obvious roguery of Richard's character.

Take turns to speak the lines with actions that might be used to provoke laughter.

---

by Saint John
Richard swears an oath
packed with post-horse
sent as quickly as possible
steeled strengthened

secret close intent hidden purpose
(What project do you think Richard has in mind?)
I run before my horse to market I am getting too far ahead of myself

HASTINGS No news so bad abroad as this at home:
        The king is sickly, weak, and melancholy,
        And his physicians fear him mightily.
RICHARD Now by Saint John, that news is bad indeed.
        Oh, he hath kept an evil diet long   140
        And over-much consumed his royal person.
        'Tis very grievous to be thought upon.
        Where is he, in his bed?
HASTINGS He is.
RICHARD Go you before, and I will follow you.   145

Exit Hastings

        He cannot live, I hope, and must not die
        Till George be packed with post-horse up to heaven.
        I'll in to urge his hatred more to Clarence
        With lies well steeled with weighty arguments,
        And if I fail not in my deep intent,   150
        Clarence hath not another day to live:
        Which done, God take King Edward to his mercy
        And leave the world for me to bustle in!
        For then I'll marry Warwick's youngest daughter.
        What though I killed her husband and her father?   155
        The readiest way to make the wench amends
        Is to become her husband and her father,
        The which will I, not all so much for love
        As for another secret close intent
        By marrying her which I must reach unto.   160
        But yet I run before my horse to market.
        Clarence still breathes, Edward still lives and reigns;
        When they are gone, then must I count my gains.

Exit

Lady Anne mourns over the corpse of King Henry VI.
She curses Richard for killing Henry and her husband,
Prince Edward, Henry's son.

1 Anne's grief and anger (in pairs)

The death of the Lancastrian King Henry VI has made possible 'the glorious summer' (Act 1 Scene 1, line 2) of the house of York. Henry VI was Anne's intended father-in-law who was killed by Richard after the decisive Battle of Tewkesbury. Anne now accompanies the body to its burial. She uses the language of mourning (solemn, ritualistic and formal) reinforcing her grief through the repetition of phrases in lines 14–16, 21 and 26. Anne also reveals her deep anger against Richard as she repeats the same word but with different meanings. For example, 'blood' can mean: family (line 7); gore, rage or Yorkists (line 16). One person slowly speaks lines 1–30; the other person echoes all the words of grief and anger.

2 'Shrouded in a hearse'

Henry's corpse is on stage throughout Scene 2. The body is royal, has to be transported, and is on view for some time as Anne grieves and weeps over it. Imagine you are the stage designer and create your solution to how the corpse could be presented on stage.

3 Justifiable curses? (in small groups)

In lines 14–28, Anne curses not only Richard but also his unborn children and any future wife. Do you think Anne's pleas for such punishment are fair? Take sides and argue that her curses are justifiable or that they are morally wrong. As you work through the play you will discover the ironic consequences of Anne's curses.

Halberds soldiers
hearse bier or coffin
obsequiously as a mourner
blood family
invocate pray to
windows wounds

More direful hap betide
  a more dreadful fate fall upon
abortive monster-like
Prodigious abnormal
thee (line 28) King Henry VI
interrèd buried

ACT 1 SCENE 2
Near the Tower of London

The corpse of KING HENRY VI is carried in accompanied by LADY
ANNE, HALBERDS, TRESSEL, BERKELEY and other gentlemen

ANNE Set down, set down your honourable load,
　　　　If honour may be shrouded in a hearse,
　　　　Whilst I awhile obsequiously lament
　　　　Th'untimely fall of virtuous Lancaster.
　　　　Poor key-cold figure of a holy king,　　　　　　　　　5
　　　　Pale ashes of the house of Lancaster,
　　　　Thou bloodless remnant of that royal blood,
　　　　Be it lawful that I invocate thy ghost
　　　　To hear the lamentations of poor Anne,
　　　　Wife to thy Edward, to thy slaughtered son,　　　　10
　　　　Stabbed by the selfsame hand that made these wounds.
　　　　Lo, in these windows that let forth thy life,
　　　　I pour the helpless balm of my poor eyes.
　　　　Oh, cursèd be the hand that made these holes,
　　　　Cursed the heart that had the heart to do it,　　　　15
　　　　Cursed the blood that let this blood from hence.
　　　　More direful hap betide that hated wretch
　　　　That makes us wretched by the death of thee
　　　　Than I can wish to wolves, to spiders, toads,
　　　　Or any creeping venomed thing that lives.　　　　　20
　　　　If ever he have child, abortive be it,
　　　　Prodigious, and untimely brought to light,
　　　　Whose ugly and unnatural aspèct
　　　　May fright the hopeful mother at the view,
　　　　And that be heir to his unhappiness.　　　　　　　　25
　　　　If ever he have wife, let her be made
　　　　More miserable by the death of him
　　　　Than I am made by my young lord and thee.
　　　　Come now towards Chertsey with your holy load,
　　　　Taken from Paul's to be interrèd there.　　　　　　　30
　　　　And still as you are weary of this weight,
　　　　Rest you while I lament King Henry's corpse.

Richard orders the guards to set down the coffin. He threatens violence if disobeyed. Anne accuses Richard of being a devil. Henry's wounds open and begin to bleed. Anne calls for Richard's death.

1 Power-play (in groups of any size)

Richard's entrance changes the mood of the scene. Use some of the following questions to help you experiment with ways of staging lines 33–45 to bring out the struggle for power between Richard and the others.

- How many people accompany Anne?
- How many of the procession are armed?
- What actions might Richard make as he commands them to 'Stay' (line 33)?
- How does the procession react to Richard's words?
- How does Anne react both to Richard and to what her followers do?

2 The wooing scene (in pairs)

Lines 46–228 are often called the wooing scene because in them Richard tries to persuade Anne to become his wife. Take parts as Richard and Anne, and speak the lines to gain a first impression of the episode. Afterwards, work on the activity below and on the following pages.

Holinshed (see page 2) writes that Henry's corpse was seen to bleed both at St Paul's and Blackfriars. Shakespeare adds to this the popular superstition that a murdered body bleeds again in the presence of the murderer (lines 55–6). What does Anne do at these lines, and how does Richard react?

spurn stamp	**heinous** evil
Avaunt be gone	**exhales** draws out
(used to banish supernatural beings)	**deluge** flood
curst spiteful	**quick** alive
exclaims outcries	**charity** christian belief

Enter RICHARD DUKE OF GLOUCESTER

RICHARD Stay, you that bear the corpse, and set it down.

ANNE What black magician conjures up this fiend
  To stop devoted charitable deeds? 35

RICHARD Villains, set down the corpse, or by Saint Paul,
  I'll make a corpse of him that disobeys.

GENTLEMAN My lord, stand back and let the coffin pass.

RICHARD Unmannered dog, stand thou when I command.
  Advance thy halberd higher than my breast, 40
  Or by Saint Paul, I'll strike thee to my foot
  And spurn upon thee, beggar, for thy boldness.

ANNE What, do you tremble? Are you all afraid?
  Alas, I blame you not, for you are mortal,
  And mortal eyes cannot endure the devil. 45
  Avaunt, thou dreadful minister of hell.
  Thou hadst but power over his mortal body;
  His soul thou canst not have. Therefore be gone.

RICHARD Sweet saint, for charity, be not so curst.

ANNE Foul devil, for God's sake hence, and trouble us not, 50
  For thou hast made the happy earth thy hell,
  Filled it with cursing cries and deep exclaims.
  If thou delight to view thy heinous deeds,
  Behold this pattern of thy butcheries.
  Oh gentlemen, see, see, dead Henry's wounds 55
  Open their congealed mouths and bleed afresh.
  Blush, blush, thou lump of foul deformity,
  For 'tis thy presence that exhales this blood
  From cold and empty veins where no blood dwells.
  Thy deeds inhuman and unnatural 60
  Provokes this deluge most unnatural.
  Oh God, which this blood mad'st, revenge his death.
  Oh earth, which this blood drink'st, revenge his death.
  Either heav'n with lightning strike the murd'rer dead,
  Or earth gape open wide and eat him quick, 65
  As thou dost swallow up this good king's blood,
  Which his hell-governed arm hath butcherèd.

RICHARD Lady, you know no rules of charity,
  Which renders good for bad, blessings for curses.

Anne continues to curse Richard, accusing him of murder. He asks for an opportunity to defend himself. He denies killing her husband but admits trying to kill Queen Margaret and killing King Henry.

1 Tennis-match language (in pairs)

In lines 68–118, words are returned back and forth rather like the ball in a tennis rally. The technical term for this alternating exchange of lines is stichomythia (see page 242).

The exchange uses repetition of words, phrases and rhythms; later they often seize on each other's words and use directly contrasting words in reply. Anne's language of hell and vengeance contrasts with Richard's of heaven and forgiveness, (for example, 'Fairer' contrasts with 'Fouler' in lines 81–3). The repeated patterns of punctuation add to the rhythm of the dialogue.

a Speak lines 68–118, emphasising the repeated or contrasting words, phrases and rhythms.

b Discuss whether you find Richard's attitude friendly, aloof or obviously insincere during the exchange.

c How would you stage the episode?

2 Who's who?

Anne accuses Richard of killing Prince Edward and King Henry VI. Richard denies his guilt, even though in Act 1 Scene 1, line 54 he claimed to have killed Anne's 'husband'. He blames Edward IV, his own brother, for Prince Edward's death. Anne says Queen Margaret was a witness to Richard's murderous actions and accuses Richard of being prevented from killing Margaret herself only by the intervention of his brothers Clarence and Edward. Richard admits to killing King Henry VI, Anne's father-in-law (line 104).

Vouchsafe allow
diffused shapeless
leave permission
circumstance evidence

excuse current genuine excuse
falchion broadsword
bend aim
hedgehog see page 66

ANNE   Villain, thou know'st nor law of God nor man.   70
        No beast so fierce but knows some touch of pity.
RICHARD   But I know none, and therefore am no beast.
ANNE   Oh, wonderful, when devils tell the truth!
RICHARD   More wonderful, when angels are so angry.
        Vouchsafe, divine perfection of a woman,   75
        Of these supposèd crimes to give me leave
        By circumstance but to acquit myself.
ANNE   Vouchsafe, diffused infection of man,
        Of these known evils but to give me leave
        By circumstance to curse thy cursèd self.   80
RICHARD   Fairer than tongue can name thee, let me have
        Some patient leisure to excuse myself.
ANNE   Fouler than heart can think thee, thou canst make
        No excuse current but to hang thyself.
RICHARD   By such despair I should accuse myself.   85
ANNE   And by despairing shalt thou stand excused
        For doing worthy vengeance on thyself,
        That didst unworthy slaughter upon others.
RICHARD   Say that I slew them not.
ANNE   Then say they were not slain.   90
        But dead they are, and, devilish slave, by thee.
RICHARD   I did not kill your husband.
ANNE   Why, then he is alive.
RICHARD   Nay, he is dead, and slain by Edward's hands.
ANNE   In thy foul throat thou liest. Queen Margaret saw   95
        Thy murd'rous falchion smoking in his blood,
        The which thou once didst bend against her breast,
        But that thy brothers beat aside the point.
RICHARD   I was provokèd by her sland'rous tongue,
        That laid their guilt upon my guiltless shoulders.   100
ANNE   Thou wast provokèd by thy bloody mind,
        That never dream'st on aught but butcheries.
        Didst thou not kill this king?
RICHARD   I grant ye.
ANNE   Dost grant me, hedgehog? Then God grant me too   105
        Thou mayst be damnèd for that wicked deed.
        Oh, he was gentle, mild, and virtuous.

Anne wishes Richard in hell but he offers himself as her new husband.
He claims her beauty caused him to kill. She curses her beauty and
him, hoping for revenge.

1 Audacious Richard (in pairs)

Having admitted to a series of crimes against her family, in a single audacious move Richard artfully suggests that Anne should share her bed with him.

Work out how Richard's tactic at line 115 could become an explosive moment of drama on stage.

2 Anne's view (in pairs)

Richard describes their meeting as a 'keen encounter of our wits' – an intellectual game. Is that how Anne sees it? The pace of the exchange could give an audience the clue to her feelings. Take parts as Anne and Richard and speak lines 68–119, first as quickly and unemotionally as possible, and then slowly, with Anne showing grief. Discuss which style of speaking seems more effective, or suggest a version of your own.

3 'A slower method'

Richard, by his own admission at line 121, adopts another tactic in his battle to win Anne over. In an attempt to dictate the pace of the argument, he now blames Anne's beauty for being the cause of his murderous acts. He begins with the question at lines 122–4. Suggest why you think Richard changes the pace and topic of his wooing strategy at this point.

holp helped
Ill rest betide bad sleep visit
timeless untimely
homicide murderer

rend tear
wrack ruin
bereft robbed

RICHARD The better for the king of heaven that hath him.
ANNE He is in heaven, where thou shalt never come.
RICHARD Let him thank me, that holp to send him thither,   110
    For he was fitter for that place than earth.
ANNE And thou unfit for any place but hell.
RICHARD Yes, one place else, if you will hear me name it.
ANNE Some dungeon.
RICHARD Your bedchamber.   115
ANNE Ill rest betide the chamber where thou liest.
RICHARD So will it, madam, till I lie with you.
ANNE I hope so.
RICHARD I know so. But gentle Lady Anne,
    To leave this keen encounter of our wits   120
    And fall something into a slower method,
    Is not the causer of the timeless deaths
    Of these Plantagenets, Henry and Edward,
    As blameful as the executioner?
ANNE Thou wast the cause and most accursed effect.   125
RICHARD Your beauty was the cause of that effect:
    Your beauty, that did haunt me in my sleep
    To undertake the death of all the world,
    So I might live one hour in your sweet bosom.
ANNE If I thought that, I tell thee, homicide,   130
    These nails should rend that beauty from my cheeks.
RICHARD These eyes could not endure that beauty's wrack.
    You should not blemish it if I stood by.
    As all the world is cheerèd by the sun,
    So I by that. It is my day, my life.   135
ANNE Black night o'ershade thy day, and death thy life.
RICHARD Curse not thyself, fair creature; thou art both.
ANNE I would I were, to be revenged on thee.
RICHARD It is a quarrel most unnatural
    To be revenged on him that loveth thee.   140
ANNE It is a quarrel just and reasonable
    To be revenged on him that killed my husband.
RICHARD He that bereft thee, lady, of thy husband
    Did it to help thee to a better husband.
ANNE His better doth not breathe upon the earth.   145

Richard tells Anne that he could love her better than Edward, her former husband. He claims Anne has the power to make him weep when other griefs leave him unmoved. He continues to woo her.

1 'Why Plantagenet'?

Plantagenet was the family name of the kings of England between 1154 and 1485. Both the houses of York and Lancaster who fought against each other in the Wars of the Roses were Plantagenets. This is the second time in the wooing scene that Richard has used his family name, Plantagenet, (the first use is in line 123). Suggest why he uses it again to refer to himself.

2 'Why dost thou spit at me?' (in small groups)

Richard's 'Here' (line 149) seems to be the trigger for Anne's strong reaction. Is it this word alone which so angers Anne, or are there other reasons for her contemptuous response?

Brainstorm and list what the action of spitting at someone means and its meanings in different cultures. How might some of the items on your list help you to advise Anne how to play her line 150?

3 More audacity (in pairs)

Delighting in wordplay, Richard's lines 156–71 turn Anne's image of the eyes of a monster into his own eyes which weep for Anne's beauty but are unable to weep at tragic events: the death of Rutland and of his father.

Rutland (line 162) was Richard's younger brother, murdered by Clifford in 1470; 'thy warlike father' is Anne's father, Warwick.

Take parts and speak lines 150–9 showing how Richard reverses Anne's intended insults ('poison' 'infect' 'dead' 'die' 'kill' and 'eyes') in his audacious attempt to win her affection.

---

mortal fatal
basilisks monsters that killed with a look
aspècts appearances
bedashed drenched

exhale draw out
sued to asked favours of
smoothing flattering
proposed offered as
sues begs, implores, pleads with

RICHARD   He lives that loves thee better than he could.
ANNE   Name him.
RICHARD   Plantagenet.
ANNE   Why, that was he.
RICHARD   The selfsame name, but one of better nature.
ANNE   Where is he?
RICHARD   Here.

She spits at him

                 Why dost thou spit at me?
ANNE   Would it were mortal poison for thy sake.   150
RICHARD   Never came poison from so sweet a place.
ANNE   Never hung poison on a fouler toad.
           Out of my sight. Thou dost infect mine eyes.
RICHARD   Thine eyes, sweet lady, have infected mine.
ANNE   Would they were basilisks', to strike thee dead.   155
RICHARD   I would they were, that I might die at once,
           For now they kill me with a living death.
           Those eyes of thine from mine have drawn salt tears,
           Shamed their aspècts with store of childish drops.
           These eyes, which never shed remorseful tear,   160
           No, when my father York and Edward wept
           To hear the piteous moan that Rutland made
           When black-faced Clifford shook his sword at him,
           Nor when thy warlike father, like a child,
           Told the sad story of my father's death   165
           And twenty times made pause to sob and weep,
           That all the standers-by had wet their cheeks
           Like trees bedashed with rain. In that sad time
           My manly eyes did scorn an humble tear.
           And what these sorrows could not thence exhale   170
           Thy beauty hath, and made them blind with weeping.
           I never sued to friend nor enemy.
           My tongue could never learn sweet smoothing word.
           But now thy beauty is proposed my fee,
           My proud heart sues and prompts my tongue to speak.   175

She looks scornfully at him

           Teach not thy lip such scorn, for it was made
           For kissing, lady, not for such contempt.

25

Richard offers Anne the opportunity to stab him. He admits he killed King Henry and Prince Edward. Anne refuses to use the dagger, so Richard offers to kill himself. He places his ring on Anne's finger.

'Look how my ring encompasseth thy finger.' Richard attempts to win the hand of Anne in marriage as part of his plan to gain the English throne. Do you think Anne is fooled completely by Richard?

dissembler hypocrite
àccessary guilty party, accomplice
figured represented

Vouchsafe accept
Look how just as
encompasseth encircles, rings

If thy revengeful heart cannot forgive,
Lo, here I lend thee this sharp-pointed sword,
Which if thou please to hide in this true breast   180
And let the soul forth that adoreth thee,
I lay it naked to the deadly stroke
And humbly beg the death upon my knee.

He lays his breast open; she offers at with his sword

Nay, do not pause, for I did kill King Henry,
But 'twas thy beauty that provokèd me.   185
Nay, now dispatch; 'twas I that stabbed young Edward,
But 'twas thy heavenly face that set me on.

She falls the sword

Take up the sword again, or take up me.
ANNE Arise, dissembler; though I wish thy death,
      I will not be thy executioner.   190
RICHARD Then bid me kill myself, and I will do it.
ANNE I have already.
RICHARD   That was in thy rage.
      Speak it again, and even with the word,
      This hand, which for thy love did kill thy love,
      Shall for thy love kill a far truer love.   195
      To both their deaths shalt thou be accessary.
ANNE I would I knew thy heart.
RICHARD 'Tis figured in my tongue.
ANNE I fear me both are false.
RICHARD Then never man was true.   200
ANNE Well, well, put up your sword.
RICHARD Say then my peace is made.
ANNE That shalt thou know hereafter.
RICHARD But shall I live in hope?
ANNE All men, I hope, live so.   205
RICHARD Vouchsafe to wear this ring.
      Look how my ring encompasseth thy finger.
      Even so thy breast encloseth my poor heart.
      Wear both of them, for both of them are thine.
      And if thy poor devoted servant may   210
      But beg one favour at thy gracious hand,
      Thou dost confirm his happiness forever.
ANNE What is it?

Richard persuades Anne to stop mourning and allow him to take charge of King Henry's funeral. He exults at his success but predicts he will soon abandon Anne.

1 Richard the hypocrite (in small groups)

Richard reveals through his words and actions that his wooing of Anne was an artfully designed game.

a As soon as Anne has left the stage Richard drops his public mask, and becomes the schemer and master planner. Instead of fulfilling his promise to take the body of Henry to Chertsey, he commands that it should be carried to Whitefriars. Work out how you would stage the removal of Henry VI's body (lines 229–30) to underline the abrupt change of mood.

b In his soliloquy (lines 231–67), Richard revels in his triumph in successfully wooing the woman whose handsome husband-to-be, Edward, he has murdered. Despite his physical deformity and his evil deeds, he has won Anne through an artful display of verbal brilliance. The rhythm and energy of the lines reveals his pleasure at having carried off such a coup. Take turns to explore ways of speaking the soliloquy to bring out Richard's sense of joy in his own cleverness.

2 Advice to Anne

After the engagement of Anne and Richard, a friend of Anne's writes to her pointing out all the reasons why she should not marry Richard. Imagine you are the friend and write the letter.

sad designs mourning (for Henry VI)
presently immediately
interred buried
expedient swift
divers several
unknown secret

boon wish
humour mood
bars obstacles
suit wooing
Framed in the prodigality of nature excessively gifted

RICHARD   That it may please you leave these sad designs
                    To him that hath most cause to be a mourner   215
                    And presently repair to Crosby House,
                    Where, after I have solemnly interred
                    At Chertsey monast'ry this noble king
                    And wet his grave with my repentant tears,
                    I will with all expedient duty see you.   220
                    For divers unknown reasons, I beseech you,
                    Grant me this boon.
ANNE With all my heart, and much it joys me, too,
                    To see you are become so penitent.
                    Tressel and Berkeley, go along with me.   225
RICHARD   Bid me farewell.
ANNE   'Tis more than you deserve,
                    But since you teach me how to flatter you,
                    Imagine I have said farewell already.

                                                    Exeunt two with Anne

GENTLEMAN   Towards Chertsey, noble lord?
RICHARD   No, to Whitefriars; there attend my coming.   230

                              Exeunt all but Richard with the corpse

                    Was ever woman in this humour wooed?
                    Was ever woman in this humour won?
                    I'll have her, but I will not keep her long.
                    What, I that killed her husband and his father,
                    To take her in her heart's extremest hate,
                    With curses in her mouth, tears in her eyes,   235
                    The bleeding witness of my hatred by,
                    Having God, her conscience, and these bars against me,
                    And I no friends to back my suit withal
                    But the plain devil and dissembling looks?
                    And yet to win her, all the world to nothing!   240
                    Ha!
                    Hath she forgot already that brave prince,
                    Edward, her lord, whom I some three months since
                    Stabbed in my angry mood at Tewkesbury?
                    A sweeter and a lovelier gentleman,   245
                    Framed in the prodigality of nature,
                    Young, valiant, wise, and (no doubt) right royal,
                    The spacious world cannot again afford.

Richard marvels at Anne's acceptance of him, in spite of his unattractive outward appearance. Elizabeth and her relatives discuss King Edward's illness.

1 The mask slips? (in pairs)

The actor playing Richard argues that in lines 250–8 Richard reveals genuine feelings of self-disgust and should speak the lines to gain sympathy from the audience. The director disagrees and wants Richard's feeling of triumph to continue as he mocks his own appearance. One person reads the lines as the actor suggests, the other as the director feels is right. Talk together about which style seems the more successful.

2 In triumph or disgust? (in pairs)

Richard's final two lines are full of irony directed principally at himself. Work out how to deliver his final couplet and departure to show what he really thinks about his appearance.

3 'In that you brook it ill' (in groups of three)

King Edward's wife, Elizabeth, and her relatives are Woodvilles, the rival faction to Richard. Rivers is Elizabeth's brother, Grey and Dorset are her sons by an earlier marriage.

Grey accuses Elizabeth of making Edward's health deteriorate because she is showing her grief. 'In that you brook it ill' (line 3) means that in bearing your grief badly you make him worse. Take parts as Grey, Rivers and Elizabeth. Act lines 1–10 as if Elizabeth is selfish, concerned only with her own future. Then perform the lines as if she is beside herself with grief and anxiety and the men respond sympathetically. Decide which you think is the more appropriate way of staging the episode.

---

abase lower, debase
cropped cut off
Edward's moiety
  a tiny fraction of his worth
halts limps

denier worthless coin
proper handsome
be at charges for buy
entertain employ
betide on happen to

And will she yet abase her eyes on me,   250
That cropped the golden prime of this sweet prince
And made her widow to a woeful bed?
On me, whose all not equals Edward's moiety?
On me, that halts and am misshapen thus?
My dukedom to a beggarly denier,   255
I do mistake my person all this while.
Upon my life, she finds (although I cannot)
Myself to be a marv'lous proper man.
I'll be at charges for a looking-glass
And entertain a score or two of tailors   260
To study fashions to adorn my body.
Since I am crept in favour with myself,
I will maintain it with some little cost.
But first I'll turn yon fellow in his grave
And then return lamenting to my love.   265
Shine out, fair sun, till I have bought a glass,
That I may see my shadow as I pass.

Exit

ACT 1 SCENE 3
London: a room in King Edward's palace

Enter QUEEN ELIZABETH, LORD RIVERS, LORD GREY
and the MARQUESS OF DORSET

RIVERS Have patience, madam. There's no doubt his majesty
        Will soon recover his accustomed health.
GREY In that you brook it ill, it makes him worse.
        Therefore, for God's sake, entertain good comfort,
        And cheer his grace with quick and merry eyes.   5
ELIZABETH If he were dead, what would betide on me?
GREY No other harm but loss of such a lord.
ELIZABETH The loss of such a lord includes all harms.
GREY The heavens have blessed you with a goodly son
        To be your comforter when he is gone.   10

Elizabeth claims that Richard, soon to be Protector, hates her and her family. Buckingham says that the dying King Edward wants reconciliation between the factions. Richard condemns those who complain of him to the king.

1 Concerns for the future

The enmity between the factions is exposed, as the Woodvilles discuss Richard's hatred of them for their influence over the dying King Edward. Elizabeth wants to maintain power after her husband's death through her son. She fears if Richard were formally nominated his nephew's Protector, he would exert a powerful influence over the boy.

The Woodvilles are joined by Buckingham (it is not yet clear who he will support) and Stanley, whose wife is the Countess of Richmond. Her son by an earlier marriage will eventually become Henry VII. Stanley tries to reassure Queen Elizabeth that his wife does not really hate the Woodvilles.

All on stage hope for King Edward's recovery. Buckingham says the king wants to reconcile Richard and the Woodvilles ('your brothers') and Hastings and the Woodvilles. Queen Elizabeth fears for the future as Richard enters.

List all the troubles on Queen Elizabeth's mind. Which is her greatest concern?

2 Hopes dashed, fears confirmed (in pairs)

The hopes for reconciliation between the factions and Elizabeth's fears for the future are brought into sharp focus by the sudden entrance of Richard. Typically, he carries the attack to his enemies, accusing those present of being against him. Explore ways of speaking lines 42–53 to identify how Richard uses his acting skills and physical appearance to try to throw his enemies off balance.

---

determined, not concluded yet agreed, but not finalised
miscarry die
envious malicious

wayward sickness depression
amendment recovery
atonement reconciliation
warn call

ELIZABETH   Ah, he is young, and his minority
       Is put unto the trust of Richard Gloucester,
       A man that loves not me nor none of you.
RIVERS   Is it concluded he shall be Protector?
ELIZABETH   It is determined, not concluded yet,   15
       But so it must be if the king miscarry.

Enter BUCKINGHAM *and* STANLEY EARL OF DERBY

GREY   Here come the lords of Buckingham and Derby.
BUCKINGHAM   Good time of day unto your royal grace.
STANLEY   God make your majesty joyful, as you have been.
ELIZABETH   The Countess Richmond, good my lord of Derby,   20
       To your good prayer will scarcely say amen.
       Yet Derby, not withstanding she's your wife
       And loves not me, be you, good lord, assured
       I hate not you for her proud arrogance.
STANLEY   I do beseech you, either not believe   25
       The envious slanders of her false accusers,
       Or if she be accused on true report,
       Bear with her weakness, which I think proceeds
       From wayward sickness and no grounded malice.
ELIZABETH   Saw you the king today, my lord of Derby?   30
STANLEY   But now the Duke of Buckingham and I
       Are come from visiting his majesty.
ELIZABETH   What likelihood of his amendment, lords?
BUCKINGHAM   Madam, good hope. His grace speaks cheerfully.
ELIZABETH   God grant him health. Did you confer with him?   35
BUCKINGHAM   Ay, madam. He desires to make atonement
       Between the Duke of Gloucester and your brothers,
       And between them and my Lord Chamberlain,
       And sent to warn them to his royal presence.
ELIZABETH   Would all were well, but that will never be.   40
       I fear our happiness is at the height.

Enter RICHARD *and* HASTINGS

RICHARD   They do me wrong, and I will not endure it.
       Who is it that complains unto the king
       That I, forsooth, am stern and love them not?
       By holy Paul, they love his grace but lightly   45
       That fill his ears with such dissentious rumours.

Richard claims the Woodvilles report ill of him to the king.
Elizabeth says the king sends for him to find the truth.
Richard implies the Woodvilles are commoners. Elizabeth denies
responsibility for Clarence's imprisonment.

1 A change of clothes? (in pairs)

The designer wants Richard's costume to be different from his last appearance because of Richard's reference to 'tailors' at the end of the wooing scene. The director disagrees, arguing that a costume change means a long unhelpful break between scenes.

Discuss which view you support and identify any compromise which may be reached.

2 Who is telling the truth? (small groups)

From line 58, Richard makes accusations against the Woodvilles which Elizabeth refutes. Identify the lines in which the following accusations and refutations are made:

- What wrongs have I ever done to your dishonest family?
- Your faction has complained against me to the dying king.
- It was the king's own wish to send for you to find the reason for the hatred you show to my family.
- Commoners are being ennobled.
- You're envious that my supporters have achieved higher social status.
- Clarence is imprisoned because of you, I'm in disgrace, nobles are scorned, and people of no rank or wealth are becoming nobles.
- I swear by God I never provoked Edward against Clarence. I've argued against his imprisonment.

When you have identified the lines, decide which statements are true, which false and which unproveable.

cog cheat	**lewd** vile
French nods	**Makes him to send**
falsely elegant manners	makes him send (for you)
silken effeminate	**the ground** the reason
jacks knaves	**noble** small coin
scarce a breathing while	**hap** life
for hardly a short time	

Because I cannot flatter and look fair,
Smile in men's faces, smooth, deceive, and cog,
Duck with French nods and apish courtesy,
I must be held a rancorous enemy.   50
Cannot a plain man live and think no harm,
But thus his simple truth must be abused
With silken, sly, insinuating jacks?

GREY To who in all this presence speaks your grace?

RICHARD To thee, that hast nor honesty nor grace.   55
When have I injured thee? When done thee wrong?
Or thee? Or thee? Or any of your faction?
A plague upon you all. His royal grace,
Whom God preserve better than you would wish,
Cannot be quiet scarce a breathing while   60
But you must trouble him with lewd complaints.

ELIZABETH Brother of Gloucester, you mistake the matter.
The king, on his own royal disposition,
And not provoked by any suitor else,
Aiming, belike, at your interior hatred,   65
That in your outward action shows itself
Against my children, brothers, and myself,
Makes him to send, that he may learn the ground.

RICHARD I cannot tell. The world is grown so bad
That wrens make prey where eagles dare not perch.   70
Since every jack became a gentleman,
There's many a gentle person made a jack.

ELIZABETH Come, come, we know your meaning, brother Gloucester.
You envy my advancement and my friends'.
God grant we never may have need of you.   75

RICHARD Meantime, God grants that I have need of you.
Our brother is imprisoned by your means,
My self disgraced, and the nobility
Held in contempt, while great promotions
Are daily given to ennoble those   80
That scarce some two days since were worth a noble.

ELIZABETH By Him that raised me to this careful height
From that contented hap which I enjoyed,
I never did incense his majesty
Against the Duke of Clarence, but have been   85
An earnest advocate to plead for him.

Richard continues to accuse and insult Elizabeth. She swears to inform the king of his scornful behaviour. Queen Margaret enters silently, and quietly rails against both Richard and Elizabeth.

1 Marry (in groups of three)

Richard's continuing taunting of Elizabeth is too much for Grey and Rivers to bear. Richard turns Rivers' protest to his advantage by punning on 'marry' (line 97) with its several meanings (by the Virgin Mary/indeed/to wed). He launches into a further personal attack on how Elizabeth became queen. Richard's echoing and repetition of Rivers' words underlines the strength of his feelings.

Take parts as Richard, Rivers and Queen Elizabeth and speak lines 89–109, emphasising Richard's repetitions and Elizabeth's indignant response.

2 Queen Margaret: Greek chorus, Nemesis

Queen Margaret was the widow of King Henry VI. Shakespeare gives her an important role in the play, but historically she remained in Burgundy and never returned to England after the deaths of her son and husband.

Dramatically, Margaret has much in common with the chorus in Greek tragedies, commenting on the action and expressing her viewpoint in her asides to the audience. Her formal echoing of the language used by others helps make her a choric figure.

A further role of the chorus was as Nemesis, or fate, to call for the avenging of past wrongs. Some critics see Margaret as a Nemesis figure, demanding justice and revenge. A modern interpretation depicts her as a symbol of the powerlessness of women.

As you read on, keep in mind these interpretations of Margaret's role in the play.

---

injury injustice
suspècts suspicions
I wis certainly
upbraidings insults
with this condition
  in this situation

is due to me mine by right
avouch't swear it
pains efforts
pack-horse beast of burden,
  toiling worker

My lord, you do me shameful injury
Falsely to draw me in these vile suspècts.
RICHARD You may deny that you were not the mean
Of my Lord Hastings' late imprisonment.   90
RIVERS She may, my lord, for –
RICHARD She may, Lord Rivers, why, who knows not so?
She may do more, sir, than denying that.
She may help you to many fair preferments,
And then deny her aiding hand therein,   95
And lay those honours on your high desert.
What may she not? She may, ay, marry, may she.
RIVERS Marry, may she?
RICHARD What, marry, may she? Marry with a king,
A bachelor, and a handsome stripling too.   100
I wis your grandam had a worser match.
ELIZABETH My lord of Gloucester, I have too long borne
Your blunt upbraidings and your bitter scoffs.
By heaven, I will acquaint his majesty
Of those gross taunts that oft I have endured.   105
I had rather be a country servant maid
Than a great queen with this condition,
To be so baited, scorned, and stormèd at.
Small joy have I in being England's queen.

Enter old QUEEN MARGARET

MARGARET [*Aside*] And lessened be that small, God I beseech him.   110
Thy honour, state, and seat is due to me.
RICHARD What? Threat you me with telling of the king?
I will avouch't in presence of the king.
I dare adventure to be sent to th'Tower.
'Tis time to speak. My pains are quite forgot.   115
MARGARET [*Aside*] Out, devil. I do remember them too well.
Thou killd'st my husband, Henry, in the Tower,
And Edward, my poor son, at Tewkesbury.
RICHARD Ere you were queen, ay, or your husband king,
I was a pack-horse in his great affairs,   120
A weeder-out of his proud adversaries,
A liberal rewarder of his friends.
To royalise his blood I spent mine own.

Richard accuses Elizabeth of treachery. He claims to feel pity for the imprisoned Clarence and professes that he would not want to be king. Margaret finally makes her presence known.

1 A question of loyalty (in groups of three)

Richard continues his accusations against Elizabeth (lines 125–40). In the Wars of the Roses, Elizabeth and Rivers had formerly supported the house of Lancaster, and Elizabeth's husband, Grey, was killed fighting against the Yorkists at the Battle of St Albans. Clarence, who changed sides to support King Edward, is now imprisoned in the Tower on suspicion of plotting against the king. Richard alone remained loyal to the Yorkist cause. To discover the pattern and nature of his claims, one person read lines 125–37 (omitting Margaret's asides) aloud very slowly, pausing at the end of each line. Another, echo each time a word of personal conflict, hate or misery is mentioned. The third person does the same with monarchy, kingdom or country.

2 Close-ups

The changed loyalties of the other characters on stage is a perfect opportunity for Richard to expose their hypocrisy without revealing his own. Richard seizes the chance. At line 146, Rivers says to Richard 'if you should be our king'; Richard replies 'If I should be?'. Speak Richard's line four times, emphasising a different word in the sentence each time. Decide which facial expression best accompanies each of the four versions and which version best fits Richard's intention at this moment.

---

factious fighting
battle army
forswore perjured
  (broke his oath to the king)
meed reward

childish-foolish childishly simple
cacodemon evil spirit
pirates thieves
pilled plundered

MARGARET [*Aside*] Ay, and much better blood than his or thine.
RICHARD In all which time, you and your husband Grey   125
        Were factious for the house of Lancaster,
        And, Rivers, so were you. Was not your husband
        In Margaret's battle at Saint Albans slain?
        Let me put in your minds, if you forget,
        What you have been ere this, and what you are;   130
        Withal, what I have been, and what I am.
MARGARET [*Aside*] A murderous villain, and so still thou art.
RICHARD Poor Clarence did forsake his father Warwick,
        Ay, and forswore himself, which Jesu pardon.
MARGARET [*Aside*] Which God revenge.   135
RICHARD To fight on Edward's party for the crown.
        And for his meed, poor lord, he is mewed up.
        I would to God my heart were flint, like Edward's,
        Or Edward's soft and pitiful, like mine.
        I am too childish-foolish for this world.   140
MARGARET [*Aside*] Hie thee to hell for shame, and leave this world,
        Thou cacodemon. There thy kingdom is.
RIVERS My lord of Gloucester, in those busy days
        Which here you urge to prove us enemies,
        We followed then our lord, our sovereign king.   145
        So should we you, if you should be our king.
RICHARD If I should be? I had rather be a pedlar.
        Far be it from my heart, the thought thereof.
ELIZABETH As little joy, my lord, as you suppose
        You should enjoy were you this country's king,
        As little joy you may suppose in me   150
        That I enjoy, being the queen thereof.
MARGARET [*Aside*] As little joy enjoys the queen thereof,
        For I am she, and altogether joyless.
        I can no longer hold me patient –   155
        Hear me, you wrangling pirates, that fall out
        In sharing that which you have pilled from me.
        Which of you trembles not that looks on me?
        If not that I am queen, you bow like subjects,
        Yet that by you deposed, you quake like rebels.   160
        Ah, gentle villain, do not turn away.
RICHARD Foul wrinkled witch, what mak'st thou in my sight?

Margaret demands the return of her throne. Richard tells how she pitilessly taunted his father. Everyone condemns that deed, but Margaret begins to curse them, prophesying deaths and sorrows ahead.

1 The family picture gallery

In lines 172–9, Richard gives a powerful description of why his father, the Duke of York, cursed Margaret after the Battle of Wakefield. After her victory, Margaret had crowned the defeated York with a paper crown and given him a cloth ('clout') soaked in the blood of his dead son, Rutland, with which to dry his tears. Hastings, Rivers, Dorset and Buckingham join in condemning Margaret, adding detail to Richard's description (lines 181–5).

Work out how to block lines 181–5 to show how the characters are grouped on stage. Would the Woodvilles physically change their position to line up with Richard against Margaret?

2 'Quick curses' (I)

As a Nemesis figure, Margaret spits out her living curses ('quick curses'), just as in the past Richard's father had cursed her. She prophesies that, as she and her family have suffered, so now will the supporters of the house of York.

Lines 195–6: Because of his excessive lifestyle King Edward will die to pay for King Henry's murder.

Lines 197–9: Prince Edward, the king's son, will die violently in his youth, just as Margaret's own son had died.

Lines 200–7: Elizabeth, like Margaret, will suffer a grief-filled life without any power or status, losing her children, husband and position as queen of England.

You will find an activity on Margaret's curses on page 42.

---

repetition telling aloud
marred spoilt
abode staying here
usurp falsely claim
faultless innocent

plagued punished
No man but everybody
catch each other by the throat quarrel viciously
surfeit over-indulgence

MARGARET But repetition of what thou hast marred,
     That will I make before I let thee go.
RICHARD Wert thou not banishèd on pain of death?   165
MARGARET I was. But I do find more pain in banishment
     Than death can yield me here by my abode.
     A husband and a son thou ow'st to me –
     And thou a kingdom – all of you allegiance.
     This sorrow that I have by right is yours,   170
     And all the pleasures you usurp are mine.
RICHARD The curse my noble father laid on thee
     When thou didst crown his warlike brows with paper
     And with thy scorns drew'st rivers from his eyes,
     And then to dry them gav'st the duke a clout   175
     Steeped in the faultless blood of pretty Rutland –
     His curses then, from bitterness of soul
     Denounced against thee, are all fall'n upon thee,
     And God, not we, hath plagued thy bloody deed.
ELIZABETH So just is God, to right the innocent.   180
HASTINGS Oh, 'twas the foulest deed to slay that babe,
     And the most merciless, that e'er was heard of.
RIVERS Tyrants themselves wept when it was reported.
DORSET No man but prophesied revenge for it.
BUCKINGHAM Northumberland, then present, wept to see it.   185
MARGARET What? were you snarling all before I came,
     Ready to catch each other by the throat,
     And turn you all your hatred now on me?
     Did York's dread curse prevail so much with heaven
     That Henry's death, my lovely Edward's death,   190
     Their kingdom's loss, my woeful banishment,
     Should all but answer for that peevish brat?
     Can curses pierce the clouds, and enter heaven?
     Why then, give way, dull clouds, to my quick curses.
     Though not by war, by surfeit die your king,   195
     As ours by murder to make him a king.
     Edward thy son, that now is Prince of Wales,
     For Edward our son, that was Prince of Wales,
     Die in his youth by like untimely violence.
     Thyself a queen, for me that was a queen,   200
     Outlive thy glory, like my wretched self.

Margaret continues her prophetic cursing, wishing grief on Elizabeth and early deaths on Rivers, Dorset and Hastings. Her most powerful curse is on Richard. He turns her words against her.

1 'Quick curses' (II) (in pairs)

Margaret continues her cursing.

Lines 208–12: Rivers, Hastings and Dorset will die prematurely and unexpectedly.

Lines 220–5: Richard will be wracked by conscience, suspect his friends of being traitors, be befriended by traitors and be unable to sleep for nightmares.

Lines 226–31: She pours insults on Richard.

Take turns to speak Margaret's lines 193–231 to bring out the passion of her hatred.

2 Raspberry Ripple

In the UK, a committee, comprised of the disabled, awards prizes called 'Raspberry Ripples' (which is cockney rhyming slang for 'cripples'). They are given to films, plays and TV programmes that have portrayed the disabled most accurately. The awards also censure those that have portrayed the handicapped badly or ignored the problem of physical disability.

Margaret's lines (226–31) are very 'politically incorrect', equating Richard's disability with his evil nature. Write a letter to the Raspberry Ripple committee in which you complain about the offensive nature of the lines. Also write the reply that the Raspberry Ripple Committee might make.

Decked dressed
stalled installed
charm spell, cursing
elvish-marked
 disfigured by evil fairies
abortive disfigured

rooting hog earth-eating pig
 (a white boar was Richard's badge)
sealed branded
rag worthless fragment
I cry thee mercy I
 beg your pardon
period end, full stop

Long mayst thou live to wail thy children's death
And see another, as I see thee now,
Decked in thy rights, as thou art stalled in mine.
Long die thy happy days before thy death,   205
And after many lengthened hours of grief,
Die neither mother, wife, nor England's queen.
Rivers and Dorset, you were standers-by,
And so wast thou, Lord Hastings, when my son
Was stabbed with bloody daggers. God I pray him,   210
That none of you may live his natural age,
But by some unlooked accident cut off.

RICHARD Have done thy charm, thou hateful, withered hag.
MARGARET And leave out thee? Stay, dog, for thou shalt hear me.
If heaven have any grievous plague in store   215
Exceeding those that I can wish upon thee,
Oh, let them keep it till thy sins be ripe
And then hurl down their indignation
On thee, the troubler of the poor world's peace.
The worm of conscience still begnaw thy soul.   220
Thy friends suspect for traitors while thou liv'st,
And take deep traitors for thy dearest friends.
No sleep close up that deadly eye of thine,
Unless it be while some tormenting dream
Affrights thee with a hell of ugly devils.   225
Thou elvish-marked, abortive, rooting hog,
Thou that wast sealed in thy nativity
The slave of nature and the son of hell.
Thou slander of thy heavy mother's womb,
Thou loathèd issue of thy father's loins,   230
Thou rag of honour, thou detested –

RICHARD   Margaret.
MARGARET Richard.
RICHARD Ha?
MARGARET I call thee not.
RICHARD I cry thee mercy then, for I did think   235
That thou hadst called me all these bitter names.
MARGARET Why so I did, but looked for no reply.
Oh, let me make the period to my curse.
RICHARD 'Tis done by me, and ends in 'Margaret'.

Margaret predicts Elizabeth will come to curse Richard.
She rebukes Hastings, Rivers and Dorset, and sorrows for her dead
son. She calls on God to punish the house of York.

1 Who's who? (in groups of five)

Elizabeth's intervention at line 240 diverts Margaret's venom from
Richard to her, which in turn provokes a reaction from Rivers,
Dorset and Hastings. Take parts as Margaret, Hastings, Rivers,
Dorset and Richard. Speak lines 240–63 slowly, and as each person
(or persons) is mentioned in any way, point to them.

2 Lancaster or York: the right to rule?

In lines 255–61, Margaret and Richard briefly become unlikely allies
as they turn on Dorset, Queen Elizabeth's son, only recently raised
to high status.

Margaret observes the greater the rank, the greater the
consequences of a fall (lines 259–60). In lines 263–5, Richard refers
to the house of York's position at the top of the tree. An 'aerie' is
a nest of young eagles, birds of prey. Like those eagles, the house
of York 'scorns the sun'. It was believed to be a sign of the eagle's
noble nature that it could gaze into the sun unblinded. Margaret
ends her brief allegiance with Richard saying that he and the house
of York 'turns the sun to shade' (line 266), causing the death of her
son. She accuses the house of York of unjustly stealing Lancaster's
high status ('Your aerie buildeth in our aerie's nest.').

As you work through the play, keep in mind the question of who
really has the right to rule England.

painted unreal	**malapert** impudent
vain flourish empty show	**blasts** winds
False-boding false prophesying	**dallies** plays with
Were you well served	**Peace** be quiet
if you got what you deserved	

ELIZABETH   Thus have you breathed your curse against yourself.   240
MARGARET   Poor painted queen, vain flourish of my fortune,
        Why strew'st thou sugar on that bottled spider
        Whose deadly web ensnareth thee about?
        Fool, fool, thou whet'st a knife to kill thyself.
        The day will come that thou shalt wish for me   245
        To help thee curse this poisonous bunch-backed toad.
HASTINGS   False-boding woman, end thy frantic curse,
        Lest to thy harm thou move our patience.
MARGARET   Foul shame upon you. You have all moved mine.
RIVERS   Were you well served, you would be taught your duty.   250
MARGARET   To serve me well, you all should do me duty,
        Teach me to be your queen, and you my subjects;
        Oh, serve me well and teach yourselves that duty.
DORSET   Dispute not with her. She is lunatic.
MARGARET   Peace, Master Marquess, you are malapert.   255
        Your fire-new stamp of honour is scarce current.
        Oh, that your young nobility could judge
        What 'twere to lose it and be miserable.
        They that stand high have many blasts to shake them,
        And if they fall, they dash themselves to pieces.   260
RICHARD   Good counsel, marry. Learn it, learn it, marquess.
DORSET   It touches you, my lord, as much as me.
RICHARD   Ay, and much more. But I was born so high.
        Our aerie buildeth in the cedar's top,
        And dallies with the wind and scorns the sun.   265
MARGARET   And turns the sun to shade, alas, alas.
        Witness my son, now in the shade of death,
        Whose bright out-shining beams thy cloudy wrath
        Hath in eternal darkness folded up.
        Your aerie buildeth in our aerie's nest.   270
        Oh God that seest it, do not suffer it;
        As it is won with blood, lost be it so.
BUCKINGHAM   Peace, peace, for shame, if not for charity.
MARGARET   Urge neither charity nor shame to me.
        Uncharitably with me have you dealt,   275
        And shamefully my hopes by you are butchered.
        My charity is outrage, life my shame,
        And in that shame still live my sorrow's rage.

Margaret extends friendship to Buckingham and warns him against Richard. He rejects her, and she prophesies his downfall. Richard expresses sympathy for Margaret and those who imprisoned Clarence.

1 Buckingham disappoints Margaret (in pairs)

Margaret, having accused everyone of responsibility for the bloody deeds of the civil war, now turns to Buckingham. She says he had no part in harming her family and therefore is the only one she does not curse. She calls him 'princely Buckingham' because he was a descendant of Thomas, Duke of Gloucester, the youngest son of King Edward III.

Take parts as Buckingham and Margaret and speak what they say in lines 279–94, indicating how Margaret pleads with Buckingham in her first two speeches. Then speak their lines 296–304, exploring how Margaret's tone could change as Buckingham does not respond as she hopes he will.

2 Richard plays the innocent again (in pairs)

Actors playing Richard try to bring out Richard's humorous delight in clever play-acting unnoticed by those on stage. Part of his style is mock innocence and false piety (pretending to be very religious), often tinged with menace.

Take turns to speak everything Richard says on the opposite page, exploring different uses of tone to influence meaning. Line 310 is about Elizabeth taking over Margaret's position as queen, and lines 311–12 are about the dying King Edward.

You will find another activity on his 'mock innocent' style on page 48.

---

league allegiance, bonding
amity friendship
fair befall good fortune come to
rankle fester
ministers devils
counsel advice

soothe conciliate, flatter
muse wonder
hot eager
franked up styed like a pig
scathe injury

BUCKINGHAM Have done, have done.

MARGARET Oh princely Buckingham, I'll kiss thy hand   280
       In sign of league and amity with thee.
       Now fair befall thee and thy noble house.
       Thy garments are not spotted with our blood,
       Nor thou within the compass of my curse.

BUCKINGHAM Nor no one here, for curses never pass   285
       The lips of those that breathe them in the air.

MARGARET I will not think but they ascend the sky
       And there awake God's gentle sleeping peace.
       Oh Buckingham, take heed of yonder dog.
       Look when he fawns, he bites; and when he bites,   290
       His venom tooth will rankle to the death.
       Have not to do with him; beware of him.
       Sin, death, and hell have set their marks on him,
       And all their ministers attend on him.

RICHARD What doth she say, my lord of Buckingham?   295

BUCKINGHAM Nothing that I respect, my gracious lord.

MARGARET What, dost thou scorn me for my gentle counsel
       And soothe the devil that I warn thee from?
       Oh, but remember this another day,
       When he shall split thy very heart with sorrow,   300
       And say poor Margaret was a prophetess.
       Live each of you the subjects to his hate,
       And he to yours, and all of you to God's.

                                                   Exit

BUCKINGHAM My hair doth stand on end to hear her curses.

RIVERS And so doth mine. I muse why she's at liberty.   305

RICHARD I cannot blame her, by God's holy mother,
       She hath had too much wrong, and I repent
       My part thereof that I have done to her.

ELIZABETH I never did her any to my knowledge.

RICHARD Yet you have all the vantage of her wrong.   310
       I was too hot to do somebody good
       That is too cold in thinking of it now.
       Marry, as for Clarence, he is well repaid;
       He is franked up to fatting for his pains.
       God pardon them that are the cause thereof.   315

RIVERS A virtuous and a Christian-like conclusion,
       To pray for them that have done scathe to us.

47

Catesby informs the queen and courtiers that King Edward has sent for them. Alone on stage, Richard discloses his techniques for deceiving others. He instructs the murderers to kill Clarence quickly, without pity.

1 Mock innocence and false piety (in pairs)

In lines 324–38, Richard admits to the audience that the plots ('mischiefs') he has instigated ('set abroach') he blames on the evil actions of others. He uses Derby, Hastings and Buckingham as dupes ('gulls') persuading them that the queen has caused Clarence's imprisonment. When his 'gulls' urge him to take revenge on the Woodvilles, he uses the bible ('scripture', 'holy writ') to pretend he pardons his enemies.

Improvise a conversation between Richard and one of his 'gulls' to imitate Richard's style of saintly innocence and forgiveness.

2 'The warrant': Richard's forward planning (in pairs)

The fact that Richard already possesses the warrant (line 344) which officially orders Clarence's death demonstrates the well-planned and premeditated nature of his 'secret mischiefs'. Use lines 342–4 to work out some stage business with the warrant that Richard might use in order to make the audience smile, and to remind them of his duplicity.

3 Inferiors, equals or conspirators? (in pairs)

Richard welcomes the murderers and begs them not to be moved by Clarence's persuasive speech. Mime three ways in which he might greet them: as a master to servants; as equals; very secretly and furtively. Then speak lines 339–55 and discuss which style of greeting is the most effective.

---

well advised careful how I speak
brawl quarrel
charge action
beweep weep for
whet encourage

Crosby Place
 Richard's London home
sudden quick
obdurate unbending
mark listen to

RICHARD So do I ever, being well advised.
       (*Speaks to himself*) For had I cursed now, I had cursed
       myself.

Enter CATESBY

CATESBY Madam, his majesty doth call for you,   320
       And for your grace, and you, my gracious lord.
ELIZABETH Catesby, I come. Lords, will you go with me?
RIVERS We wait upon your grace.

Exeunt all but Richard

RICHARD I do the wrong, and first begin to brawl.
       The secret mischiefs that I set abroach   325
       I lay unto the grievous charge of others.
       Clarence, who I indeed have cast in darkness,
       I do beweep to many simple gulls,
       Namely to Derby, Hastings, Buckingham,
       And tell them 'tis the queen and her allies   330
       That stir the king against the duke my brother.
       Now they believe it, and withal whet me
       To be revenged on Rivers, Dorset, Grey.
       But then I sigh, and with a piece of scripture
       Tell them that God bids us do good for evil.   335
       And thus I clothe my naked villainy
       With odd old ends stol'n forth of holy writ,
       And seem a saint when most I play the devil.

Enter two MURDERERS

       But soft, here come my executioners –
       How now, my hardy, stout, resolvèd mates,   340
       Are you now going to dispatch this thing?
FIRST MURDERER We are, my lord, and come to have the warrant
       That we may be admitted where he is.
RICHARD Well thought upon, I have it here about me.
       When you have done, repair to Crosby Place.   345
       But, sirs, be sudden in the execution,
       Withal obdurate. Do not hear him plead,
       For Clarence is well spoken and perhaps
       May move your hearts to pity if you mark him.

Richard dismisses the murderers to kill Clarence. In the Tower, Clarence recounts his dream of escaping to Burgundy by boat, from which he was struck overboard by Richard.

1 'Go, go, dispatch'

The word 'dispatch' is a pun which can mean either 'kill' or 'go quickly'. Invent gestures that Richard might use to accompany his words.

2 Symbolising the Tower

In modern theatres, as on Shakespeare's own stage, one scene flows quickly into the next with no long delay for changing the set. Imagine you are set designer. Sketch how you would present the Tower to symbolise its atmosphere and gruesome associations.

3 Clarence's nightmare

In lines 9–63, Clarence recounts his dream that he escaped from the Tower, and while sailing to Burgundy was pushed into the sea by Richard. Drowning, he experiences the terrors of death as he goes to hell. There, he is accused of perjury and murder and taken to be tortured. He wakes, thinking he is in hell.

The episode shows Clarence awakening from a dream which he can scarcely believe. It presents the nature of conscience and retribution within the context of England's bloody civil war: the Wars of the Roses. Its series of vivid pictures provides one of the most poetic moments in the play. The dream sequence captures a moment of self-revelation as Clarence begins to realise the terrifying consequences of his actions. You will find activities on Clarence's dream on pages 52 and 54.

prate chat
millstones blocks of granite
heavily sadly
Christian faithful man
  devout and religious man

Burgundy the Low Countries,
  a Yorkist sanctuary
hatches deck
cited up recalled
stay steady, save

SECOND MURDERER   Tut, tut, my lord, we will not stand to prate;   350
        Talkers are no good doers. Be assured
        We go to use our hands and not our tongues.
RICHARD   Your eyes drop millstones when fools' eyes fall tears.
        I like you, lads. About your business straight.
        Go, go, dispatch.
MURDERERS   We will, my noble lord.   355

Exeunt

ACT 1 SCENE 4
A room in the Tower of London

Enter CLARENCE and KEEPER

KEEPER   Why looks your grace so heavily today?
CLARENCE   Oh, I have passed a miserable night,
        So full of fearful dreams, of ugly sights,
        That as I am a Christian faithful man,
        I would not spend another such a night   5
        Though 'twere to buy a world of happy days,
        So full of dismal terror was the time.
KEEPER   What was your dream, my lord? I pray you, tell me.
CLARENCE   Methoughts that I had broken from the Tower,
        And was embarked to cross to Burgundy,   10
        And in my company my brother Gloucester,
        Who from my cabin tempted me to walk
        Upon the hatches. Thence we looked toward England
        And cited up a thousand heavy times
        During the wars of York and Lancaster   15
        That had befall'n us. As we paced along
        Upon the giddy footing of the hatches,
        Methought that Gloucester stumbled, and in falling
        Struck me, that thought to stay him, overboard
        Into the tumbling billows of the main.   20

Clarence tells the Keeper of the agony of drowning. He recounts how his soul goes to hell, where Warwick accuses him of betrayal. Prince Edward, whom he killed, adds another accusation.

1 Dreams of drowning (in pairs)

Clarence's dream of drowning divides into four sections. Lines 21–5 tell of the physical pain of drowning; lines 26–8 describe the wealth on the sea bed; lines 29–33 mock the worthlessness of that wealth; and lines 36–41 return to the pain Clarence feels as he wishes to die but cannot.

For each section, one person speaks the lines while the other echoes the key words: for example, words signifying 'pain' in the first section, 'wealth' in the second, and so on.

2 Dreams of hell (in pairs)

Hell was a real and terrifying place for the Elizabethans (see page 230). Clarence describes the journey of his tormented soul to hell in lines 43–63. He crosses the River Styx ('melancholy flood') ferried by Charon ('that sour ferryman') to hell ('the kingdom of perpetual night') where his soul is judged. There, he is first accused of perjury by his father-in-law Warwick (Clarence had betrayed Warwick when he changed his allegiance in the Wars of the Roses). His second accuser is Edward, Prince of Wales, still covered in his own blood, murdered by Richard and Clarence after the Battle of Tewkesbury. He demands that Clarence be taken by devils and tortured in hell. The shrieking of the 'foul fiends' (see line 58) convinces Clarence he is still in hell even after he awakes.

Step into role as Clarence and the Keeper (lines 43–65). In your own words, describe your journey through hell to the Keeper, then exchange roles.

Inestimable unable to be counted	**shadow** shade
yield the ghost die	(the ghost of Prince Edward)
bulk body	**fleeting** inconstant, fickle
perjury oath breaking	**furies** avenging goddesses

Oh Lord, methought what pain it was to drown,
What dreadful noise of water in mine ears,
What sights of ugly death within mine eyes.
Methoughts I saw a thousand fearful wracks,
A thousand men that fishes gnawed upon,   25
Wedges of gold, great anchors, heaps of pearl,
Inestimable stones, unvalued jewels,
All scattered in the bottom of the sea.
Some lay in dead men's skulls, and in the holes
Where eyes did once inhabit there were crept,   30
As 'twere in scorn of eyes, reflecting gems,
That wooed the slimy bottom of the deep
And mocked the dead bones that lay scattered by.

KEEPER   Had you such leisure in the time of death
To gaze upon these secrets of the deep?   35

CLARENCE   Methought I had, and often did I strive
To yield the ghost; but still the envious flood
Stopped in my soul and would not let it forth
To find the empty, vast, and wandering air,
But smothered it within my panting bulk,   40
Who almost burst to belch it in the sea.

KEEPER   Awaked you not in this sore agony?

CLARENCE   No, no, my dream was lengthened after life.
Oh, then began the tempest to my soul.
I passed, methought, the melancholy flood,   45
With that sour ferryman which poets write of,
Unto the kingdom of perpetual night.
The first that there did greet my stranger-soul
Was my great father-in-law, renownèd Warwick,
Who spake aloud, 'What scourge for perjury   50
Can this dark monarchy afford false Clarence?'
And so he vanished. Then came wandering by
A shadow like an angel, with bright hair
Dabbled in blood, and he shrieked out aloud,
'Clarence is come: false, fleeting, perjured Clarence,   55
That stabbed me in the field by Tewkesbury.
Seize on him, furies, take him unto torment.'

Clarence, recalling his dream, confesses his misdeeds. He prays for mercy from God for his family, then sleeps. Brakenbury reflects on how outward appearance often hides inner turmoil. The murderers bring Richard's warrant.

1 After the dream (in groups of three)

Clarence admits committing horrific acts during the civil war, and his conversation with the Keeper reveals his troubled state of mind.

Talk together about how far (if at all) Clarence's dream journey of self-exploration and confession has changed your opinion of him. Then take parts as Clarence and the Keeper and speak lines 64–75. The third person, as director, advise on the tone and the action to express:

- the fear in both men;
- the confessional and religious tone of Clarence;
- the Keeper's sympathy for Clarence.

2 The cares of high office (in pairs)

The actor playing Brakenbury asks you for help. He finds some of lines 76–83 unclear, and is unsure what he should do as he speaks. He is confident in his interpretation of the first four lines (that sorrow destroys the borders between the seasons, sleep, day and night; and that even the title 'prince' cannot prevent the consequences of sorrow).

Advise the actor of your interpretation of the meaning of the second part of Brakenbury's speech (lines 80–3), and suggest how this will affect his behaviour towards the sleeping Clarence. 'Unfelt imaginations' could mean 'things imagined but not experienced', or 'ordinary people imagine a happiness that princes have never felt'.

---

legion battalion	**appease** pacify
Environed imprisoned	**inward toil** unrest of mind
season time	**brief** rude
requites rewards	**commission** warrant

With that, methought, a legion of foul fiends
Environed me, and howlèd in mine ears
Such hideous cries that with the very noise   60
I trembling waked, and for a season after
Could not believe but that I was in hell,
Such terrible impression made my dream.
KEEPER   No marvel, lord, though it affrighted you.
I am afraid, methinks, to hear you tell it.   65
CLARENCE   Ah keeper, keeper, I have done these things
That now give evidence against my soul
For Edward's sake, and see how he requites me.
Oh God, if my deep prayers cannot appease thee,
But thou wilt be avenged on my misdeeds,   70
Yet execute thy wrath in me alone.
Oh, spare my guiltless wife and my poor children.
Keeper, I prithee sit by me awhile.
My soul is heavy, and I fain would sleep.
KEEPER   I will, my lord. God give your grace good rest.   75

Enter BRAKENBURY, *the Lieutenant*

BRAKENBURY   Sorrow breaks seasons and reposing hours,
Makes the night morning and the noontide night.
Princes have but their titles for their glories,
An outward honour for an inward toil,
And for unfelt imaginations   80
They often feel a world of restless cares;
So that between their titles and low name
There's nothing differs but the outward fame.

Enter two MURDERERS

FIRST MURDERER   Ho, who's here?
BRAKENBURY   What wouldst thou, fellow? And how cam'st thou   85
hither?
SECOND MURDERER   I would speak with Clarence, and I came hither on
my legs.
BRAKENBURY   What, so brief?
FIRST MURDERER   'Tis better, sir, than to be tedious.   90
Let him see our commission, and talk no more.

Brakenbury leaves the two murderers alone with Clarence. They discuss whether to kill Clarence immediately. The Second Murderer fears that he will be damned for killing Clarence, but is tempted by the thought of reward.

1 Brakenbury's motives (in pairs)

Brakenbury has received Richard's warrant. In contrast to the ambiguity of his first speech, he is now very clear about what he must do to protect himself from blame. Take turns to speak lines 92–8, then talk together about Brakenbury's reaction to the warrant. Why does he want to tell King Edward how he has acted? Suggest three or four possible motives.

2 The pangs of conscience? (I) (in pairs)

Conscience is a major theme of the play. Characters delight in or are tortured by thoughts of their misdeeds. Both Clarence and Brakenbury have listened anxiously to their consciences, and now Shakespeare presents the murderers wrestling with their sense of right and wrong in a witty and clever way as they balance conscience and payment. The Second Murderer is worried that Clarence's murder could damn his soul but is persuaded by the reward he will be given by Richard. Even the First Murderer seems to briefly feel the pangs of conscience.

To gain a first impression of this 'wrestling with conscience' episode take parts as the two murderers and speak lines 100–44. Try to bring out both the brutality and the wit.

deliver hand over	**passionate** compassionate
reason discuss	**wont** accustomed
urging putting forward an idea	**tells** counts
remorse pity	**entertain** want

[Brakenbury] reads

BRAKENBURY   I am in this commanded to deliver
               The noble Duke of Clarence to your hands.
               I will not reason what is meant hereby,
               Because I will be guiltless from the meaning.   95
               There lies the duke asleep, and there the keys.
               I'll to the king and signify to him
               That thus I have resigned to you my charge.

                              Exeunt Brakenbury and Keeper

FIRST MURDERER   You may, sir, 'tis a point of wisdom. Fare you well.
SECOND MURDERER   What, shall we stab him as he sleeps?   100
FIRST MURDERER   No. He'll say 'twas done cowardly, when he wakes.
SECOND MURDERER   Why, he shall never wake until the great
     judgement day.
FIRST MURDERER   Why, then he'll say we stabbed him sleeping.
SECOND MURDERER   The urging of that word judgement hath bred a   105
     kind of remorse in me.
FIRST MURDERER   What? Art thou afraid?
SECOND MURDERER   Not to kill him, having a warrant,
               But to be damned for killing him, from the which
               No warrant can defend me.   110
FIRST MURDERER   I thought thou hadst been resolute.
SECOND MURDERER   So I am, to let him live.
FIRST MURDERER   I'll back to the Duke of Gloucester and tell him so.
SECOND MURDERER   Nay, I prithee stay a little.
               I hope this passionate humour of mine will change.   115
               It was wont to hold me but while one tells twenty.
FIRST MURDERER   How dost thou feel thyself now?
SECOND MURDERER   Some certain dregs of conscience are yet within
     me.
FIRST MURDERER   Remember our reward when the deed's done.   120
SECOND MURDERER   Come, he dies. I had forgot the reward.
FIRST MURDERER   Where's thy conscience now?
SECOND MURDERER   Oh, in the Duke of Gloucester's purse.
FIRST MURDERER   When he opens his purse to give us our reward, thy
     conscience flies out.   125
SECOND MURDERER   'Tis no matter; let it go. There's few or none will
     entertain it.
FIRST MURDERER   What if it come to thee again?

The murderers reject the claims of conscience. They decide to strike Clarence on the head and throw his body in a barrel of wine. Clarence wakes and guesses correctly that they have come to murder him.

1 The pangs of conscience (II) (in pairs)

Lines 129–37 are the Second Murderer's catalogue of how conscience constrains man's behaviour. One person speak the lines while the other acts out what conscience makes men do.

2 Get on with it! (in groups of three)

Some critics argue that the two murderers' lines 100–44 are irrelevant to the plot. The director wants to cut the lines to reduce the play's running time. The actors playing the murderers disagree, arguing that the episode expresses major themes of the play. Improvise the discussion which takes place.

3 On stage – or off stage? (in pairs)

The stage designer wants to cut the words: 'in the next room' from line 146 because s/he is adamant that 'the malmsey butt' (a huge barrel of wine) should be visible to the audience as a strong physical presence of Clarence's fear of drowning. The director disagrees. Step into role as designer and director and argue your point of view.

4 Different attitudes to killing? (in pairs)

Do the two murderers have different attitudes towards killing Clarence? Check through lines 100–64, with one person examining the attitude of the First Murderer while the other does the same for the Second Murderer.

---

shamefaced bashful, ashamed
bosom heart
beggars impoverishes
Take the devil
  resist or stop the devil

insinuate be friendly with
tall brave
Take him on the costard
  hit him on the head
sop bread or cake soaked in wine

SECOND MURDERER I'll not meddle with it; it makes a man a coward.
    A man cannot steal but it accuseth him. A man cannot swear but   130
    it checks him. A man cannot lie with his neighbour's wife, but it
    detects him. 'Tis a blushing, shamefaced spirit that mutinies in a
    man's bosom. It fills a man full of obstacles. It made me once
    restore a purse of gold that by chance I found. It beggars any man
    that keeps it. It is turned out of towns and cities for a dangerous   135
    thing, and every man that means to live well endeavours to trust
    to himself and live without it.
FIRST MURDERER 'Tis even now at my elbow, persuading me not to kill
    the duke.
SECOND MURDERER Take the devil in thy mind, and believe him not.   140
    He would insinuate with thee but to make thee sigh.
FIRST MURDERER I am strong framed, he cannot prevail with me.
SECOND MURDERER Spoke like a tall man that respects thy reputation.
    Come, shall we fall to work?
FIRST MURDERER Take him on the costard with the hilts of thy sword,   145
    and then throw him into the malmsey butt in the next room.
SECOND MURDERER Oh, excellent device. And make a sop of him.
FIRST MURDERER Soft, he wakes.
SECOND MURDERER Strike!
FIRST MURDERER No, we'll reason with him.   150
CLARENCE Where art thou, keeper? Give me a cup of wine.
SECOND MURDERER You shall have wine enough, my lord, anon.
CLARENCE In God's name, what art thou?
FIRST MURDERER A man, as you are.
CLARENCE But not, as I am, royal.   155
FIRST MURDERER Nor you, as we are, loyal.
CLARENCE Thy voice is thunder, but thy looks are humble.
FIRST MURDERER My voice is now the king's, my looks mine own.
CLARENCE How darkly and how deadly dost thou speak!
    Your eyes do menace me. Why look you pale?   160
    Who sent you hither? Wherefore do you come?
SECOND MURDERER To, to, to –
CLARENCE To murder me?
BOTH Ay, ay.
CLARENCE You scarcely have the hearts to tell me so,   165
    And therefore cannot have the hearts to do it.
    Wherein, my friends, have I offended you?
FIRST MURDERER Offended us you have not, but the king.

Clarence argues that he has not been convicted of any crime, and that only God can punish. He claims that he murdered Prince Edward for the sake of his brother, King Edward.

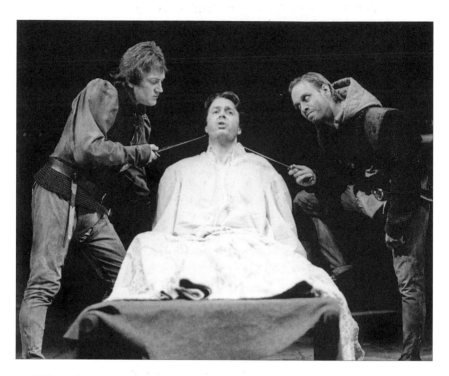

'Therefore prepare to die.' Clarence, to save his life, appeals to the Christian beliefs of damnation (being punished forever in hell for one's sins on earth) and the supreme authority of God's law. He argues the religious law of God ('The great King of kings') is above the secular power of the earthly king.

quest jury
is damnable condemns you to hell
Erroneous vassals mistaken slaves
table of his law the ten
  commandments
Spurn at his edict reject his law

receive the sacrament
  religiously vow
thy sovereign's son
  Henry VI's son, Prince Edward
dear important

CLARENCE I shall be reconciled to him again.

SECOND MURDERER Never, my lord. Therefore prepare to die.   170

CLARENCE Are you drawn forth among a world of men
      To slay the innocent? What is my offence?
      Where is the evidence that doth accuse me?
      What lawful quest have given their verdict up
      Unto the frowning judge? Or who pronounced   175
      The bitter sentence of poor Clarence' death
      Before I be convict by course of law?
      To threaten me with death is most unlawful.
      I charge you, as you hope for any goodness,
      That you depart and lay no hands on me.   180
      The deed you undertake is damnable.

FIRST MURDERER What we will do, we do upon command.

SECOND MURDERER And he that hath commanded is our king.

CLARENCE Erroneous vassals! The great King of kings
      Hath in the table of his law commanded   185
      That thou shalt do no murder. Will you then
      Spurn at his edict and fulfil a man's?
      Take heed, for he holds vengeance in his hand
      To hurl upon their heads that break his law.

SECOND MURDERER And that same vengeance doth he hurl on thee   190
      For false forswearing and for murder, too.
      Thou didst receive the sacrament to fight
      In quarrel of the House of Lancaster.

FIRST MURDERER And, like a traitor to the name of God,
      Didst break that vow, and with thy treacherous blade   195
      Unripped'st the bowels of thy sovereign's son.

SECOND MURDERER Whom thou wast sworn to cherish and defend.

FIRST MURDERER How canst thou urge God's dreadful law to us
      When thou hast broke it in such dear degree?

CLARENCE Alas! For whose sake did I that ill deed?   200
      For Edward, for my brother, for his sake.
      He sends you not to murder me for this,
      For in that sin he is as deep as I.
      If God will be avengèd for the deed,
      Oh, know you yet, he doth it publicly.   205
      Take not the quarrel from his powerful arm.
      He needs no indirect or lawless course
      To cut off those that have offended him.

Clarence, believing King Edward seeks his death, claims Richard will reward the murderers for letting him live. Refusing to believe Richard has ordered his murder, he argues that the murderers will be damned for killing him.

1 Who's who? (in groups of six)

Lines 209–29 are filled with references to the Plantagenet family: Prince Edward (son of King Henry VI); King Edward; Richard (Duke of Gloucester); the Duke of York. Take parts as Clarence (himself a Plantagenet) and those four characters. The sixth person speaks all the lines slowly, and each person raises their hand as their character is mentioned. The remainder should point to the character they believe is referred to. Try to reconcile any disagreements. You will find the family tree of the Plantagenets on page 252 helpful.

2 A brother's love (in groups of three)

Clarence cannot believe that his brother Richard wants him murdered, but the two murderers know the truth: Richard is scheming and duplicitous.

Abruptly, Clarence abandons his belief that Richard loves him. Shakespeare leaves it up to the actor to work out between lines 237 and 241 what triggers Clarence's realisation of the truth and how he responds to the news that his brother seeks his death. Step into the roles of Clarence and the murderers and discuss what each man might do to show the audience what brings about Clarence's sudden realisation that his brother seeks his death.

minister activist, actor
gallant-springing ... novice courageous young Prince Edward
meed reward
lessoned taught

labour my delivery work for my release
thraldom slavery
set you on instructed you

FIRST MURDERER   Who made thee, then, a bloody minister
    When gallant-springing brave Plantagenet,   210
    That princely novice, was struck dead by thee?
CLARENCE   My brother's love, the devil, and my rage.
FIRST MURDERER   Thy brother's love, our duty, and thy faults
    Provoke us hither now to slaughter thee.
CLARENCE   If you do love my brother, hate not me.   215
    I am his brother, and I love him well.
    If you are hired for meed, go back again,
    And I will send you to my brother Gloucester,
    Who shall reward you better for my life
    Than Edward will for tidings of my death.   220
SECOND MURDERER   You are deceived. Your brother Gloucester hates
  you.
CLARENCE   Oh, no, he loves me, and he holds me dear.
    Go you to him from me.
FIRST MURDERER   Ay, so we will.   225
CLARENCE   Tell him, when that our princely father York
    Blessed his three sons with his victorious arm,
    He little thought of this divided friendship.
    Bid Gloucester think of this, and he will weep.
FIRST MURDERER   Ay, millstones, as he lessoned us to weep.   230
CLARENCE   Oh, do not slander him, for he is kind.
FIRST MURDERER   Right, as snow in harvest.
    Come, you deceive yourself,
    'Tis he that sends us to destroy you here.
CLARENCE   It cannot be, for he bewept my fortune,   235
    And hugged me in his arms, and swore with sobs
    That he would labour my delivery.
FIRST MURDERER   Why, so he doth, when he delivers you
    From this earth's thraldom to the joys of heaven.
SECOND MURDERER   Make peace with God, for you must die, my lord.   240
CLARENCE   Have you that holy feeling in your souls
    To counsel me to make my peace with God,
    And are you yet to your own souls so blind
    That you will war with God by murdering me?
    Oh sirs, consider, they that set you on   245
    To do this deed will hate you for the deed.
SECOND MURDERER   What shall we do?

Clarence begs the murderers to have pity, but he is stabbed by the First Murderer, who drags off the body and throws it in the malmsey butt. The Second Murderer wishes he had saved Clarence.

1 Staging Clarence's murder (in small groups)

The murder of Clarence is the dramatic climax of the act. Work out how to stage the episode to greatest dramatic effect using the following to help you.

a Clarence's words 'My friend, I spy some pity in thy looks' (line 256), and the following 'Look behind you, my lord' suggest that the Second Murderer tries to prevent the killing (but there are alternative interpretations). One person speaks lines 255–61; the others play Clarence and the two murderers. In very slow motion, devise the most dramatically effective method for the stabbing of Clarence.

b The actor playing the First Murderer wants Clarence alive after the stabbing so he can be drowned in the malmsey butt. He argues that this will make the scene even more horrific. The actor playing the Second Murderer disagrees, saying that if Clarence were still alive, his remorse would make him intervene to save Clarence from drowning. Talk together about which actor's suggestion you find the more convincing.

c The First Murderer plans to find a temporary hiding place for Clarence's body and make his escape before the deed is discovered. The Second Murderer distances himself from the killing (lines 269–71), wishing he had tried to save Clarence and refusing his share of the reward. Work out how to stage the exits of the two murderers, emphasising their contrasting characters.

---

pent from liberty imprisoned
entreat beg
if thine eye be not a flatterer
  if your appearance is not false
desperately recklessly

fain happily
Pilate Pontius Pilate (who took no
  responsibility for the death of Jesus)
will out
  will become common knowledge

CLARENCE   Relent, and save your souls.
          Which of you, if you were a prince's son,
          Being pent from liberty, as I am now,   250
          If two such murderers as yourselves came to you,
          Would not entreat for life as you would beg,
          Were you in my distress?
FIRST MURDERER Relent? No. 'Tis cowardly and womanish.
CLARENCE Not to relent is beastly, savage, devilish.   255
          My friend, I spy some pity in thy looks.
          Oh, if thine eye be not a flatterer,
          Come thou on my side and entreat for me;
          A begging prince, what beggar pities not?
SECOND MURDERER Look behind you, my lord.   260
FIRST MURDERER Take that, and that.

                    (*Stabs him*)

                                         If all this will not do,
          I'll drown you in the malmsey butt within.

                              Exit [with Clarence's body]

SECOND MURDERER A bloody deed, and desperately dispatched.
          How fain, like Pilate, would I wash my hands
          Of this most grievous murder.   265

                    Enter FIRST MURDERER

FIRST MURDERER How now? What mean'st thou that thou help'st me
          not?
          By heaven, the duke shall know how slack you have been.
SECOND MURDERER I would he knew that I had saved his brother.
          Take thou the fee, and tell him what I say,   270
          For I repent me that the duke is slain.   *Exit*
FIRST MURDERER So do not I. Go, coward as thou art.
          Well, I'll go hide the body in some hole
          Till that the duke give order for his burial;
          And when I have my meed, I will away,   275
          For this will out, and then I must not stay.   *Exit*

Looking back at Act 1
Activities for groups or individuals

1 A dramatic opening

Many productions attempt to establish the play's atmosphere and concerns in its opening moments through a striking dramatic image. Ian McKellen's film begins (before Richard speaks) with an eight-minute sequence that includes a battle followed by Yorkist celebrations. Laurence Olivier's film has a five-minute portrayal of King Edward's coronation before Richard's opening soliloquy. Before Richard speaks what dramatic image or brief sequence would you use to suggest an important theme of the play?

2 Richard insulted

In Scenes 2 and 3, many characters insult and abuse Richard. List as many insults directed at Richard as you can. Suggest what each might mean and identify what common themes and images they share in revealing what others feel about Richard. For example, 'hedgehog' (Scene 2, line 105) could refer to Richard's emblem of the hog or boar, his hunch back, or as a general term for a person without feelings.

3 Richard's secret agenda

Richard makes clear his secret thoughts and intentions through soliloquies or apparently innocuous remarks addressed to characters on stage. For example, in Scene 1, he openly reveals his plot against Clarence and finds ways to insult and arouse suspicions about Queen Elizabeth, the Woodvilles and Jane Shore. Quickly read through Scenes 1, 2 and 3 and identify where he reveals his secret thoughts. Jot down the objectives he has for the future at these moments. Which have been achieved by the end of the Act?

4 Everlasting suffering or eternal happiness?

A major preoccupation of the play is the individual's spiritual state. Throughout the play characters think about their fate after death. They will be judged by their deeds in life and sent to either the bliss of heaven or horrors of hell. Clarence fears hell as a place of perpetual physical and mental torment. Many Elizabethan churches were decorated with terrifying paintings of hell. Either find a medieval depiction of hell, or draw, or describe your own version. (It need not be Elizabethan.)

5 Social status

Make a list of everyone who appears in Act 1 and put them in order of social status. What does the list reveal about Richard's position in the social hierarchy?

Richard's physical appearance is vital to the play. Directors have to decide how to present his disabilities to the audience. Step into roles as director and actor playing Richard and discuss some possible ways of presenting Richard's physical appearance. Study the picture of Richard before you begin your discussion.

> *King Edward attempts to reconcile the quarrelling nobles. Queen Elizabeth, Rivers and Dorset (the Woodvilles) swear love and friendship with Hastings. The king asks Buckingham to join the peace pact.*

1 Actions speak louder than words? (in groups of six)

King Edward attempts to reconcile the Woodville family (Queen Elizabeth, Dorset her son and Rivers her brother) with those who oppose them (Hastings and Buckingham). The episode is full of dramatic irony because it occurs immediately after the scene of Clarence's murder. King Edward, unaware of that event, uses the language of piety, love and peace. The irony can also be underlined by how the characters behave, using actions that contrast with their words of peace.

a One person speak all lines 1–40. The others echo all the words and phrases of friendship and religion.

b How genuine is the reconciliation? Take parts as King Edward, Rivers, Hastings, Queen Elizabeth, Dorset and Buckingham. Act out lines 1–40 using all actions that are mentioned or indicated, for example, 'Rivers and Hastings, take each other's hand' (line 7); 'So thrive I, as I truly swear the like' (line 11). Perform the lines twice, the first time so that an audience would see it as a sincere agreement of friendship. In your second version, act out the episode in a way that shows all the reconciliations are insincere and that enmity still exists between the characters.

c King Edward warns Rivers and Hastings not to be insincere ('dally') in front of him, because God ('the King of kings') will see through their deceit and ensure they kill each other ('end'). You can find out more on page 230–2 about how Shakespeare makes Christian beliefs a central preoccupation of the play.

---

peers lords
united league friendship
embassage message
my redeemer to redeem me
  hence my Christ to save me
  (Edward expects to die)
Dissemble not do not pretend

purged cleansed
thrive flourish
unfeignedly
  genuinely, without pretence
inviolable permanent, unbreakable
princely Buckingham
  (see page 46)

ACT 2 SCENE 1
London: a room in King Edward's palace

Flourish. Enter KING EDWARD (sick), QUEEN ELIZABETH,
LORD MARQUESS DORSET, RIVERS, HASTINGS, CATESBY,
BUCKINGHAM and others

KING EDWARD Why, so. Now have I done a good day's work.
    You peers, continue this united league.
    I every day expect an embassage
    From my redeemer to redeem me hence.
    And more to peace my soul shall part to heaven,   5
    Since I have made my friends at peace on earth.
    Rivers and Hastings, take each other's hand.
    Dissemble not your hatred; swear your love.
RIVERS By heaven, my soul is purged from grudging hate,
    And with my hand I seal my true heart's love.   10
HASTINGS So thrive I, as I truly swear the like.
KING EDWARD Take heed you dally not before your king,
    Lest he that is the supreme King of kings
    Confound your hidden falsehood and award
    Either of you to be the other's end.   15
HASTINGS So prosper I, as I swear perfect love.
RIVERS And I, as I love Hastings with my heart.
KING EDWARD Madam, yourself is not exempt from this,
    Nor you, son Dorset, Buckingham, nor you;
    You have been factious one against the other.   20
    Wife, love Lord Hastings, let him kiss your hand,
    And what you do, do it unfeignedly.
ELIZABETH There, Hastings, I will never more remember
    Our former hatred, so thrive I and mine.
KING EDWARD Dorset, embrace him. Hastings, love Lord Marquess.   25
DORSET This interchange of love, I here protest,
    Upon my part shall be inviolable.
HASTINGS And so swear I.
KING EDWARD Now, princely Buckingham, seal thou this league
    With thy embracements to my wife's allies,   30
    And make me happy in your unity.

Buckingham pledges his love and loyalty to King Edward.
The king wishes for Richard to arrive to complete the peace process.
Richard enters and expresses peace and goodwill to everyone present.

1 Asking for trouble

Buckingham's speech is full of dramatic irony. The fate that he wishes on himself if he is disloyal to Edward is exactly what happens to him later in the play. As you read on, watch out for how he is betrayed by 'a friend' (line 36) who is crafty ('Deep'), false ('hollow') and 'treacherous, and full of guile'.

2 Enter Ratcliffe and Richard

In some productions, Richard and Ratcliffe are already on stage and hear King Edward's wish that Gloucester (line 43) were present. Suggest what dramatic effects might be achieved by having Richard and Ratcliffe enter unobserved by others much earlier in the scene.

3 Sincere friendship?

Richard asks to be reconciled with those he might have offended. But he suggests that people's hostility arises from wrong information ('false intelligence') and incorrect conclusions ('wrong surmise'). He suggests that if he did do anything that was resented by others ('hardly borne'), it was done 'unwillingly, or in my rage'.

a How might an actor playing Richard make it clear to an audience that his words are not sincere?

b 'Lord Woodville' and 'Lord Scales' (line 68) are other titles of 'Lord Rivers'. How might Richard make a joke of line 68?

c Suggest how each character reacts to Richard's offer of friendship.

---

but (line 33) except
cordial medicine
wanteth is only missing
period finish

swelling angry
wrong-incensèd wrongly angered
heap company
without desert without cause

BUCKINGHAM Whenever Buckingham doth turn his hate
      Upon your grace, but with all duteous love
      Doth cherish you and yours, God punish me
      With hate in those where I expect most love.   35
      When I have most need to employ a friend,
      And most assurèd that he is a friend,
      Deep, hollow, treacherous, and full of guile
      Be he unto me. This do I beg of heaven,
      When I am cold in love to you or yours.   40

Embrace

KING EDWARD A pleasing cordial, princely Buckingham,
      Is this thy vow unto my sickly heart.
      There wanteth now our brother Gloucester here
      To make the blessèd period of this peace.
BUCKINGHAM And in good time,   45
      Here comes Sir Richard Ratcliffe and the Duke.

Enter RATCLIFFE *and* RICHARD

RICHARD Good morrow to my sovereign king and queen;
      And princely peers, a happy time of day.
KING EDWARD Happy indeed, as we have spent the day.
      Gloucester, we have done deeds of charity,   50
      Made peace of enmity, fair love of hate,
      Between these swelling, wrong-incensèd peers.
RICHARD A blessèd labour, my most sovereign lord.
      Among this princely heap, if any here
      By false intelligence or wrong surmise   55
      Hold me a foe; if I unwillingly, or in my rage
      Have aught committed that is hardly borne
      To any in this presence, I desire
      To reconcile me to his friendly peace.
      'Tis death to me to be at enmity;   60
      I hate it and desire all good men's love.
      First, madam, I entreat true peace of you,
      Which I will purchase with my duteous service;
      Of you, my noble cousin Buckingham,
      If ever any grudge were lodged between us;   65
      Of you and you, Lord Rivers, and of Dorset,
      That all without desert have frowned on me;
      Of you, Lord Woodville, and Lord Scales, of you;
      Dukes, earls, lords, gentlemen, indeed of all.

Richard claims to be free of all thoughts of enmity. Elizabeth requests pardon for Clarence. Richard announces Clarence's death and casts suspicion on the Woodvilles. Derby asks a favour of Edward.

1 'They all start' (in large groups)

The mood of reconciliation continues with more words of religion and redemption. Richard says he feels as much at peace with the world as a new-born might. Elizabeth wants the day to be remembered ('kept hereafter') as a 'holy day' when all the differences were reconciled ('all strifes were well compounded'). But when Elizabeth asks the king to include Clarence in the mood of forgiveness 'To take our brother Clarence to your grace' (line 77), the mood is abruptly changed by Richard's announcement of Clarence's death.

Suggest how you would stage lines 70–88 to make the shift in mood as dramatically effective as possible.

2 Who killed Clarence? (in pairs)

Edward admits that he had ordered Clarence's death but then countermanded the order. Richard seizes the chance to throw suspicion on the Woodvilles. In lines 93–6, Richard hints that the Woodvilles, not of Royal blood but murderously inclined ('less noble ... not in blood'), deserve death (like Clarence's), even though they are not at the moment suspected of his murder. One person speaks lines 89–96 very slowly, pausing at the end of each line. In the pause, the other suggests how Richard can use actions and expressions to throw suspicion on others.

What is the significance of Buckingham's comment (line 85)?

---

jot small portion
at odds in conflict
grace favour
flouted misused, insulted
in the presence present
wingèd Mercury in classical
  mythology, a messenger of the
  gods who wore a winged helmet
  and sandals

tardy cripple slow and
  incapacitated (see page 42)
lag late
go current escape
forfeit sparing

        I do not know that Englishman alive   70
        With whom my soul is any jot at odds
        More than the infant that is born tonight.
        I thank my God for my humility.
ELIZABETH A holy day shall this be kept hereafter.
        I would to God all strifes were well compounded.   75
        My sovereign lord, I do beseech your highness
        To take our brother Clarence to your grace.
RICHARD Why, madam, have I offered love for this,
        To be so flouted in this royal presence?
        Who knows not that the gentle duke is dead?   80

They all start

        You do him injury to scorn his corpse.
KING EDWARD Who knows not he is dead?
        Who knows he is?
ELIZABETH All-seeing heaven, what a world is this?
BUCKINGHAM Look I so pale, Lord Dorset, as the rest?   85
DORSET Ay, my good lord, and no man in the presence
        But his red colour hath forsook his cheeks.
KING EDWARD Is Clarence dead? The order was reversed.
RICHARD But he (poor man) by your first order died,
        And that a wingèd Mercury did bear;   90
        Some tardy cripple bare the countermand,
        That came too lag to see him burièd.
        God grant that some, less noble and less loyal,
        Nearer in bloody thoughts and not in blood,
        Deserve not worse than wretched Clarence did,   95
        And yet go current from suspicion.

Enter [STANLEY] EARL OF DERBY

STANLEY A boon, my sovereign, for my service done.
KING EDWARD I prithee, peace, my soul is full of sorrow.
STANLEY I will not rise unless your highness hear me.
KING EDWARD Then say at once what is it thou requests.   100
STANLEY The forfeit, sovereign, of my servant's life,
        Who slew today a riotous gentleman
        Lately attendant on the Duke of Norfolk.

*King Edward contrasts Stanley's plea with the lack of pleas for mercy
for Clarence. Edward remembers Clarence's many favours to him.
He grants pardon, but fears God's revenge. Richard blames the
Woodvilles for Clarence's death.*

1 Why didn't you all plead for Clarence? (in pairs)

In lines 104–34, King Edward admits responsibility for Clarence's
death. Match the following summary to King Edward's lines. Talk
together about how convinced you are by Edward's explanation of
his behaviour. Then speak the lines as persuasively as you can.

- Why should I pardon a slave, when I ordered my own brother's death?
- Clarence killed no one, yet he was killed.
- Why didn't anyone plead for him and remind me of all he did for me?
- In my anger, I forgot Clarence's good deeds and none of you reminded me.
- But when one of your servants ('waiting vassals') offend, you immediately plead for mercy for them.
- I have to grant the plea for a servant though neither I nor you pleaded for Clarence, even though we were all indebted to him.
- We and our children will be punished for his death.

2 Seizing the opportunity

Richard hints both at Edward's poor judgement and his loose living
('the fruits of rashness') and directly blames the Woodvilles. Does
Richard involve the audience? Speak his lines 137–42, making clear
who he engages in eye contact sentence by sentence.

---

to doom to be responsible for
his fault was thought
  he never acted in a traitorous way
Oxford an enemy nobleman
lap wrap
thin thinly covered

straight immediately
ungracious lacking grace
beholding indebted
closet private room
still always

KING EDWARD   Have I a tongue to doom my brother's death,
And shall that tongue give pardon to a slave?   105
My brother killed no man; his fault was thought,
And yet his punishment was bitter death.
Who sued to me for him? Who (in my wrath)
Kneeled at my feet and bid me be advised?
Who spoke of brotherhood? Who spoke of love?   110
Who told me how the poor soul did forsake
The mighty Warwick and did fight for me?
Who told me, in the field at Tewkesbury,
When Oxford had me down, he rescued me
And said 'Dear brother, live, and be a king'?   115
Who told me, when we both lay in the field,
Frozen almost to death, how he did lap me
Even in his garments and did give himself
(All thin and naked) to the numb cold night?
All this from my remembrance brutish wrath   120
Sinfully plucked, and not a man of you
Had so much grace to put it in my mind.
But when your carters or your waiting vassals
Have done a drunken slaughter and defaced
The precious image of our dear redeemer,   125
You straight are on your knees for pardon, pardon,
And I, unjustly too, must grant it you.
But for my brother not a man would speak,
Nor I, ungracious, speak unto myself
For him, poor soul. The proudest of you all   130
Have been beholding to him in his life,
Yet none of you would once beg for his life.
Oh God, I fear thy justice will take hold
On me and you, and mine and yours, for this.
Come, Hastings, help me to my closet.   135
Ah, poor Clarence!   *Exeunt some with King and Queen*
RICHARD   This is the fruits of rashness. Marked you not
How that the guilty kindred of the queen
Looked pale when they did hear of Clarence' death?
Oh, they did urge it still unto the king.   140
God will revenge it. Come, lords, will you go
To comfort Edward with our company?
BUCKINGHAM   We wait upon your grace.   *Exeunt*

Clarence's children suspect their father is dead, but the
Duchess of York, their grandmother, says she grieves for
King Edward's illness. She admits Clarence is dead and warns the
children not to be fooled by Richard.

1 The language of deceit (in groups of three)

The Duchess of York begins with a lie, and Clarence's son has difficulties in perceiving what is true. Take parts as the duchess, the son and the daughter. Speak lines 1–33, pausing at the end of each sentence. In the pause, talk together about whether what is said is true, false or unproven (impossible to judge).

2 Revenge

Clarence's son says 'God will revenge it', echoing Richard's words 16 lines earlier in the previous scene. As you work through the play, keep thinking about how far different characters are motivated by a desire for revenge, and how revenge becomes an increasingly important theme.

3 Richard the actor (in groups of three)

The Duchess of York is in no doubt about Richard's ability to 'dissemble': to pretend, act a part, and lie. His talent to deceive is demonstrated by the way he behaves towards Clarence's son. As one person speaks lines 20–6, the others mime the actions.

4 A mother's judgement (in groups of three)

Richard's mother, the Duchess of York, gives her unflattering view of her son's character in lines 27–30. Give some examples of the deep vices that you know Richard is hiding under his mask of goodness ('virtuous visor') up to this moment in the play.

---

cousins grandchildren
loath unwilling
lost sorrow futile grief
importune beg
Incapable and shallow innocents
  young children lacking knowledge

impeachments
  accusations of treason
gentle shape kindly actions
dugs breasts

ACT 2 SCENE 2
London: a room in King Edward's palace

Enter the old DUCHESS OF YORK with Clarence's two children
[BOY and GIRL]

BOY Good grandam, tell us, is our father dead?
DUCHESS No, boy.
GIRL Why do you weep so oft, and beat your breast,
        And cry, 'Oh Clarence, my unhappy son'?
BOY Why do you look on us, and shake your head,   5
        And call us orphans, wretches, castaways,
        If that our noble father were alive?
DUCHESS My pretty cousins, you mistake me both.
        I do lament the sickness of the king,
        As loath to lose him, not your father's death.   10
        It were lost sorrow to wail one that's lost.
BOY Then you conclude, my grandam, he is dead.
        The king mine uncle is to blame for it.
        God will revenge it, whom I will importune
        With earnest prayers all to that effect.   15
GIRL And so will I.
DUCHESS Peace, children, peace. The king doth love you well.
        Incapable and shallow innocents,
        You cannot guess who caused your father's death.
BOY Grandam, we can, for my good uncle Gloucester   20
        Told me the king, provoked to it by the queen,
        Devised impeachments to imprison him.
        And when my uncle told me so, he wept,
        And pitied me, and kindly kissed my cheek;
        Bade me rely on him as on my father,   25
        And he would love me dearly as a child.
DUCHESS Ah, that deceit should steal such gentle shape
        And with a virtuous visor hide deep vice.
        He is my son, ay, and therein my shame,
        Yet from my dugs he drew not this deceit.   30
BOY Think you my uncle did dissemble, grandam?
DUCHESS Ay, boy.

The grieving Queen Elizabeth brings news of King Edward's death. The duchess laments the loss of two sons and Richard's false character. She and Clarence's children seem to lack sympathy for Elizabeth.

1 Elizabeth's grief (in pairs)

Queen Elizabeth enters with '*her hair about her ears*'. The same traditional symbol of grief is used in Shakespeare's *King John* when a mother, Constance, hears of the death of her young son. Discuss how you could use the stage direction to create a strong visual image of Elizabeth's grief as she enters.

2 Images of mourning (in pairs)

Lines 1–88 are full of references to death, loss and grief. Two children are left fatherless, Queen Elizabeth is widowed and the Duchess of York has lost two sons. Each character expresses their own grief and loss. The mourning is expressed in formal language with even the children using an 'adult' style.

Elizabeth and the duchess use a great deal of imagery. The 'branches' and 'root' (line 41) are images of the family tree of King Edward, a tree which will now die. In lines 50–4, the 'two mirrors' are the Duchess of York's sons, King Edward and Clarence, and the 'false glass' is Richard. With Edward and Clarence dead, her support ('two crutches') has gone. In lines 66–70, Queen Elizabeth asks for her eyes to be like the ocean so she may flood the world with her tears.

Identify all the images used on the opposite page and make your own judgement about whether you find them false and exaggerated or imaginatively truthful.

chide reprimand, rebuke	**moiety** small portion
rude rough, barbarous	**moan** grief
brief quick	**overgo** exceed
ne'er-changing night death	**widow-dolour** grief of widowhood
interest personal concern	**reduce** bring
title right (as a mother)	

BOY   I cannot think it. Hark, what noise is this?

Enter the QUEEN ELIZABETH *with her hair about her ears,*
RIVERS and DORSET *after her*

ELIZABETH   Ah, who shall hinder me to wail and weep,
      To chide my fortune and torment myself?   35
      I'll join with black despair against my soul,
      And to myself become an enemy.
DUCHESS   What means this scene of rude impatience?
ELIZABETH   To make an act of tragic violence.
      Edward, my lord, thy son, our king, is dead.   40
      Why grow the branches when the root is gone?
      Why wither not the leaves that want their sap?
      If you will live, lament; if die, be brief,
      That our swift-wingèd souls may catch the king's,
      Or, like obedient subjects, follow him   45
      To his new kingdom of ne'er-changing night.
DUCHESS   Ah, so much interest have I in thy sorrow
      As I had title in thy noble husband.
      I have bewept a worthy husband's death
      And lived with looking on his images,   50
      But now two mirrors of his princely semblance
      Are cracked in pieces by malignant death,
      And I for comfort have but one false glass,
      That grieves me when I see my shame in him.
      Thou art a widow, yet thou art a mother   55
      And hast the comfort of thy children left.
      But death hath snatched my husband from mine arms
      And plucked two crutches from my feeble hands,
      Clarence and Edward. Oh, what cause have I,
      Thine being but a moiety of my moan,   60
      To overgo thy woes and drown thy cries.
BOY   Ah, aunt, you wept not for our father's death.
      How can we aid you with our kindred tears?
GIRL   Our fatherless distress was left unmoaned.
      Your widow-dolour likewise be unwept.   65
ELIZABETH   Give me no help in lamentation.
      I am not barren to bring forth complaints.
      All springs reduce their currents to mine eyes,

The women and children echo each other's grief. Dorset attempts to comfort his mother. Rivers urges Queen Elizabeth to arrange that young Prince Edward is crowned king immediately. Richard says weeping is unhelpful.

1 The ritual language of mourning (in small groups)

The formal and ritualistic language continues. In some performances, the many repetitions are emphasised sometimes for comic effect, sometimes to create a solemn and choric sense of grief. Other productions speak the lines in a way that brings out the helplessness that overcomes the women and children with the loss of the important men in their lives.

Take parts as the children, the Duchess of York and Queen Elizabeth. Speak lines 71–85, emphasising the exact repetition and pattern of the words. Bring out the humour in your first version and the tragedy in the second. Discuss which style seems the more appropriate.

Criticism or comfort?: The language of Dorset contrasts with the highly patterned style of the women and children. Lines 89–95 refer to the Christian belief in the power of God over human life. How do you think he speaks the lines? Is he rebuking or comforting his mother?

Power broking: After the very personal sorrowing of the duchess, and Dorset's religious tone, Rivers gives practical advice. He is alert to the political implications of King Edward's death and the need to maintain power in the hands of the Woodvilles by immediately crowning Elizabeth's son. Suggest how River's actions and tone could underline the political urgency of the power vacuum caused by King Edward's death.

---

stay support
parcelled individual, particular
threefold distressed (she grieves for her husband and two sons)
pamper care for
opposite with hostile to

requires calls in, wants return of
dead Edward Edward IV
living Edward Prince of Wales, Edward IV's son
Sister sister-in-law

That I, being governed by the watery moon,
May send forth plenteous tears to drown the world.   70
Ah, for my husband, for my dear lord Edward.
CHILDREN Ah, for our father, for our dear lord Clarence.
DUCHESS Alas for both, both mine Edward and Clarence.
ELIZABETH What stay had I but Edward? And he's gone.
CHILDREN What stay had we but Clarence? And he's gone.   75
DUCHESS What stays had I but they? And they are gone.
ELIZABETH Was never widow had so dear a loss.
CHILDREN Were never orphans had so dear a loss.
DUCHESS Was never mother had so dear a loss.
    Alas, I am the mother of these griefs;   80
    Their woes are parcelled, mine is general.
    She for an Edward weeps, and so do I;
    I for a Clarence weep, so doth not she.
    These babes for Clarence weep, and so do I;
    I for an Edward weep, so do not they.   85
    Alas, you three, on me, threefold distressed,
    Pour all your tears; I am your sorrow's nurse,
    And I will pamper it with lamentation.
DORSET Comfort, dear mother. God is much displeased
    That you take with unthankfulness his doing.   90
    In common worldly things 'tis called ungrateful
    With dull unwillingness to repay a debt
    Which with a bounteous hand was kindly lent;
    Much more to be thus opposite with heaven,
    For it requires the royal debt it lent you.   95
RIVERS Madam, bethink you like a careful mother
    Of the young prince your son. Send straight for him.
    Let him be crowned. In him your comfort lives.
    Drown desperate sorrow in dead Edward's grave
    And plant your joys in living Edward's throne.   100

    Enter RICHARD, BUCKINGHAM, [STANLEY EARL OF] DERBY,
        HASTINGS, *and* RATCLIFFE

RICHARD Sister, have comfort. All of us have cause
    To wail the dimming of our shining star,
    But none can help our harms by wailing them.
    Madam, my mother, I do cry you mercy;

Richard comments ironically on his mother's blessing.
Buckingham argues that a small escort should bring Prince Edward to
London for his coronation because a large one might provoke unrest.
His advice is accepted.

1 Mother and son (in pairs)

The duchess blesses Richard but his aside shows he does not take her words seriously. He says that the 'butt-end' of her blessing would be that he would die naturally in old age, a reformed character. The 'butt-end' is the unpleasant dregs left in a barrel of drink. Take parts as Richard and the duchess and speak lines 104–11. Then invent an aside for the duchess to speak to the audience before line 107. Remember that her earlier image of Richard as a 'false glass' (line 53) shows what she really thinks of him.

2 Buckingham's persuasive powers (in groups)

Buckingham seems to take the initiative. To strengthen his argument he uses a series of metaphors (see page 243) to describe the fragile nature of the power structure of the kingdom ('estate'). He says that a small escort should be sent to Ludlow (see the map on page 3) to escort Prince Edward to London for his coronation. Talk together about how successfully the following metaphors add to his persuasive powers: harvest is coming (lines 115–16); healing fractures (lines 117–19); and anarchy (lines 129–30).

3 Hidden motives

Richard seems to hope for a peaceful future and Buckingham succeeds in having his proposal accepted: only a small escort will fetch Prince Edward from Ludlow. Write a sentence about what you think are their true intentions.

---

cloudy gloomy
spent lost
Me seemeth it seems to me
train escort
fet fetched
multitude large escort
green weak, new

compact pact of friendship
apparent likelihood
 obvious possibility
breach break up
meet right, appropriate
straight shall post
 immediately ride

I did not see your grace. Humbly on my knee   105
I crave your blessing.
DUCHESS   God bless thee and put meekness in thy breast,
Love, charity, obedience, and true duty.
RICHARD   Amen. [*Aside*] And make me die a good old man,
That is the butt-end of a mother's blessing;   110
I marvel that her grace did leave it out.
BUCKINGHAM   You cloudy princes and heart-sorrowing peers
That bear this heavy mutual load of moan,
Now cheer each other in each other's love.
Though we have spent our harvest of this king,   115
We are to reap the harvest of his son.
The broken rancour of your high-swoll'n hates,
But lately splintered, knit, and joined together,
Must gently be preserved, cherished, and kept.
Me seemeth good that with some little train   120
Forthwith from Ludlow the young prince be fet
Hither to London, to be crowned our king.
RIVERS   Why with some little train,
My lord of Buckingham?
BUCKINGHAM   Marry, my lord, lest by a multitude   125
The new-healed wound of malice should break out,
Which would be so much the more dangerous
By how much the estate is green and yet ungoverned.
Where every horse bears his commanding rein
And may direct his course as please himself,   130
As well the fear of harm, as harm apparent,
In my opinion, ought to be prevented.
RICHARD   I hope the king made peace with all of us,
And the compact is firm and true in me.
RIVERS   And so in me, and so, I think, in all.   135
Yet since it is but green, it should be put
To no apparent likelihood of breach,
Which haply by much company might be urged.
Therefore I say with noble Buckingham
That it is meet so few should fetch the prince.   140
HASTINGS   And so say I.
RICHARD   Then be it so, and go we to determine
Who they shall be that straight shall post to Ludlow.

Buckingham promises to separate the Woodvilles from Prince Edward. Richard applauds his aims which are exactly his own. Three citizens discussing King Edward's death see trouble ahead for England.

1 Showing the power struggle

Richard appears to be empowering Queen Elizabeth and the Duchess of York by asking them to give their opinions ('censures') on who should escort Edward, Prince of Wales, to London for his coronation. Lines 151–4 reveal he has quite different plans in mind. The exit of the queen's 'proud kindred', leaving Richard and Buckingham alone on stage, is a great opportunity for actors to show the struggle for power between the Woodvilles and Richard and Buckingham.

Write notes on how to perform the stage direction at line 145, so that the audience can appreciate this power struggle.

2 'My other self' (in pairs)

In line 151, Richard states that he and Buckingham are utterly alike ('My other self') and that they think as one ('my counsel's consistory'). An Elizabethan audience would recognise Richard's hyperbolic description of Buckingham as characteristic language of the Vice of morality plays (see page 246) who would flatter to deceive. Take parts as Buckingham and Richard and enact lines 151–4 in the following ways:

• Richard really means what he says.

• Richard is quite insincere.

• Richard speaks the lines as an aside to the audience as Buckingham strides away.

In each case, show Buckingham's response.

---

sort occasion make an opportunity
index introduction
story plan
consistory council chamber
oracle someone who foretells the future

promise assure
abroad being spread
by'r Lady by the Virgin Mary
giddy crazy, unstable
while present time

Madam, and you my sister, will you go
To give your censures in this business?   145

Exeunt [all but] Buckingham and Richard

BUCKINGHAM My lord, whoever journeys to the prince,
            For God's sake let not us two stay at home,
            For by the way I'll sort occasion,
            As index to the story we late talked of,
            To part the queen's proud kindred from the prince.   150
RICHARD My other self, my counsel's consistory,
         My oracle, my prophet, my dear cousin,
         I, as a child, will go by thy direction.
         Toward Ludlow then, for we'll not stay behind.

Exeunt

ACT 2 SCENE 3
London: a street

Enter FIRST CITIZEN and SECOND CITIZEN

FIRST CITIZEN Good morrow, neighbour. Whither away so fast?
SECOND CITIZEN I promise you, I scarcely know myself.
            Hear you the news abroad?
FIRST CITIZEN Yes, that the king is dead.
SECOND CITIZEN Ill news, by'r Lady; seldom comes the better.   5
            I fear, I fear, 'twill prove a giddy world.

Enter another [THIRD] CITIZEN

THIRD CITIZEN Neighbours, God speed.
FIRST CITIZEN Give you good morrow, sir.
THIRD CITIZEN Doth the news hold of good King Edward's death?
SECOND CITIZEN Ay, sir, it is too true, God help the while.   10
THIRD CITIZEN Then, masters, look to see a troublous world.
FIRST CITIZEN No, no, by God's good grace his son shall reign.
THIRD CITIZEN Woe to that land that's governed by a child.

*The citizens hope for a peaceful future under the new young king.
The Third Citizen fears that rivalry between Richard and the
Woodvilles will bring dangerous and harsh times.*

1 The voice of the people (in groups of three)

The Second and Third Citizens have a very pessimistic view of a
future England under the rule of the young Prince Edward. The
Third Citizen has just lamented 'Woe to that land that's governed
by a child' (line 13), and the citizens continue to discuss Prince
Edward who is only a child ('in his nonage'). They know that
England will now be ruled by a group of nobles and members of the
royal family ('council'), and they fear the coming struggle between
Richard and the Woodvilles.

As you speak Scene 3, try to bring out the differing view points
of each citizen. Discuss which citizen you think has the clearest view
of England's future.

2 Formal verse (in pairs)

Although the citizens are the ordinary people of England, they
speak in the stylised and formal verse usually reserved for the
nobility. The Third Citizen uses a good deal of imagery in lines
34–7 and 44–6. Identify these images and discuss how effective you
find them in conveying the Third Citizen's meaning.

3 Present rivalry, future strife

As Prince Edward's uncles, Richard and Rivers will be the most
powerful influence on the new king. The Third Citizen foresees
their rivalry ('emulation') will seriously harm everyone ('touch us all
too near'). Keep the Third Citizen's prophecy in mind as you read
on to discover what happens in England's 'sickly land' (line 32).

---

wot knows
politic grave counsel
  wise, solemn advice
by from
queen's sons Dorset and Grey
haught haughty
solace have comfort

dearth famine
sort orders
heavily worriedly
Ensuing danger
  forthcoming disasters
proof experience

SECOND CITIZEN In him there is a hope of government,
       Which in his nonage, council under him,   15
       And in his full and ripened years, himself
       No doubt shall then, and till then, govern well.
FIRST CITIZEN So stood the state when Henry the Sixth
       Was crowned in Paris but at nine months old.
THIRD CITIZEN Stood the state so? No, no, good friends, God wot,   20
       For then this land was famously enriched
       With politic grave counsel. Then the king
       Had virtuous uncles to protect his grace.
FIRST CITIZEN Why, so hath this, both by his father and mother.
THIRD CITIZEN Better it were they all came by his father,   25
       Or by his father there were none at all.
       For emulation who shall now be nearest
       Will touch us all too near, if God prevent not.
       Oh, full of danger is the Duke of Gloucester,
       And the queen's sons and brothers haught and proud.   30
       And were they to be ruled, and not to rule,
       This sickly land might solace as before.
FIRST CITIZEN Come, come, we fear the worst; all will be well.
THIRD CITIZEN When clouds are seen, wise men put on their cloaks;
       When great leaves fall, then winter is at hand;   35
       When the sun sets, who doth not look for night?
       Untimely storms makes men expect a dearth.
       All may be well, but if God sort it so,
       'Tis more than we deserve or I expect.
SECOND CITIZEN Truly the hearts of men are full of fear.   40
       You cannot reason almost with a man
       That looks not heavily and full of dread.
THIRD CITIZEN Before the days of change, still is it so.
       By a divine instinct, men's minds mistrust
       Ensuing danger, as by proof, we see   45
       The water swell before a boisterous storm.
       But leave it all to God. Whither away?
SECOND CITIZEN Marry, we were sent for to the justices.
THIRD CITIZEN And so was I. I'll bear you company.

Exeunt

The Archbishop reports the progress to London of Prince Edward and his escort. The Duchess of York recalls Richard's slow growth in childhood and her doubts about his character.

1 Calm or storm (in groups of four)

- *The calm.* Three generations – a grandmother (the Duchess of York), a mother (Queen Elizabeth) and her son (the young Duke of York) look forward to Prince Edward's arrival.

- *The storm.* But the audience knows (from the previous scene) that Richard and Buckingham have plotted to isolate the Woodvilles from Prince Edward.

Take parts and speak lines 1–37. Discuss whether you would play the scene as one of 'calm' (a happy domestic scene) or of 'storm' (unease, especially at the mention of Richard). In the picture below, the scene began with grieving over the dead body of King Edward (centre).

herbs plants	**leisurely** slowly
grace (line 13) good qualities	**gracious** virtuous
apace quickly	**grace (line 24)** prayer at a meal
did not hold was not true	**flout** rebuff, mocking reply
object say, assert	**touch** strike at, criticise

London: a room in King Edward's palace

Enter the ARCHBISHOP OF YORK, *the young* DUKE OF YORK,
QUEEN ELIZABETH, *and the* DUCHESS OF YORK

ARCHBISHOP Last night, I heard, they lay at Stony Stratford,
    And at Northampton they do rest tonight.
    Tomorrow, or next day, they will be here.
DUCHESS I long with all my heart to see the prince.
    I hope he is much grown since last I saw him. 5
ELIZABETH But I hear no. They say my son of York
    Has almost overta'en him in his growth.
YORK Ay, mother, but I would not have it so.
DUCHESS Why, my good cousin? It is good to grow.
YORK Grandam, one night as we did sit at supper, 10
    My uncle Rivers talked how I did grow
    More than my brother. 'Ay', quoth my uncle Gloucester,
    'Small herbs have grace; great weeds do grow apace.'
    And since, methinks, I would not grow so fast,
    Because sweet flowers are slow, and weeds make haste. 15
DUCHESS Good faith, good faith, the saying did not hold
    In him that did object the same to thee.
    He was the wretched'st thing when he was young,
    So long a-growing, and so leisurely,
    That if his rule were true, he should be gracious. 20
YORK And so no doubt he is, my gracious madam.
DUCHESS I hope he is, but yet let mothers doubt.
YORK Now, by my troth, if I had been remembered,
    I could have given my uncle's grace a flout
    To touch his growth nearer than he touched mine. 25
DUCHESS How, my young York? I prithee, let me hear it.

York says Richard was born with teeth. A messenger brings news of the imprisonment of Rivers, Grey and Vaughan. Elizabeth foresees the end of the Woodvilles under the tyranny of Richard.

1 Mischievous boy? (in pairs)

In lines 27–30, the young Duke of York, measuring his own slow growth against that of his uncle, wishes that he had made an effective joke ('biting jest') of the comparison. Many rumours were spread about Richard of Gloucester's unusual growth and development in childhood. For example, in this scene, Richard's mother does not deny his unusually fast growth and being born with teeth (lines 27–37).

To find if you agree with his mother's judgement that the Duke of York is mischievous ('parlous') and sharp-tongued ('shrewd'), speak all that he says between lines 10–34.

2 Bad news (in groups of four)

Lines 38–51 convey the bad news in sharp, short phrases and sentences. Take parts as the Archbishop, the messenger, Queen Elizabeth and the Duchess of York. Speak the lines in as rapid and staccato fashion as possible. Do you think this is the most appropriate way of delivering the lines? What do their questions reveal about the concerns of the Archbishop, the queen and the duchess?

3 The hunter and the prey

Elizabeth foresees the forthcoming destruction of the Woodvilles. Indentify who is the 'tiger' and who 'the gentle hind' in line 53.

---

biting effective
Pitchers jugs
  (proverb: children overhear what
  they are not supposed to)
sum total

disclosed told
gentle hind defenceless deer
jut encroach
aweless throne
  vulnerable young king

YORK   Marry, they say my uncle grew so fast
      That he could gnaw a crust at two hours old.
      'Twas full two years ere I could get a tooth.
      Grandam, this would have been a biting jest.   30
DUCHESS   I prithee, pretty York, who told thee this?
YORK   Grandam, his nurse.
DUCHESS   His nurse? Why, she was dead ere thou wast born.
YORK   If 'twere not she, I cannot tell who told me.
ELIZABETH   A parlous boy; go to, you are too shrewd.   35
DUCHESS   Good madam, be not angry with the child.
ELIZABETH   Pitchers have ears.

Enter a MESSENGER

ARCHBISHOP   Here comes a messenger. What news?
MESSENGER   Such news, my lord, as grieves me to report.
ELIZABETH   How doth the prince?   40
MESSENGER   Well, madam, and in health.
DUCHESS   What is thy news?
MESSENGER   Lord Rivers and Lord Grey
      Are sent to Pomfret, and with them
      Sir Thomas Vaughan, prisoners.   45
DUCHESS   Who hath committed them?
MESSENGER   The mighty dukes, Gloucester and Buckingham.
ARCHBISHOP   For what offence?
MESSENGER   The sum of all I can, I have disclosed.
      Why or for what the nobles were committed   50
      Is all unknown to me, my gracious lord.
ELIZABETH   Aye me! I see the ruin of my house.
      The tiger now hath seized the gentle hind;
      Insulting tyranny begins to jut
      Upon the innocent and aweless throne.   55
      Welcome, destruction, blood, and massacre.
      I see, as in a map, the end of all.

The Duchess of York remembers past battles and how,
in peacetime, her sons quarrelled. Elizabeth decides to seek sanctuary
for herself and York. The Archbishop pledges his loyalty and
vows to share the queen's fate.

1 The Wars of the Roses: a woman's view (in pairs)

The Duchess of York bemoans the constant fighting ('Accursèd and unquiet wrangling days') she has witnessed in the battle for the throne (see page 1 'The context of the play'). She describes her conflicting emotions at her husband's death and her sons' defeats and victories.

Even after their success, when enthroned ('being seated') and the civil war over, they continue to fight within the family. Speak lines 58–68 to show the mixture of emotions that the duchess feels.

2 Sanctuary

Queen Elizabeth wants to take the Duke of York and herself to the safety of Westminster Abbey. In medieval times, church law guaranteed that a fugitive from justice or debt was immune from arrest if they sought sanctuary in a church or other sacred place. You can find more on sanctuary on page 98.

3 Performance decisions (in pairs)

The Archbishop's lines 73–8 are open to a range of different interpretations. Who is he addressing as 'gracious lady' and 'your grace'? Does he, the keeper of the 'seal' of England, the symbol of sovereignty (line 76), actually hand it over?

Every production has to decide precisely how these lines will be staged and to whom he speaks. Step into role as director and advise the Archbishop, line by line, how he should deliver his speech.

---

wrangling quarrelling
domestic broils/Clean over-
  blown the civil war over
Make war upon themselves
  fight amongst the family

preposterous ridiculous, unnatural
spleen anger
so betide to me
  may similar fortune befall me
tender have high regard for

DUCHESS Accursèd and unquiet wrangling days,
         How many of you have mine eyes beheld?
         My husband lost his life to get the crown,   60
         And often up and down my sons were tossed
         For me to joy and weep their gain and loss.
         And being seated, and domestic broils
         Clean over-blown, themselves the conquerors
         Make war upon themselves, brother to brother,   65
         Blood to blood, self against self. Oh, preposterous
         And frantic outrage, end thy damnèd spleen,
         Or let me die, to look on earth no more.
ELIZABETH Come, come, my boy, we will to sanctuary.
         Madam, farewell.   70
DUCHESS Stay, I will go with you.
ELIZABETH You have no cause.
ARCHBISHOP My gracious lady, go,
         And thither bear your treasure and your goods.
         For my part, I'll resign unto your grace   75
         The seal I keep, and so betide to me
         As well I tender you and all of yours.
         Go, I'll conduct you to the sanctuary.

                                                      Exeunt

Looking back at Act 2
Activities for groups or individuals

King Edward IV's only appearance in the play is in Scene 1. In his final moving speech, the dying king shows remorse for Clarence's death and fear of God's judgement and punishment. But Richard has already spoken of Edward's dissolute past. Identify Edward's actions and the opinions others have of him in Acts 1 and 2 and say whether you think he has good cause to fear God's judgement. Which aspects of King Edward's character are suggested in the production illustrated above?

1 Two scenes with children

Read again the two scenes in which children play an important role. In Scene 2, the Duchess of York unsuccessfully attempts to hide from Clarence's children their father's murder; and in Scene 4, the young Duke of York makes witty comments about his uncle Richard. Do they talk and act like children? Suggest how the children affect the mood and atmosphere of the play and how they might be played to create different moods (for example, humour, pathos).

2 The people speak

Scene 3 provides the only occasion in the play when ordinary people, unobserved by their social superiors, voice their fears for the future. Step into role as the director of a modern, contemporary interpretation of the play. Write your set of director's notes giving your reasons for how the citizens dress and speak. Begin by considering their individual and group motivation.

3 Is the duchess in danger?

Queen Elizabeth realises her danger when she learns of the arrest of her son (Grey), brother (Rivers) and Sir Thomas Vaughan. She determines to escape danger, but comments that the Duchess of York has 'no cause' (Scene 4, line 72) to join her in seeking sanctuary. Step into role as the Duchess of York. Describe your feelings to show your understanding of the significance of the present situation and then give your reply to Elizabeth's comment.

4 Increasing tyranny

Buckingham's decision to assist Richard begins a relationship which brings with it increasing tyranny and menace for all those who oppose them. Look back at the exchanges between Richard and Buckingham and chart the growth of their relationship during the Act. List the characters who feel threatened by them.

5 Appearance and reality

An important theme in the play is whether outside appearance is a true guide to a person's inner nature. Some characters see Richard's true nature and others are fooled by him. List the names of those characters who see Richard for what he is and make a second list of those who are fooled by him.

Arriving in London, Prince Edward is saddened by the arrest of Rivers and Grey, disagreeing with Richard that they were disloyal. He seems puzzled that his mother and brother have not yet arrived.

1 Royal entrance (in large groups)

Richard has plotted with Buckingham and intends to proclaim himself king. There is no hint of this intention as Richard and Buckingham welcome Prince Edward, the heir to the throne, to his capital ('chamber'). The stage directions lists the others who enter with the prince. Try out ways that the entrance could be staged which would show Edward's importance: he is now, in all but name, King of England.

2 More duplicity (in pairs)

Richard welcomes Prince Edward with superficial courtesy, but once again his words have sinister double meanings. 'My thoughts' sovereign' could mean both 'king of my thoughts' and 'my overriding thought of your death'. Richard adopts the tactics he accuses Rivers and Grey of using on Edward: he tells the young prince they are untrustworthy. Talk together about ways in which Richard's tone and actions could bring out the dramatic irony of his own 'sugared words'.

3 Prince Edward's troubles (in pairs)

Prince Edward blames troubles on his journey ('crosses on the way') as the reason for his sadness ('melancholy'). He is also unhappy at the arrest of his uncles and does not believe they are traitors ('false friends'). He seems further troubled by the absence of his mother and brother and by Hastings' late arrival. Suggest ways in which the young Prince Edward's unease, and consequently his vulnerability, could be made obvious on stage.

want lack
untainted pure
jumpeth agrees
heart character
slug slow person

ACT 3 SCENE 1
London: a street

The Trumpets sound. Enter young PRINCE EDWARD,
RICHARD DUKE OF GLOUCESTER, BUCKINGHAM, LORD CARDINAL
BOURCHIER, CATESBY, with others

BUCKINGHAM Welcome, sweet prince, to London, to your chamber.
RICHARD Welcome, dear cousin, my thoughts' sovereign.
    The weary way hath made you melancholy.
PRINCE EDWARD No, uncle, but our crosses on the way
    Have made it tedious, wearisome, and heavy.   5
    I want more uncles here to welcome me.
RICHARD Sweet prince, the untainted virtue of your years
    Hath not yet dived into the world's deceit.
    Nor more can you distinguish of a man
    Than of his outward show, which God he knows,   10
    Seldom or never jumpeth with the heart.
    Those uncles which you want were dangerous.
    Your grace attended to their sugared words
    But looked not on the poison of their hearts.
    God keep you from them and from such false friends.   15
PRINCE EDWARD God keep me from false friends, but they were none.
RICHARD My lord, the Mayor of London comes to greet you.

Enter LORD MAYOR

MAYOR God bless your grace with health and happy days.
PRINCE EDWARD I thank you, good my lord, and thank you all.
    I thought my mother and my brother York   20
    Would long ere this have met us on the way.
    Fie, what a slug is Hastings, that he comes not
    To tell us whether they will come or no.

Enter LORD HASTINGS

BUCKINGHAM And in good time, here comes the sweating lord.
PRINCE EDWARD Welcome, my lord. What, will our mother come?   25

Hastings says the queen has taken sanctuary, so preventing the Duke of York from meeting his brother. Buckingham recommends bringing the boy by force. The Cardinal disagrees, but is persuaded to fetch the prince.

---

1 Can York claim sanctuary? (in pairs)

The argument between the Cardinal and Buckingham is prompted by Hastings' statement that the Duke of York ('The tender prince') wanted to meet his brother but was prevented ('perforce withheld') by his mother. Buckingham's reaction to Hastings' message is robust – the queen must be persuaded to send the Duke of York, or Hastings must take him by force.

The Cardinal says he will try to persuade to queen to change her mind, but he refuses to break the 'holy privilege/Of blessèd sanctuary'. Sanctuary was granted to those who felt persecuted and claimed the right of shelter in a church.

Buckingham accuses the Cardinal of being old-fashioned, claiming the present violent times ('the grossness of this age') justifies forceful action. He says that sanctuary is always granted to those who have the intelligence ('wit') to claim it if their circumstances deserve it; but he asserts that the Duke of York neither deserved or claimed sanctuary as he was taken into it by his mother. The Cardinal agrees to carry out Buckingham's instructions.

Take parts as Buckingham and the Cardinal and speak lines 31–57 to express their different attitudes. Remember that the Cardinal is a man of the church while Buckingham is a politician and man of action trying to be as persuasive as he possibly can. In the theatre, Buckingham often makes the audience laugh with his delivery of lines 55–6.

On what occasion for what reason
tender young
Would fain have wished to
peevish perverse
presently immediately
oratory pleading, persuasion

Anon at once
obdurate stubborn
senseless foolishly
charter warrant of immunity
sojourn stay

HASTINGS On what occasion God he knows, not I,
   The queen your mother and your brother York
   Have taken sanctuary. The tender prince
   Would fain have come with me to meet your grace,
   But by his mother was perforce withheld.   30
BUCKINGHAM Fie, what an indirect and peevish course
   Is this of hers. Lord Cardinal, will your grace
   Persuade the queen to send the Duke of York
   Unto his princely brother presently?
   If she deny, Lord Hastings, go with him,   35
   And from her jealous arms pluck him perforce.
CARDINAL My lord of Buckingham, if my weak oratory
   Can from his mother win the Duke of York,
   Anon expect him here; but if she be obdurate
   To mild entreaties, God forbid   40
   We should infringe the holy privilege
   Of blessèd sanctuary. Not for all this land
   Would I be guilty of so great a sin.
BUCKINGHAM You are too senseless obstinate, my lord,
   Too ceremonious and traditional.   45
   Weigh it but with the grossness of this age:
   You break not sanctuary in seizing him.
   The benefit thereof is always granted
   To those whose dealings have deserved the place
   And those who have the wit to claim the place.   50
   This prince hath neither claimed it nor deserved it,
   And therefore, in mine opinion, cannot have it.
   Then taking him from thence that is not there,
   You break no privilege nor charter there.
   Oft have I heard of sanctuary men,   55
   But sanctuary children ne'er till now.
CARDINAL My lord, you shall o'er-rule my mind for once.
   Come on, Lord Hastings, will you go with me?
HASTINGS I go, my lord.

           Exit Cardinal and Hastings

PRINCE EDWARD Good lords, make all the speedy haste you may.   60
   Say, uncle Gloucester, if our brother come,
   Where shall we sojourn till our coronation?

Richard's suggestion that Prince Edward stay in the Tower dismays the prince. As Edward reflects on the nature of fame and reputation, Richard hints that the young prince has not long to live.

1 Richard's 'asides': to whom? (in pairs)

Prince Edward's words ('I do not like the Tower, of any place') can remind a modern audience of its sinister reputation – the Tower was both a royal castle and a state prison. The sense of impending tragedy and the vulnerability of the young prince is reinforced by Richard's three asides (lines 79, 82–3 and 94), reminding the audience he intends Prince Edward's death.

The theatrical convention of 'asides' is that they are made to the audience, and not heard by the other characters on stage. Might Richard speak all three asides to Buckingham? Talk together about the dramatic consequences of delivering the asides in this way.

2 Lies, truth and fame

More of Edward's character is revealed. Buckingham tells him two untruths about the Tower of London (it was not built by Julius Caesar and there is no written record that he did). Buckingham's words prompt Prince Edward to reflect on the nature of history and truth, saying that he thinks truth comes through both written records ('registered') and oral tradition ('retailed'). Edward's reaction to Buckingham's answers heightens the sense of irony in the episode as it unwittingly forecasts his own fate. Julius Caesar was a brave man but was murdered by the men he trusted. What do you think are Shakespeare's dramatic purposes in this episode? Give your reply as a written list.

fit apt
re-edified repaired
the general ending day judgement day
characters written records

moralise explain
wit wisdom
lightly often
forward early, precocious
my dear lord my dear king

RICHARD Where it think'st best unto your royal self.
　　　　If I may counsel you, some day or two
　　　　Your highness shall repose you at the Tower,　　　　　　65
　　　　Then where you please and shall be thought most fit
　　　　For your best health and recreation.
PRINCE EDWARD I do not like the Tower, of any place.
　　　　Did Julius Caesar build that place, my lord?
BUCKINGHAM He did, my gracious lord, begin that place,　　　70
　　　　Which since, succeeding ages have re-edified.
PRINCE EDWARD Is it upon record, or else reported
　　　　Successively from age to age, he built it?
BUCKINGHAM Upon record, my gracious lord.
PRINCE EDWARD But say, my lord, it were not registered,　　　75
　　　　Methinks the truth should live from age to age,
　　　　As 'twere retailed to all posterity,
　　　　Even to the general ending day.
RICHARD [Aside] So wise so young, they say, do never live long.
PRINCE EDWARD What say you, uncle?　　　　　　　　　　　80
RICHARD I say, without characters fame lives long.
　　　　[Aside] Thus, like the formal Vice, Iniquity,
　　　　I moralise two meanings in one word.
PRINCE EDWARD That Julius Caesar was a famous man.
　　　　With what his valour did enrich his wit,　　　　　　　85
　　　　His wit set down to make his valour live.
　　　　Death makes no conquest of his conqueror,
　　　　For now he lives in fame, though not in life.
　　　　I'll tell you what, my cousin Buckingham.
BUCKINGHAM What, my gracious lord?　　　　　　　　　　90
PRINCE EDWARD And if I live until I be a man,
　　　　I'll win our ancient right in France again
　　　　Or die a soldier, as I lived a king.
RICHARD [Aside] Short summers lightly have a forward spring.

　　　　Enter young YORK, HASTINGS, *and* CARDINAL

BUCKINGHAM Now in good time, here comes the Duke of York.　95
PRINCE EDWARD Richard of York, how fares our noble brother?
YORK Well, my dear lord, so must I call you now.
PRINCE EDWARD Ay, brother, to our grief, as it is yours.
　　　　Too late he died that might have kept that title,
　　　　Which by his death hath lost much majesty.　　　　　100

The young Duke of York, in a witty conversation, taunts his uncle Richard whose responses are filled with menacing double meanings. Richard invites the princes to the Tower.

1 Innocence and menace (in groups of four)

The Duke of York is reunited with his brother, Prince Edward. He seems a more exuberant child, as revealed in his exchanges with his uncle, Richard. Take parts and work out a performance of lines 95–151. Use the following to help you.

a How do the two brothers greet each other at lines 96–7? (With an embrace? Very formally? Or ...?)

b Identify lines where Richard's avuncular manner hides his sinister intentions.

c York's reference to 'idle weeds' refers to Richard's remark that weeds grow quickly (Act 2 Scene 4, lines 13–15). Work out how York recalls this remark at lines 102–4: for example, puzzled, or accusingly, or in some other way.

d In lines 118–19, Richard and York pun (use a word with more than one meaning) on 'light', meaning both valueless and lacking weight. York also puns on 'weightier' and 'bear'. Suggest how Richard reacts to a young boy outsmarting him at his own verbal game.

e In many productions, York leaps on Richard's back at line 132. Say what you think of the dramatic effect of that action, and suggest how Richard might react.

f Is Buckingham genuine in his admiration of York in lines 133–6? Explore ways of speaking the lines: for example, sincerely, sarcastically, menacingly, or in some other way.

---

idle useless
kinsman relation, relative
toy trifle
cross contradictory
bear with (line 128) tolerate

bear (line 129) carry
sharp-provided ready, quick
mitigate lessen
pass come

RICHARD How fares our cousin, noble lord of York?
YORK I thank you, gentle uncle. Oh my lord,
  You said that idle weeds are fast in growth;
  The prince my brother hath outgrown me far.
RICHARD He hath, my lord.   105
YORK And therefore is he idle?
RICHARD Oh my fair cousin, I must not say so.
YORK Then he is more beholding to you than I.
RICHARD He may command me as my sovereign,
  But you have power in me as in a kinsman.   110
YORK I pray you, uncle, give me this dagger.
RICHARD My dagger, little cousin? With all my heart.
PRINCE EDWARD A beggar, brother?
YORK Of my kind uncle, that I know will give,
  And being but a toy, which is no grief to give.   115
RICHARD A greater gift than that I'll give my cousin.
YORK A greater gift? Oh, that's the sword to it.
RICHARD Ay, gentle cousin, were it light enough.
YORK Oh, then I see you will part but with light gifts.
  In weightier things you'll say a beggar nay.   120
RICHARD It is too weighty for your grace to wear.
YORK I weigh it lightly, were it heavier.
RICHARD What, would you have my weapon, little lord?
YORK I would, that I might thank you as you call me.
RICHARD How?   125
YORK Little.
PRINCE EDWARD My lord of York will still be cross in talk.
  Uncle, your grace knows how to bear with him.
YORK You mean to bear me, not to bear with me.
  Uncle, my brother mocks both you and me: 130
  Because that I am little, like an ape,
  He thinks that you should bear me on your shoulders.
BUCKINGHAM With what a sharp-provided wit he reasons.
  To mitigate the scorn he gives his uncle,
  He prettily and aptly taunts himself.   135
  So cunning and so young is wonderful.
RICHARD My lord, will't please you pass along?
  Myself and my good cousin Buckingham
  Will to your mother, to entreat of her
  To meet you at the Tower and welcome you.   140

The two princes go reluctantly to the Tower. Buckingham and Richard criticise young York. Catesby is instructed to find out whether Hastings will support Richard's bid to be crowned king.

1 Changes of mood

The mood of foreboding is heightened in the repeated references to the Tower (lines 140, 141, 143 and 151), York's fear of Clarence's ghost, and Edward's thought of the possible fate of Grey and Rivers ('And if they live').

Does Edward have some suspicions about his uncle's intentions? His reference to Richard as 'My Lord Protector' acknowledges Richard's powerful position. Advise Edward how to speak all his lines opposite to reveal his true feelings about his uncle Richard.

2 The princes' exit (in groups of any size)

A *sennet* is a trumpet call played at the approach or departure of a procession. The departure of the princes for the Tower is the last time they appear alive in the play. Stage their exit with Hastings. You may wish to contrast the sennet (ceremonial associated with high office) with the vulnerability of the two young princes. Think about what York might do as his final action that prompts Richard's six descriptions of him in lines 155–6.

3 Instructions to Catesby

Buckingham has told Catesby of the scheme to make Richard king. He now sends him to discover what Hastings thinks of the plan. Imagine Buckingham has also written a letter of instructions for Catesby. Write the letter based on lines 158–82.

---

in quiet peacefully
prating talkative
incensèd incited
perilous dangerous
capable intelligent
effect do

of our mind agree with us
as it were far off
  casually, as a future possibility
doth stand affected is disposed
tractable to in agreement with

YORK What, will you go unto the Tower, my lord?
PRINCE EDWARD My Lord Protector will have it so.
YORK I shall not sleep in quiet at the Tower.
RICHARD Why, what should you fear?
YORK Marry, my uncle Clarence' angry ghost.   145
      My grandam told me he was murdered there.
PRINCE EDWARD I fear no uncles dead.
RICHARD Nor none that live, I hope.
PRINCE EDWARD And if they live, I hope I need not fear.
      But come, my lord, and with a heavy heart,   150
      Thinking on them, go I unto the Tower.

      A sennet. Exeunt Prince, York, Hastings, [and others, except]
                        Richard, Buckingham, and Catesby

BUCKINGHAM Think you, my lord, this little prating York
      Was not incensèd by his subtle mother
      To taunt and scorn you thus opprobriously?
RICHARD No doubt, no doubt. Oh, 'tis a perilous boy,   155
      Bold, quick, ingenious, forward, capable.
      He is all the mother's, from the top to toe.
BUCKINGHAM Well, let them rest. Come hither, Catesby.
      Thou art sworn as deeply to effect what we intend
      As closely to conceal what we impart.   160
      Thou know'st our reasons urged upon the way.
      What think'st thou? Is it not an easy matter
      To make William Lord Hastings of our mind
      For the instalment of this noble duke
      In the seat royal of this famous isle?   165
CATESBY He for his father's sake so loves the prince
      That he will not be won to aught against him.
BUCKINGHAM What think'st thou, then, of Stanley? Will not he?
CATESBY He will do all in all as Hastings doth.
BUCKINGHAM Well then, no more but this: 170
      Go, gentle Catesby, and as it were far off,
      Sound thou Lord Hastings
      How he doth stand affected to our purpose,
      And summon him tomorrow to the Tower
      To sit about the coronation.   175
      If thou dost find him tractable to us,
      Encourage him, and tell him all our reasons.

Buckingham tells Catesby to bring news of Hastings' intentions.
Richard threatens to behead Hastings if he refuses his support.
He promises Buckingham the Earldom of Hereford.
Hastings receives a messenger from Stanley.

1 'Divided councils'

No one is quite clear what Buckingham means by 'divided councils' but it may be that Richard will summon two councils. The first will meet at Crosby Place (Richard's London home) to offer him the crown. The second council, mainly the supporters of Edward IV, will meet at the Tower to plan Prince Edward's coronation. Scenes 2 and 4 will show how that second council is also 'divided'.

2 Richard takes the initiative (in pairs)

Richard's greeting to Hastings ('Lord William') seems clear and favourable: Hastings' enemies are to be killed ('let blood'), Hastings is to rejoice in the news with his mistress. But is there a threatening meaning behind the good news?

Speak lines 183–7 in two ways: first, as a friendly greeting with 'good news'; and second, in a tone of menace that hints at future trouble for Hastings. Say which one you prefer, or whether you recommend a quite different delivery.

3 Outside Hastings' house (in pairs)

In one production, Hastings appeared in a nightshirt at an upstairs window, with Jane Shore visible behind him. Step into role as set designer and director. Suggest how you would signal to an audience the change of location from a street in London to Hastings' house.

---

highly in an important position
soundly effectively
heed speed
complots plots
determine arrange

movables personal property
 (not land and houses)
betimes early
digest arrange
form order

If he be leaden, icy, cold, unwilling,
Be thou so too, and so break off the talk,
And give us notice of his inclination.   180
For we tomorrow hold divided councils,
Wherein thyself shalt highly be employed.

RICHARD   Commend me to Lord William. Tell him, Catesby,
His ancient knot of dangerous adversaries
Tomorrow are let blood at Pomfret Castle;   185
And bid my lord, for joy of this good news,
Give Mistress Shore one gentle kiss the more.

BUCKINGHAM   Good Catesby, go, effect this business soundly.

CATESBY   My good lords both, with all the heed I can.

RICHARD   Shall we hear from you, Catesby, ere we sleep?   190

CATESBY   You shall, my lord.

RICHARD   At Crosby House, there shall you find us both.

Exit Catesby

BUCKINGHAM   Now, my lord,
What shall we do if we perceive
Lord Hastings will not yield to our complots?   195

RICHARD   Chop off his head.
Something we will determine.
And look when I am king, claim thou of me
The earldom of Hereford and all the movables
Whereof the king my brother was possessed.   200

BUCKINGHAM   I'll claim that promise at your grace's hand.

RICHARD   And look to have it yielded with all kindness.
Come, let us sup betimes, that afterwards
We may digest our complots in some form.   *Exeunt*

ACT 3 SCENE 2
Outside the house of Lord Hastings

Enter a MESSENGER *who knocks on the door of Hastings*

MESSENGER   My lord! My lord!

HASTINGS   [*Within*] Who knocks?

MESSENGER   One from the Lord Stanley.

The messenger warns Hastings that Stanley has dreamt that Richard revealed his cruel nature and danger threatens at tomorrow's councils. He urges Hastings to flee. Hastings mocks his fears and says Richard is friendly.

1 The boar

The boar was Richard's emblem. Stanley's dream that the boar has removed his helmet ('razèd off his helm') reveals his fear that Richard will turn on Hastings and himself. Hastings' reply continues the image, and mocks Stanley's dream.

Find a way for the actors to make clear to the audience that the 'boar' refers to Richard.

2 Naive Hastings (in pairs)

Shakespeare builds a good deal of dramatic irony into Hastings' lines 19–33. Only a few minutes earlier the audience has heard Richard's intention towards Hastings: 'Chop off his head'. Now Shakespeare makes Hastings appear naive and trusting by giving him language that stands in ironic contrast to what the play has revealed. Hastings speaks of his 'good friend Catesby' (line 22) and his confidence that 'the boar will use us kindly': 'kindly' can mean gentle, or after his own nature (what is the nature of a boar?)

Take parts as Hastings and the messenger and speak lines 4–33 to bring out Hastings' confident, but ill-founded trust.

3 Dreams

Hastings rebukes Stanley for believing in dreams. Dreams carried great significance to an Elizabethan audience, and they play an important part in *Richard III*. See page 233 for more information on dreams.

---

tedious wearisome
certifies swears
rue regret
the north (Stanley's power base)
divines foretells

toucheth affects
intelligence information
shallow unfounded
instance reason, cause
simple foolish

HASTINGS [*Within*] What is't o'clock?
MESSENGER Upon the stroke of four.   5

Enter LORD HASTINGS

HASTINGS Cannot my Lord Stanley sleep these tedious nights?
MESSENGER So it appears by that I have to say.
        First, he commends him to your noble self.
HASTINGS What then?
MESSENGER Then certifies your lordship that this night   10
        He dreamt the boar had razèd off his helm.
        Besides, he says there are two councils kept,
        And that may be determined at the one
        Which may make you and him to rue at th'other.
        Therefore he sends to know your lordship's pleasure,   15
        If you will presently take horse with him
        And with all speed post with him toward the north,
        To shun the danger that his soul divines.
HASTINGS Go, fellow, go, return unto thy lord;
        Bid him not fear the separated council.   20
        His honour and myself are at the one,
        And at the other is my good friend Catesby,
        Where nothing can proceed that toucheth us
        Whereof I shall not have intelligence.
        Tell him his fears are shallow, without instance.   25
        And for his dreams, I wonder he's so simple
        To trust the mockery of unquiet slumbers.
        To fly the boar before the boar pursues
        Were to incense the boar to follow us
        And make pursuit where he did mean no chase.   30
        Go, bid thy master rise and come to me,
        And we will both together to the Tower,
        Where he shall see the boar will use us kindly.
MESSENGER I'll go, my lord, and tell him what you say.   *Exit*

Enter CATESBY

CATESBY Many good morrows to my noble lord.   35
HASTINGS Good morrow, Catesby. You are early stirring.
        What news, what news, in this our tott'ring state?

Hastings refuses to support Richard's bid for the crown, but welcomes news of the fate of Rivers, Grey and Vaughan. He feels confident of Richard's friendship, but Catesby's words have ominous meaning.

1 Hastings' fatal mistakes (in pairs)

Take parts as Hastings and Catesby and speak lines 35–71, bringing out as clearly as possible the menace and dramatic irony of the situation. Use the following points to help you.

a Hastings is unaware that almost all he says is sealing his own fate. Catesby probes Hastings' intentions, continuing the metaphor of 'our tott'ring state' (line 37) to strengthen the impression of a country drunk and out of control with a crowned Richard the only solution. Hastings disagrees with Catesby's conclusion that Richard should be king, arguing he would rather first lose his own head ('this crown'). In what tone might he speak 'the crown' (line 41)?

b Try to bring out the dramatic irony as Hastings parades his self-assurance, totally unaware of the peril of his situation. He constantly refers to death, both his own and his enemies (lines 43–4, 50, 55 and 61).

c Catesby's replies are full of double meanings. Explore ways of showing how Catesby's sinister implications are hidden from the self-confident Hastings, but not the audience.

d In line 70, Catesby's aside refers to the grisly custom of displaying the heads of traitors on poles at London Bridge. If Catesby addresses line 70 directly to the audience, what gestures and expressions might he use? 'The princes' (line 69) are Richard and Buckingham.

---

reeling tottering, spinning
forward/Upon supporting
adversaries enemies
bar prevent

to the death at the risk of death
send some packing kill
account (line 69) regard
account (line 70) count on

CATESBY It is a reeling world indeed, my lord,
And I believe will never stand upright
Till Richard wear the garland of the realm.   40
HASTINGS How, wear the garland? Dost thou mean the crown?
CATESBY Ay, my good lord.
HASTINGS I'll have this crown of mine cut from my shoulders
Before I'll see the crown so foul misplaced.
But canst thou guess that he doth aim at it?   45
CATESBY Ay, on my life, and hopes to find you forward
Upon his party for the gain thereof.
And thereupon he sends you this good news,
That this same very day your enemies,
The kindred of the queen, must die at Pomfret.   50
HASTINGS Indeed, I am no mourner for that news,
Because they have been still my adversaries.
But that I'll give my voice on Richard's side
To bar my master's heirs in true descent,
God knows I will not do it, to the death.   55
CATESBY God keep your lordship in that gracious mind.
HASTINGS But I shall laugh at this a twelvemonth hence,
That they which brought me in my master's hate,
I live to look upon their tragedy.
Well, Catesby, ere a fortnight make me older,   60
I'll send some packing that yet think not on't.
CATESBY 'Tis a vile thing to die, my gracious lord,
When men are unprepared and look not for it.
HASTINGS Oh, monstrous, monstrous! And so falls it out
With Rivers, Vaughan, Grey; and so 'twill do   65
With some men else that think themselves as safe
As thou and I, who, as thou know'st, are dear
To princely Richard and to Buckingham.
CATESBY The princes both make high account of you.
[*Aside*] For they account his head upon the bridge.   70
HASTINGS I know they do, and I have well deserved it.

Enter LORD STANLEY [EARL OF DERBY]

Come on, come on, where is your boar spear, man?
Fear you the boar and go so unprovided?

Stanley is troubled by the separate meetings of the two councils and the executions at Pomfret. He agrees to go with Hastings to the Tower. Hastings recalls his own former imprisonment there.

1 Changing fortunes (in pairs)

Both Stanley and Hastings are aware of the dramatic changes in fortune experienced by those close to the throne. Hastings was himself imprisoned in the Tower. He now feels 'triumphant' (line 81) because he believes his future is secure. Stanley's warning that Rivers, Grey and Vaughan were happy ('jocund') when they rode to London to meet Prince Edward fails to shake Hastings' confidence.

Take parts and speak lines 72–95. Work out how, in speech and action, you might express Hastings' feelings of triumph in contrast to Stanley's worry about the rapid executions at Pomfret in line 86 ('This sudden stab of rancour I misdoubt').

2 Hastings' visitors

In this scene, Hastings receives visits from the messenger, Catesby and Stanley. Each brings messages and news which Hastings chooses to ignore. Consider each 'visitor' in turn, suggesting how each adds to the dramatic effect of the scene (for example, what they reveal of Hastings' character and how they deepen the dramatic irony).

3 Pursuivant and priest

Hastings' meeting with the pursuivant (line 94) and priest (line 108) appear chance encounters. You will find that Shakespeare's dramatic purpose for introducing them becomes clear in Act 3 Scene 4, lines 86–90. A pursuivant was a royal messenger with the power to make arrests.

---

rood cross	**have with you** come along
several separate (see page 106)	**Wot** know
state position	**truth** loyalty
o'ercast became dark	**wear their hats** hold office
rancour ill-will	**suggestion** instigation
spent getting late	**Gramercy** thank you

STANLEY My lord, good morrow. Good morrow, Catesby.
        You may jest on, but by the holy rood, 75
        I do not like these several councils, I.
HASTINGS My lord, I hold my life as dear as yours,
        And never in my days, I do protest,
        Was it so precious to me as 'tis now.
        Think you, but that I know our state secure, 80
        I would be so triumphant as I am?
STANLEY The lords at Pomfret, when they rode from London,
        Were jocund and supposed their states were sure,
        And they indeed had no cause to mistrust.
        But yet you see how soon the day o'ercast. 85
        This sudden stab of rancour I misdoubt.
        Pray God, I say, I prove a needless coward.
        What, shall we toward the Tower? The day is spent.
HASTINGS Come, come, have with you.
        Wot you what, my lord? 90
        Today the lords you talk of are beheaded.
STANLEY They, for their truth, might better wear their heads
        Than some that have accused them wear their hats.
        But come, my lord, let's away.

Enter a PURSUIVANT

HASTINGS Go on before, I'll talk with this good fellow. 95

Exeunt Lord Stanley and Catesby

        How now, sirrah? How goes the world with thee?
PURSUIVANT The better that your lordship please to ask.
HASTINGS I tell thee, man, 'tis better with me now
        Than when thou met'st me last, where now we meet.
        Then was I going prisoner to the Tower 100
        By the suggestion of the queen's allies.
        But now I tell thee (keep it to thyself)
        This day those enemies are put to death,
        And I in better state than e'er I was.
PURSUIVANT God hold it to your honour's good content. 105
HASTINGS Gramercy, fellow. There, drink that for me.

Throws him his purse

PURSUIVANT I thank your honour.   *Exit Pursuivant*

Hastings promises to pay the priest on the following Sunday.
Buckingham's aside reminds the audience that Hastings will die.
Rivers, Grey and Vaughan show defiance as they face death.

1 More dramatic irony

The dramatic irony of Hastings' situation continues to the end of
the scene. If Richard's plan succeeds, Hastings will not be alive to
pay the priest. The reference to 'no shriving work' is both Buckingham's cruel joke, and dramatically ironic. 'Shriving', as
Buckingham uses it, is the blessing for confessing his sins to a priest
that a condemned person receives shortly before his execution. The
confession and blessing signified that the executed person would not
suffer in hell. Buckingham's surface meaning is that Hastings is in
no need of shriving, but his aside at line 122 reminds the audience
that Hastings is doomed (he will stay for 'supper' – but he will be
dead).

Look back over Scene 2 to remind yourself of examples of irony
and dramatic irony. Choose one example of each that you think is
particularly effective on stage.

2 Executions at Pontefract Castle

The opening stage direction of Scene 3 describes the soldiers
('Halberds') taking the three men to their deaths. Think about how
an effective dramatic entrance for Rivers, Grey and Vaughan (for
example, sympathetic, cruel, thrown in, formal, or some other way)
would influence the feelings of the audience towards the three men
as they face execution.

Sir John respectful address
 to a clergyman
exercise religious service
content pay
no shriving work no need for
 confession (see above)

thence leaves there
Dispatch that's enough!
The limit of your lives is out
 you have reached your lives' end

Enter a PRIEST

PRIEST Well met, my lord. I am glad to see your honour.
HASTINGS I thank thee, good Sir John, with all my heart.
   I am in your debt for your last exercise.   110
   Come the next sabbath, and I will content you.
PRIEST I'll wait upon your lordship.

Enter BUCKINGHAM

BUCKINGHAM What, talking with a priest, Lord Chamberlain?
   Your friends at Pomfret, they do need the priest.
   Your honour hath no shriving work in hand.   115
HASTINGS Good faith, and when I met this holy man,
   The men you talk of came into my mind.
   What, go you toward the Tower?
BUCKINGHAM I do, my lord, but long I cannot stay there.
   I shall return before your lordship thence.   120
HASTINGS Nay, like enough, for I stay dinner there.
BUCKINGHAM [*Aside*] And supper too, although thou know'st it not. –
   Come, will you go?
HASTINGS I'll wait upon your lordship.   *Exeunt*

ACT 3 SCENE 3
Yorkshire: Pontefract Castle

Enter SIR RICHARD RATCLIFFE with Halberds, taking RIVERS,
GREY, and VAUGHAN to their deaths

RIVERS Sir Richard Ratcliffe, let me tell thee this:
   Today shalt thou behold a subject die
   For truth, for duty, and for loyalty.
GREY God bless the prince from all the pack of you.
   A knot you are of damnèd bloodsuckers.   5
VAUGHAN You live that shall cry woe for this hereafter.
RATCLIFFE Dispatch. The limit of your lives is out.

The Woodvilles recall past murders at Pontefract Castle.
They remember Margaret's curses and hope that Richard, Buckingham
and Hastings will also suffer. The council begins planning
Prince Edward's coronation.

1 Triple executions: on or off stage?

Grey remembers Margaret's curse, and Rivers hopes Margaret's curses will also visit revenge on Hastings, Buckingham and Richard. He requests God not to demand more deaths from the Woodville family. The stage direction clearly indicates that the Woodvilles are executed off stage, but some productions show their deaths on stage. Which would you choose? Why?

'Now Margaret's curse is fall'n upon our heads'. To heighten dramatic effect, this production staged the death of Rivers, Grey and Vaughan in semi-darkness, with hooded executioners behind each man.

slander disgrace
dismal seat sad place
is expiate has come
determine of decide on

nomination the day to be decided
Lord Protector Richard
inward intimate

RIVERS Oh Pomfret, Pomfret! Oh thou bloody prison,
    Fatal and ominous to noble peers.
    Within the guilty closure of thy walls   10
    Richard the Second here was hacked to death,
    And, for more slander to thy dismal seat,
    We give to thee our guiltless blood to drink.
GREY Now Margaret's curse is fall'n upon our heads,
    When she exclaimed on Hastings, you, and I   15
    For standing by when Richard stabbed her son.
RIVERS Then cursed she Richard,
    Then cursed she Buckingham,
    Then cursed she Hastings. Oh remember God,
    To hear her prayer for them, as now for us.   20
    And for my sister and her princely sons,
    Be satisfied, dear God, with our true blood,
    Which, as thou know'st, unjustly must be spilt.
RATCLIFFE Make haste. The hour of death is expiate.
RIVERS Come, Grey, come, Vaughan, let us here embrace.   25
    Farewell, until we meet again in heaven.   *Exeunt*

ACT 3 SCENE 4
A room in the Tower of London

Enter BUCKINGHAM, STANLEY EARL OF DERBY, HASTINGS,
BISHOP OF ELY, NORFOLK, RATCLIFFE, LOVELL, *with others*

HASTINGS Now, noble peers, the cause why we are met
    Is to determine of the coronation.
    In God's name, speak. When is the royal day?
BUCKINGHAM Is all things ready for the royal time?
STANLEY It is, and wants but nomination.   5
ELY Tomorrow, then, I judge a happy day.
BUCKINGHAM Who knows the Lord Protector's mind herein?
    Who is most inward with the noble duke?
ELY Your grace, we think, should soonest know his mind.

Buckingham denies his close association with Richard. Hastings assumes Richard will vote as he does. Richard sends Ely for strawberries, then tells Buckingham of Hastings' opposition to his plans.

1 Faces and hearts

An over-confident Hastings and the council begin planning Prince Edward's coronation. Buckingham's lines 10–13 give dramatic force to the theme of appearance and reality, the ability to correctly judge a person by external signs. Buckingham says he knows Richard's outward appearance ('faces') but not his inward thoughts ('hearts'). In sharp contrast, Hastings claims a close relationship with Richard and assumes that Richard will willingly accept his view as his own.

The play has already shown many examples of the differences between 'faces' and 'hearts'. As you read on, collect further instances of outward appearances masking inward reality.

2 Hastings' downfall (I) (in groups of five)

Lines 21–78 show the downfall of Hastings (who has shown himself to be unable to distinguish between 'faces' and 'hearts'). Take parts as Buckingham, Ely, Stanley, Hastings and Richard and work out a performance of the lines.

a In what tone does Richard speak lines 22–5?

b How might you give special emphasis to Buckingham's use of theatrical metaphors ('cue', 'pronounced', 'part', 'your voice')?

c Suggest some reasons why Richard sends Ely for strawberries.

d In what style does Richard speak to Buckingham in lines 35–40? (whispering? angrily? with humour?)

e How do Richard and Buckingham make their exit? (obviously plotting? pretending normality?)

---

purpose intention
sounded questioned
take in gentle part accept willingly
neglect cause to be neglected
design plan
voice vote

testy irate
hot angry
His master's child Prince Edward
sudden soon
provided convinced
prolonged postponed

BUCKINGHAM We know each other's faces. For our hearts,   10
    He knows no more of mine than I of yours,
    Or I of his, my lord, than you of mine.
    Lord Hastings, you and he are near in love.
HASTINGS I thank his grace, I know he loves me well.
    But for his purpose in the coronation,   15
    I have not sounded him, nor he delivered
    His gracious pleasure any way therein.
    But you, my honourable lords, may name the time,
    And in the duke's behalf I'll give my voice,
    Which I presume he'll take in gentle part.   20

            Enter RICHARD DUKE OF GLOUCESTER

ELY In happy time, here comes the duke himself.
RICHARD My noble lords and cousins all, good morrow.
    I have been long a sleeper, but I trust
    My absence doth neglect no great design
    Which by my presence might have been concluded.   25
BUCKINGHAM Had you not come upon your cue, my lord,
    William Lord Hastings had pronounced your part,
    I mean your voice for crowning of the king.
RICHARD Than my Lord Hastings no man might be bolder.
    His lordship knows me well and loves me well. –   30
    My lord of Ely, when I was last in Holborn,
    I saw good strawberries in your garden there.
    I do beseech you, send for some of them.
ELY Marry, and will, my lord, with all my heart.   *Exit Bishop*
RICHARD Cousin of Buckingham, a word with you.   35
    Catesby hath sounded Hastings in our business,
    And finds the testy gentleman so hot
    That he will lose his head ere give consent
    His master's child, as worshipfully he terms it,
    Shall lose the royalty of England's throne.   40
BUCKINGHAM Withdraw yourself a while; I'll go with you.

            Exeunt [Richard and Buckingham]

STANLEY We have not yet set down this day of triumph.
    Tomorrow, in my judgement, is too sudden,
    For I myself am not so well provided
    As else I would be, were the day prolonged.   45

Hastings claims Richard's face is filled with good will. Richard accuses Queen Elizabeth and Jane Shore of using witchcraft to wither his arm. He condemns Hastings to death as Jane Shore's protector.

1 Hastings' downfall (II) (in groups of five or more)

The dramatic irony intensifies as Hastings continues to mistakenly assume that 'faces' equal 'hearts'. He claims that Richard is unable to conceal his feelings and intentions ('I think there's never a man in Christendom/Can lesser hide his love or hate, than he'). Continue to work on your performance by thinking about:

a How might the strawberries play a part in the sentencing of Hastings?

b How Stanley speaks lines 54–5. Does his tone show that he suspects Richard of false appearance?

c At what point does Hastings realise his faith in recognising 'hearts' and 'faces' is mistaken, and how does he react to his death sentence?

d How does Richard perform the inbuilt stage direction in lines 66–8?

e Richard's command 'rise and follow me' (line 78) is an important part of his power-play. How do the nobles obey his order to desert Hastings and follow Richard? Identify how each character shows their allegiance to Richard.

f How would you direct Ely and his strawberries in this scene? Would you present Ely as a fool, or aware of the power-play?

smooth at ease
conceit idea
livelihood expression
doom judge, condemn to death

blasted struck by lightning
sapling young tree
strumpet prostitute

Enter the BISHOP OF ELY

ELY Where is my lord the Duke of Gloucester?
      I have sent for these strawberries.
HASTINGS His grace looks cheerfully and smooth this morning.
      There's some conceit or other likes him well
      When that he bids good morrow with such spirit.   50
      I think there's never a man in Christendom
      Can lesser hide his love or hate, than he,
      For by his face straight shall you know his heart.
STANLEY What of his heart perceive you in his face
      By any livelihood he showed today?   55
HASTINGS Marry, that with no man here he is offended,
      For were he, he had shown it in his looks.

Enter RICHARD *and* BUCKINGHAM

RICHARD I pray you all, tell me what they deserve
      That do conspire my death with devilish plots
      Of damnèd witchcraft and that have prevailed   60
      Upon my body with their hellish charms.
HASTINGS The tender love I bear your grace, my lord,
      Makes me most forward in this princely presence
      To doom th'offenders, whosoe'er they be.
      I say, my lord, they have deservèd death.   65
RICHARD Then be your eyes the witness of their evil.
      Look how I am bewitched. Behold, mine arm
      Is like a blasted sapling, withered up.
      And this is Edward's wife, that monstrous witch,
      Consorted with that harlot, strumpet Shore,   70
      That by their witchcraft thus have markèd me.
HASTINGS If they have done this deed, my noble lord –
RICHARD If? Thou protector of this damnèd strumpet,
      Talk'st thou to me of ifs? Thou art a traitor.
      Off with his head! Now by Saint Paul I swear,   75
      I will not dine until I see the same.
      Lovell and Ratcliffe, look that it be done.
      The rest that love me, rise and follow me.

Exeunt [all but] Lovell and Ratcliffe, with the Lord Hastings

Hastings regrets ignoring Stanley's warning, the omen of his horse's stumbling and his earlier over-confidence. He recalls Margaret's curse, reflects on the nature of fame, and prophesies a bleak future for an England under Richard.

1 Hastings has ignored the warnings (in pairs)

As Hastings reflects on his actions and decisions, he blames his own foolishness for his fate. He now realises he has ignored or misinterpreted events and has failed to respond to ominous signs. Identify each event or sign he mentions in lines 79–92, and briefly remind yourself of the particular moment that each occurred in the play and how Hastings responded to each. (Note: this is the first time his stumbling horse is mentioned.)

2 Does Hastings gain self-knowledge? (in pairs)

Hastings realises too late that in pursuing earthly fame ('momentary grace of mortal men') he has ignored the blessing of God. In an extended simile, he compares the fragility of human success ('your good looks') to a drunken sailor on the mast of sailing a ship. Discuss how convincing you find Hastings' discovery of self-knowledge as he is about to be executed.

3 Who? Us?

Lovell and Ratcliffe both take Hastings away for execution. How would you direct the actors playing Lovell and Ratcliffe – as brutal, mechanical, officious, embarrassed, or in some other way? How do they react to Hastings' final line (which appears to be directed at them)?

---

whit portion
fond foolish
rouse our helms raise our helmets
footcloth horse elaborately clothed
  horse, a symbol of wealth
lighted landed

shrift confession and absolution
in air of on the airy foundation of
the deep sea
bootless fruitless
block execution block for a
  beheading

HASTINGS   Woe, woe for England, not a whit for me,
          For I, too fond, might have prevented this.   80
          Stanley did dream the boar did rouse our helms,
          And I did scorn it and disdain to fly.
          Three times today my footcloth horse did stumble,
          And started when he looked upon the Tower,
          As loath to bear me to the slaughterhouse.   85
          Oh, now I need the priest that spake to me.
          I now repent I told the pursuivant,
          As too triumphing, how mine enemies
          Today at Pomfret bloodily were butchered,
          And I myself secure in grace and favour.   90
          Oh Margaret, Margaret, now thy heavy curse
          Is lighted on poor Hastings' wretched head.
RATCLIFFE   Come, come, dispatch. The duke would be at dinner.
          Make a short shrift; he longs to see your head.
HASTINGS   Oh momentary grace of mortal men,   95
          Which we more hunt for than the grace of God,
          Who builds his hope in air of your good looks
          Lives like a drunken sailor on a mast,
          Ready with every nod to tumble down
          Into the fatal bowels of the deep.   100
LOVELL   Come, come, dispatch; 'tis bootless to exclaim.
HASTINGS   Oh bloody Richard, miserable England,
          I prophesy the fearful'st time to thee
          That ever wretched age hath looked upon.
          Come, lead me to the block; bear him my head.   105
          They smile at me who shortly shall be dead.

                                                    Exeunt

King Richard III

> *Buckingham claims he can act terror convincingly. He and Richard pretend an attack is imminent. Richard pretends to mourn Hastings' death saying he loved him and thought him a great friend.*

1 Enjoying a crisis (in groups of six)

Richard and Buckingham reveal the techniques they will use to act convincingly in front of the Lord Mayor of London, then begin to put them into action. Take parts as Richard, Buckingham, Lovell, Ratcliffe, Catesby and the Lord Mayor. Rehearse and perform lines 1–24, playing up Richard and Buckingham's malicious sense of fun and the panic they generate. The following points may help you:

a Richard and Buckingham appear in rusty ('rotten') armour which is extremely ugly ('marvellous ill-favoured'). How might you achieve an impression of their appearance if you have no armour or costume?

b Lines 1–9 describe the techniques of actors of the great tragedies and their methods of delivering lines in Shakespeare's times. Practise each technique they describe (for example, 'quake', 'change thy colour', and so on; there are at least twelve actions).

c In lines 14–20, Richard and Buckingham stage-manage a crisis for the benefit of the Lord Mayor. They pretend they are being attacked by enemies. Using the stage directions in the language, work out your own performance that will convince the Lord Mayor that an attack is taking place.

d How and when might Hastings' head be revealed to greatest dramatic effect?

---

counterfeit imitate
pry look around suspiciously
in their offices to function
stratagems tricks
o'erlook inspect

defend thee guard yourself
plainest most honest
my book
  my diary, keeper of my secrets

Act 3 Scene 5
The courtyard of the Tower of London

Enter RICHARD *and* BUCKINGHAM *in rotten armour,*
marvellous ill-favoured

RICHARD Come, cousin, canst thou quake and change thy colour,
　　　Murder thy breath in middle of a word,
　　　And then again begin, and stop again,
　　　As if thou were distraught and mad with terror?
BUCKINGHAM Tut, I can counterfeit the deep tragedian,　　　　5
　　　Speak and look back, and pry on every side,
　　　Tremble and start at wagging of a straw.
　　　Intending deep suspicion, ghastly looks
　　　Are at my service, like enforcèd smiles.
　　　And both are ready in their offices　　　　10
　　　At any time to grace my stratagems.
　　　But what, is Catesby gone?
RICHARD He is, and see, he brings the Mayor along.

Enter the MAYOR *and* CATESBY

BUCKINGHAM Lord Mayor –
RICHARD Look to the drawbridge there!　　　　15
BUCKINGHAM Hark, a drum!
RICHARD Catesby, o'erlook the walls!
BUCKINGHAM Lord Mayor, the reason we have sent –
RICHARD Look back, defend thee, here are enemies!
BUCKINGHAM God and our innocency defend and guard us!　　　　20

Enter LOVELL *and* RATCLIFFE *with Hastings's head*

RICHARD Be patient; they are friends, Ratcliffe and Lovell.
LOVELL Here is the head of that ignoble traitor,
　　　The dangerous and unsuspected Hastings.
RICHARD So dear I loved the man that I must weep.
　　　I took him for the plainest harmless creature　　　　25
　　　That breathed upon the earth a Christian,
　　　Made him my book, wherein my soul recorded
　　　The history of all her secret thoughts.

Richard says that Hastings, apart from his affair with Jane Shore, was never suspected of evil. Buckingham claims Hastings plotted to kill himself and Richard. He pretends to regret the mayor did not hear Hastings' confession.

1 Convincing the Lord Mayor (in groups of three)

Richard and Buckingham must convince the Lord Mayor that the seemingly innocent Hastings was a clever ('subtle') traitor who plotted their deaths and deserved to die. Take parts as Richard, Buckingham and the Lord Mayor and speak lines 24–71, using the points below to help you.

a Jane Shore is mentioned by Richard in line 31 and by Buckingham (lines 50–1). Why do you think Richard and Buckingham remind the Lord Mayor of Hastings' relationship with Jane Shore?

b The Lord Mayor's response (line 40) to Buckingham's lie that Hastings intended to murder Richard and himself could be spoken in different ways. Explore ways of speaking the line (for example, doubt, shock, disbelief or amazement).

c Richard answers the Lord Mayor with rhetorical questions (lines 41–6) invoking Christian ethics, the law, the country and the importance of his and Buckingham's security ('our persons' safety'). Speak the lines giving each item different emphasis. What convinces the Lord Mayor: one particular item? the collective argument?

d The mayor seems to accept the story and is then dismissed by Buckingham. Work out how he might speak lines 62–6 and the manner of his dismissal and exit.

---

daubed plastered over	**fair befall you**
omitted excepted	good fortune come to you
conversation sexual liaison	**determined** intended
from all attainder of suspects	**meanings** intentions
free of all taint of suspicion	**prevented** forestalled
covert'st sheltered	**Misconster** misinterpret
most secret and concealed	**carping** critical

So smooth he daubed his vice with show of virtue
That his apparent open guilt omitted,   30
I mean his conversation with Shore's wife,
He lived from all attainder of suspects.
BUCKINGHAM Well, well, he was the covert'st sheltered traitor
That ever lived.
        Would you imagine, or almost believe,   35
Were't not that by great preservation
We live to tell it, that the subtle traitor
This day had plotted, in the Council House,
To murder me and my good lord of Gloucester?
MAYOR Had he done so?   40
RICHARD What. Think you we are Turks or infidels?
Or that we would, against the form of law,
Proceed thus rashly in the villain's death,
But that the extreme peril of the case,
The peace of England, and our persons' safety,   45
Enforced us to this execution?
MAYOR Now fair befall you, he deserved his death,
And your good graces both have well proceeded
To warn false traitors from the like attempts.
BUCKINGHAM I never looked for better at his hands   50
After he once fell in with Mistress Shore.
Yet had we not determined he should die
Until your lordship came to see his end,
Which now the loving haste of these our friends,
Something against our meanings, have prevented;   55
Because, my lord, I would have had you heard
The traitor speak and timorously confess
The manner and the purpose of his treasons,
That you might well have signified the same
Unto the citizens, who haply may   60
Misconster us in him and wail his death.
MAYOR But, my good lord, your graces' words shall serve
As well as I had seen and heard him speak.
And do not doubt, right noble princes both,
But I'll acquaint our duteous citizens   65
With all your just proceedings in this case.
RICHARD And to that end we wished your lordship here,
T'avoid the censures of the carping world.

Richard sends Buckingham to spread rumours about King Edward IV: the illegitimacy of his children, his uncontrolled lust, his injustice and his bastardy. If believed, Buckingham must bring the Lord Mayor and citizens to Baynard Castle.

1 Four rumours

Richard instructs Buckingham to spread rumours about Edward IV and his children which question their legal right to claim the English throne. Buckingham is to make four allegations to the Lord Mayor and leading citizens at the Guildhall.

Line 75: The illegitimacy of King Edward IV's children.

Lines 76–9: Edward ordered the unjust execution of a merchant who had told his son he would inherit his house named 'The Crown'. Edward misinterpreted the merchant's wishes, believing he referred to his 'crown', meaning kingdom.

Lines 80-84: Edward's lustful nature.

Lines 85-92: King Edward is illegitimate because the Duchess of York conceived him while her husband was fighting in France, and there was no physical resemblance between father and son.

All four allegations are untrue (with the possible exception of Edward's lustful nature: he had a reputation as a notorious womaniser). They are largely the invention of Sir Thomas More's anti-Richard history (see page 2).

In Richard's time, the equivalent of a 'press release' was a poster nailed up in public places. Use the rumours above to write the press release which Buckingham issues casting doubt on Prince Edward's legitimacy to claim the throne.

Go after follow
hies him in all post
 goes at top speed
meetest vantage of the time
 most opportune moment
Infer imply
luxury lust

prey sexual conquest
computation counting, reckoning
his begot fathered by him (York)
lineaments features
Baynard's Castle
 one of Richard's London homes

BUCKINGHAM Which, since you come too late of our intent,
        Yet witness what you hear we did intend.   70
        And so, my good lord Mayor, we bid farewell.

                       Exit Mayor

RICHARD Go after, after, cousin Buckingham.
        The Mayor towards Guildhall hies him in all post.
        There, at your meetest vantage of the time,
        Infer the bastardy of Edward's children.   75
        Tell them how Edward put to death a citizen
        Only for saying he would make his son
        Heir to the crown, meaning indeed his house,
        Which, by the sign thereof, was termèd so.
        Moreover, urge his hateful luxury   80
        And bestial appetite in change of lust,
        Which stretched unto their servants, daughters, wives,
        Even where his raging eye or savage heart,
        Without control, lusted to make a prey.
        Nay, for a need, thus far come near my person: 85
        Tell them, when that my mother went with child
        Of that insatiate Edward, noble York,
        My princely father, then had wars in France,
        And by true computation of the time
        Found that the issue was not his begot,   90
        Which well appearèd in his lineaments,
        Being nothing like the noble duke, my father.
        Yet touch this sparingly, as 'twere far off,
        Because, my lord, you know my mother lives.
BUCKINGHAM Doubt not, my lord, I'll play the orator   95
        As if the golden fee for which I plead
        Were for myself. And so, my lord, adieu.
RICHARD If you thrive well, bring them to Baynard's Castle,
        Where you shall find me well accompanied
        With reverend fathers and well-learnèd bishops.   100
BUCKINGHAM I go, and towards three or four o'clock
        Look for the news that the Guildhall affords.

                    Exit Buckingham

Richard sends for two churchmen, then plans to isolate Clarence's and Edward's children. The scrivener reflects on the deceit involved in Hastings' execution. Buckingham reports the citizens' lack of reaction to his speech.

1 The next steps (in pairs)

Richard sends Lovell to fetch two influential churchmen, Dr Shaw and Friar Penker, to help win the citizens' support for his plan to become king.

a Make a guess about how Richard intends to use the two churchmen. Check your guess in lines 94–6 in Scene 7.

b Richard intends to make secret arrangements ('some privy order') to ensure Clarence's children are kept isolated from view. He will ensure King Edward's rightful heirs, the princes in the Tower, receive no visitors. Discuss reasons why he might feel these moves are necessary to his plotting.

2 Tampering with justice (in pairs)

The scrivener, a professional writer who drafts legal documents, has written Hastings' indictment in the final, appropriate legal form ('in a set hand fairly is engrossed'). He estimates eleven hours of work have gone into the original draft. He has worked on the draft another eleven hours, yet only five hours previously Hastings had not been accused or questioned and was free ('Untainted, unexamined, free, at liberty'). He questions whether there is a person so stupid ('gross') who cannot see such obvious trickery ('palpable device'). Line 12 reveals the world Richard is creating where people are afraid of criticising obvious injustice.

This brief scene is often cut in performance. Discuss what is lost if the scene is not included in a production of the play.

---

no manner person nobody
indictment legal accusation
Paul's St Paul's, a meeting place
  of lawyers
the sequel the sequence of events

precedent original draft
the while at present
seen in thought
  only thought about

RICHARD   Go, Lovell, with all speed to Doctor Shaw.
Go thou to Friar Penker. Bid them both
Meet me within this hour at Baynard's Castle.   *Exit [Lovell]*   105
Now will I go to take some privy order
To draw the brats of Clarence out of sight,
And to give order that no manner person
Have any time recourse unto the princes.   *Exeunt*

ACT 3 SCENE 6
London: the scrivener's house

Enter a SCRIVENER

SCRIVENER   Here is the indictment of the good Lord Hastings,
Which in a set hand fairly is engrossed
That it may be today read o'er in Paul's.
And mark how well the sequel hangs together:
Eleven hours I have spent to write it over,   5
For yesternight by Catesby was it sent me;
The precedent was full as long a-doing.
And yet within these five hours Hastings lived,
Untainted, unexamined, free, at liberty.
Here's a good world the while.   10
Who is so gross that cannot see this palpable device?
Yet who so bold but says he sees it not?
Bad is the world, and all will come to naught
When such ill dealing must be seen in thought.   *Exit*

ACT 3 SCENE 7
London: the courtyard of Baynard's Castle

Enter RICHARD and BUCKINGHAM

RICHARD   How now, how now, what say the citizens?
BUCKINGHAM   Now, by the holy mother of our Lord,
The citizens are mum, say not a word.
RICHARD   Touched you the bastardy of Edward's children?

Buckingham reports that the citizens remained silent as he slandered Edward and praised Richard. He explains how he used the cheers of a few of his own men to claim that all the citizens support Richard.

1 Buckingham: an unsuccessful orator? (in pairs)

Buckingham plays an increasingly important role as Richard's chief henchman and mouthpiece, revealing a strong understanding of political double-dealing. He uses the four allegations suggested by Richard (see page 128) and adds more of his own:

Line 5: the rumour that Edward had been engaged to Elizabeth Lucy.

Line 6: the rumour that Edward dishonoured a deputy (negotiator) who had arranged for him to marry the sister-in-law of the King of France.

Lines 15–17: Richard was a brave war leader, who captured the Scottish city of Berwick in 1482 ('victories in Scotland'), but Buckingham falsely adds 'virtue, fair humility'.

Unable to rouse the citizens with his oratory, Buckingham asks the Lord Mayor for an explanation of the lack of response ('wilful silence'). The Lord Mayor replies that the people are only used to being addressed by a legal officer ('the Recorder'). Buckingham's speech is repeated, but the Lord Mayor refuses to commit himself to Richard's cause ('But nothing spoke in warrant from himself').

Buckingham has said that he will 'play the orator' but he doesn't seem to have been very successful. Take turns to speak everything Buckingham says on the opposite page. Bring out the emotions he feels as he tells how he embellished the rumours and yet could not get the citizens to support Richard.

enforcement violation
Withal also
right idea true image
discourse speech

reprehended rebuked
vantage advantage
Argues proves

BUCKINGHAM I did, with his contràct with Lady Lucy   5
        And his contràct by deputy in France;
        Th'insatiate greediness of his desire
        And his enforcement of the city wives;
        His tyranny for trifles; his own bastardy,
        As being got, your father then in France,   10
        And his resemblance being not like the duke.
        Withal, I did infer your lineaments,
        Being the right idea of your father
        Both in your form and nobleness of mind;
        Laid open all your victories in Scotland,   15
        Your discipline in war, wisdom in peace,
        Your bounty, virtue, fair humility;
        Indeed, left nothing fitting for your purpose
        Untouched or slightly handled in discourse.
        And when my oratory drew toward end,   20
        I bid them that did love their country's good
        Cry 'God save Richard, England's royal king!'
RICHARD And did they so?
BUCKINGHAM No, so God help me, they spake not a word,
        But like dumb statuès or breathing stones   25
        Stared each on other and looked deadly pale.
        Which when I saw, I reprehended them,
        And asked the Mayor what meant this wilful silence.
        His answer was, the people were not used
        To be spoke to but by the Recorder.   30
        Then he was urged to tell my tale again:
        'Thus saith the duke, thus hath the duke inferred',
        But nothing spoke in warrant from himself.
        When he had done, some followers of mine own
        At lower end of the hall hurled up their caps,   35
        And some ten voices cried 'God save King Richard!'
        And thus I took the vantage of those few:
        'Thanks, gentle citizens and friends', quoth I,
        'This general applause and cheerful shout
        Argues your wisdom and your love to Richard.'   40
        And even here broke off and came away.
RICHARD What tongueless blocks were they! Would they not speak?
        Will not the Mayor, then, and his brethren, come?

Buckingham instructs Richard to appear saintly before the Lord Mayor.
Catesby reports that Richard cannot be disturbed while he is praying.
Buckingham contrasts Richard's piety with Edward's dissolute ways.

1 Sexism?

The remainder of Scene 7 is a richly ironic episode in which
appearances are almost invariably deceptive. To fool the Lord
Mayor and the citizens, Buckingham urges Richard to pretend fear
('intend some fear') and to be interrupted only by very important
entreaties ('mighty suit') from the Lord Mayor.

The two men engage in sexual banter as they make preparations.
Buckingham jokes on the proverb which states that virgins say 'no'
to sexual advances when they mean 'yes' ('still answer nay and take
it'). Richard hopes his 'nay' will bring a successful birth ('a happy
issue'). Imagine that someone says to you: 'I think lines 50–3 should
be cut in performance. They are sexist and add nothing to the play'.
Make your reply.

2 'A holy descant' (in groups of three)

Using a musical metaphor, Buckingham describes how he will play
a variety of ingenious variations ('descant') on Richard's repeated
theme ('ground') of pretended piety. He makes a start in lines 70–9
in which he contrasts Richard with Edward. As one person speaks
Buckingham's lines slowly, the second person echoes each example
of Edward's wantonness, and the third person echoes each example
of Richard's piety.

---

leads flat roof covered in lead
dance attendance
 wait obsequiously
Divinely bent devoutly inclined
holy exercise worship
deep designs important matters

lulling lolling
brace of courtesans two whores
deep divines learned clergymen
engross fatten
watchful unsleeping
sovereignty kingship

BUCKINGHAM The Mayor is here at hand; intend some fear.
        Be not you spoke with but by mighty suit.   45
        And look you get a prayer book in your hand
        And stand between two churchmen, good my lord,
        For on that ground I'll make a holy descant.
        And be not easily won to our requests;
        Play the maid's part: still answer nay and take it.   50
RICHARD I go; and if you plead as well for them
        As I can say nay to thee for myself,
        No doubt we bring it to a happy issue.
BUCKINGHAM Go, go, up to the leads. The Lord Mayor knocks.

                               Exit [Richard]

            Enter the MAYOR *and Citizens*

        Welcome, my lord. I dance attendance here.   55
        I think the duke will not be spoke withal.

                Enter CATESBY

BUCKINGHAM Now, Catesby, what says your lord to my request?
CATESBY He doth entreat your grace, my noble lord,
        To visit him tomorrow or next day.
        He is within, with two right reverend fathers,   60
        Divinely bent to meditation,
        And in no worldly suits would he be moved
        To draw him from his holy exercise.
BUCKINGHAM Return, good Catesby, to the gracious duke.
        Tell him myself, the Mayor, and aldermen   65
        In deep designs, in matter of great moment,
        No less importing than our general good,
        Are come to have some conference with his grace.
CATESBY I'll signify so much unto him straight.   *Exit*
BUCKINGHAM Ah ha, my lord, this prince is not an Edward. 70
        He is not lulling on a lewd love-bed
        But on his knees at meditation,
        Not dallying with a brace of courtesans
        But meditating with two deep divines,
        Not sleeping to engross his idle body   75
        But praying, to enrich his watchful soul.
        Happy were England, would this virtuous prince
        Take on his grace the sovereignty thereof,
        But sure I fear we shall not win him to it.

Catesby reports that Richard fears the citizens wish him harm. Richard appears between two churchmen. Buckingham asks him to listen to the citizens' requests, but Richard says he fears he has displeased them.

Richard appears between two bishops. Identify the lines spoken.

Marry by Our Lady
at their beads
  saying their rosary, praying
much to draw them thence
  difficult to attract their attention
stay stop

know recognise
Deferred the visitation
  put off visiting
disgracious displeasing,
  unacceptable

MAYOR Marry, God defend his grace should say us nay.   80
BUCKINGHAM I fear he will. Here Catesby comes again.

Enter CATESBY

Now, Catesby, what says his grace?
CATESBY He wonders to what end you have assembled
Such troops of citizens to come to him,
His grace not being warned thereof before.   85
He fears, my lord, you mean no good to him.
BUCKINGHAM Sorry I am my noble cousin should
Suspect me that I mean no good to him.
By heaven, we come to him in perfect love,
And so once more return and tell his grace.   90

Exit [Catesby]

When holy and devout religious men
Are at their beads, 'tis much to draw them thence,
So sweet is zealous contemplation.

Enter RICHARD *aloft, between two Bishops*

MAYOR See where his grace stands, 'tween two clergymen.
BUCKINGHAM Two props of virtue for a Christian prince,   95
To stay him from the fall of vanity.
And see, a book of prayer in his hand,
True ornaments to know a holy man —
Famous Plantagenet, most gracious prince,
Lend favourable ear to our requests,   100
And pardon us the interruption
Of thy devotion and right Christian zeal.
RICHARD My lord, there needs no such apology.
I do beseech your grace to pardon me,
Who, earnest in the service of my God,   105
Deferred the visitation of my friends.
But leaving this, what is your grace's pleasure?
BUCKINGHAM Even that, I hope, which pleaseth God above
And all good men of this ungoverned isle.
RICHARD I do suspect I have done some offence   110
That seems disgracious in the city's eye,
And that you come to reprehend my ignorance.
BUCKINGHAM You have, my lord. Would it might please your grace
On our entreaties to amend your fault.

Buckingham puts forward several reasons to persuade Richard to become king. He claims it is the citizens' wish. Richard debates whether he should reply or remain silent.

1 Buckingham's rhetoric (in pairs)

The plot to fool the Lord Mayor and citizens into accepting Richard as king continues with a brilliant display of rhetoric (persuasive language).

Lines 116–21: Buckingham tells Richard that he is wrong to give up his right to the crown in favour of corrupt members of his family ('blemished stock').

Lines 122–8: he urges Richard to awake to action because England is sick and her royal family at the point of death ('almost shouldered in the swallowing gulf/Of dark forgetfulness and deep oblivion').

Lines 129–35: the people beg ('solicit') Richard to cure ('recure') England by becoming not an agent ('factor') of another, but the true king in his own right.

Lines 136–9: all this is the wish of the citizens; I speak for them.

Speak Buckingham's lines 116–39 as persuasively as you can.

2 Mock-modest Richard (I)

In lines 140–72, Richard's answer to Buckingham's offer of the crown his formal language masks his ambition. Lines 140–52 are like an internal debate that attempts to balance two opposing arguments: to be silent or to speak. On the one hand, his silence might be interpreted as acceptance of the crown; on the other, if he speaks it may seem like a reprimand to good friends.

---

sceptered office position as king
lineal glory inherited honours
blemished stock impure family
graft with united to, joined with
shouldered pushed into
empery dominion, empire
consorted associated

vehement instigation
 strong insistence
move persuade
degree status
suit request
seasoned made agreeable
checked rebuked

RICHARD   Else wherefore breathe I in a Christian land?   115
BUCKINGHAM   Know then, it is your fault that you resign
   The supreme seat, the throne majestical,
   The sceptered office of your ancestors,
   Your state of fortune and your due of birth,
   The lineal glory of your royal house,   120
   To the corruption of a blemished stock;
   While in the mildness of your sleepy thoughts,
   Which here we waken to our country's good,
   The noble isle doth want her proper limbs;
   Her face defaced with scars of infamy,   125
   Her royal stock graft with ignoble plants,
   And almost shouldered in the swallowing gulf
   Of dark forgetfulness and deep oblivion.
   Which to recure, we heartily solicit
   Your gracious self to take on you the charge   130
   And kingly government of this your land,
   Not as protector, steward, substitute,
   Or lowly factor for another's gain,
   But as successively from blood to blood,
   Your right of birth, your empery, your own.   135
   For this, consorted with the citizens,
   Your very worshipful and loving friends,
   And by their vehement instigation,
   In this just cause come I to move your grace.
RICHARD   I cannot tell if to depart in silence   140
   Or bitterly to speak in your reproof
   Best fitteth my degree or your condition.
   If not to answer, you might haply think
   Tongue-tied ambition, not replying, yielded
   To bear the golden yoke of sovereignty,   145
   Which fondly you would here impose on me.
   If to reprove you for this suit of yours,
   So seasoned with your faithful love to me,
   Then on the other side I checked my friends.
   Therefore, to speak, and to avoid the first,   150
   And then, in speaking, not to incur the last,
   Definitively thus I answer you:

Richard argues that he is unworthy to be king and that young Edward will in time become a successful monarch. Buckingham reminds Richard of the Prince of Wales' suspect family history.

1 Mock-modest Richard (II)

Lines 155–65: Richard argues he is unfit for such a high position. He compares himself to a ship ('bark') unfit to endure a great ocean ('brook no mighty sea') arguing he would rather avoid kingship ('greatness') than desire it ('covet to be hid') and be overwhelmed by such an awesome responsibility.

Lines 166–72: He asserts that the Prince of Wales is the rightful heir who will mature ('mellowed by the stealing hours of time') into a distinguished monarch. But Richard's 'no doubt' is a sting in the tail of his praise of Edward.

Use the information above and on page 138 to help you deliver Richard's lines 140–72. Try to bring out his hypocrisy.

2 Sneering at Queen Elizabeth (in pairs)

Buckingham replies that Richard's arguments are too subtle and weak ('nice and trivial'). He repeats the accusations of Prince Edward's illegitimacy and King Edward's breaking of two marriage contracts. In highly insulting language, he recalls how King Edward met Elizabeth Grey. Buckingham stresses Elizabeth's lack of status ('a poor petitioner'), lack of looks ('beauty-waning') and lack of youth ('Even in the afternoon of her best days'). He accuses her of seducing Edward ('Made prize and purchase of his wanton eye'), and accuses her of making a bigamous marriage. His final sneer is that Prince Edward is only given the title 'prince' through courtesy ('our manners'). One person speak lines 182–90 slowly while the other echoes all the words which insult Elizabeth.

---

desert/Unmeritable
 unworthy merit
shuns rejects
even smooth
As the ripe revenue and due of
 birth as what is rightly mine

need lack
defend forbid
pitch importance
degree position
base declension ignoble decline
our manners through courtesy

Your love deserves my thanks, but my desert
Unmeritable shuns your high request.
First, if all obstacles were cut away,   155
And that my path were even to the crown
As the ripe revenue and due of birth,
Yet so much is my poverty of spirit,
So mighty and so many my defects,
That I would rather hide me from my greatness,   160
Being a bark to brook no mighty sea,
Than in my greatness covet to be hid
And in the vapour of my glory smothered.
But, God be thanked, there is no need of me,
And much I need to help you, were there need.   165
The royal tree hath left us royal fruit,
Which, mellowed by the stealing hours of time,
Will well become the seat of majesty
And make (no doubt) us happy by his reign.
On him I lay that you would lay on me,   170
The right and fortune of his happy stars,
Which God defend that I should wring from him.
BUCKINGHAM My lord, this argues conscience in your grace,
But the respects thereof are nice and trivial,
All circumstances well considerèd.   175
You say that Edward is your brother's son.
So say we too, but not by Edward's wife,
For first was he contràct to Lady Lucy,
Your mother lives a witness to his vow,
And afterward by substitute betrothed   180
To Bona, sister to the King of France.
These both put off, a poor petitioner,
A care-crazed mother to a many sons,
A beauty-waning and distressèd widow,
Even in the afternoon of her best days,   185
Made prize and purchase of his wanton eye,
Seduced the pitch and height of his degree
To base declension and loathed bigamy.
By her, in his unlawful bed, he got
This Edward, whom our manners call the prince.   190

141

Buckingham says he will refrain from further criticism.
He begs Richard to accept the crown, echoed by the mayor on behalf
of the people. Richard refuses. Buckingham threatens to enthrone
another. Catesby adds his pleas.

1 Richard the unwilling king? (I) (in large groups)

The unsettling, macabre humour and dramatic irony continues to the end of the scene as Richard and his co-plotters act out their charade for the mayor and citizens. Decide whether the mayor and citizens really are deceived by Richard. Take parts as Lord Mayor and citizens, Richard, Buckingham and Catesby. Work out a performance of lines 191–245, bringing out the humour and hypocrisy in the episode.

a Use this summary of lines 191–9 to work out how Buckingham speaks as much to the mayor and citizens as he does to Richard:

'I refuse to speak further of King Edward's scandalous past and of the queen and Prince Edward ("I give a sparing limit to my tongue") to save the feelings of "some alive". I beg you to accept the crown ("take to your royal self/This proffered benefit of dignity") not only for the people and country but to rescue ("draw forth") the house of York from the dishonour King Edward and Elizabeth have brought on the true line of descent ("a lineal true-derivèd course").'

b The mayor's plea at line 200 is (probably) sincere. Buckingham's and Catesby's lines 201–2 are deeply insincere. Use tones and gestures to bring out what is really in each man's mind.

c How can Richard speak lines 203–4 to reveal his hypocrisy?

d How does Richard react to Buckingham's description of him in lines 209–10?

---

expostulate criticise	**effeminate** tender
amiss wrongly	**kindred** family
zeal enthusiasm	**all estates** people of all ranks

More bitterly could I expostulate,
Save that for reverence to some alive,
I give a sparing limit to my tongue.
Then, good my lord, take to your royal self
This proffered benefit of dignity,   195
If not to bless us and the land withal,
Yet to draw forth your noble ancestry
From the corruption of abusing times
Unto a lineal true-derivèd course.

MAYOR   Do, good my lord, your citizens entreat you.   200
BUCKINGHAM   Refuse not, mighty lord, this proffered love.
CATESBY   Oh, make them joyful. Grant their lawful suit.
RICHARD   Alas, why would you heap this care on me?
I am unfit for state and majesty.
I do beseech you, take it not amiss;   205
I cannot nor I will not yield to you.
BUCKINGHAM   If you refuse it, as in love and zeal
Loath to depose the child, your brother's son,
As well we know your tenderness of heart
And gentle, kind, effeminate remorse,   210
Which we have noted in you to your kindred
And equally indeed to all estates,
Yet know, whe'er you accept our suit or no,
Your brother's son shall never reign our king,
But we will plant some other in the throne   215
To the disgrace and downfall of your house.
And in this resolution here we leave you.
Come, citizens. We will entreat no more.

                                              Exeunt

CATESBY   Call him again, sweet prince; accept their suit.
If you deny them, all the land will rue it.   220

Richard orders Catesby to recall everyone, grudgingly accepts the burden of kingship, but says that if discord follows, he is free of blame. He is proclaimed king, the coronation to take place the following day.

1 Richard the unwilling king? (II) (in large groups)

a The stage direction *Exeunt* at line 218 implies that only Richard, the bishops and Catesby remain on stage. In some productions, after a long pause after line 221, Richard is genuinely afraid that the citizens will not come back. Use that interpretation to suggest how Richard speaks 'Call them again' to create audience laughter.

b Richard's lines 225–34 reveal more of his cunning. He says he must patiently accept the burden of kingship that they are fastening like armour ('buckle') on his back. As kingship was imposed upon him, so those who forced him to become king must acquit him of any future blame. In your delivery of the lines, show how Richard's language shifts responsibility away from himself, and reinforces his appearance of grudgingly accepting the crown (for example, in his use of 'you' and 'your' and 'I', and in the words that mean burden and faults).

c Many stage productions place the interval at this point, closing with a striking image, as a triumphant Richard achieves his aim and is proclaimed king. In one stage production, Richard threw away his prayer book and the bishops revealed themselves as armed soldiers. In the Laurence Olivier film, Richard's final action was to force Buckingham to kneel and kiss his hand in an act of submission.

Work out a final, effective dramatic image of your own to close the scene.

---

penetrable open
Albeit although it is
Attend the sequel appear as a
 result

Your mere enforcement the mere
 fact you forced me
acquittance acquit
impure blots slanders

RICHARD   Will you enforce me to a world of cares?
          Call them again. I am not made of stones,
          But penetrable to your kind entreaties,
          Albeit against my conscience and my soul.

          Enter BUCKINGHAM *and the rest*

          Cousin of Buckingham, and sage, grave men,   225
          Since you will buckle fortune on my back,
          To bear her burden, whe'er I will or no,
          I must have patience to endure the load.
          But if black scandal or foul-faced reproach
          Attend the sequel of your imposition,   230
          Your mere enforcement shall acquittance me
          From all the impure blots and stains thereof;
          For God doth know, and you may partly see,
          How far I am from the desire of this.
MAYOR   God bless your grace; we see it and will say it.   235
RICHARD   In saying so, you shall but say the truth.
BUCKINGHAM   Then I salute you with this royal title:
          Long live King Richard, England's worthy king.
ALL   Amen.
BUCKINGHAM   Tomorrow may it please you to be crowned?   240
RICHARD   Even when you please, for you will have it so.
BUCKINGHAM   Tomorrow, then, we will attend your grace,
          And so most joyfully we take our leave.
RICHARD   [*To the Bishops*] Come, let us to our holy work again. –
          Farewell, my cousins, farewell, gentle friends.   245

                                                      Exeunt

Looking back at Act 3
Activities for groups or individuals

1 Richard plays many parts

Richard takes a malicious delight in acting out a variety of parts as he plots and kills his way to the throne. Act 3 has many examples of Richard's duplicity, from his ironically warning Prince Edward to beware 'false friends' (Scene 1) to the full-scale production put on for the benefit of the Lord Mayor and citizens (Scene 7). Trace all Richard's 'performances' in the Act and discuss how they compare with other examples from Acts 1 and 2 of Richard's techniques for dissembling and cynically using others.

2 The rat, the cat, the dog

Sir Richard Ratcliffe's power and influence has steadily increased through his unquestioning loyalty to Richard since his first appearance (Act 2 Scene 1). His two friends Catesby and Lovell have similarly flourished under Richard's patronage as they carry out his sinister commands. Catesby is entrusted to sound out Hastings' loyalty, and Lovell brings in Hastings' severed head. The three men featured in the contemporary verse:

'The Cat, the Rat and Lovell the dog
Do rule all England under the Hog.'

Trace what other services the three have performed for Richard so far. Suggest how a director might emphasise their new-found status. As you read on, look out for what else they do.

3 Jane Shore

Jane Shore's name does not appear in the cast list, but she is an influential if invisible figure. The mistress of both Edward IV and Hastings, she is referred to at least five times in the first three Acts. Work out how you might stage her appearance in Scene 2, then discuss what is gained or lost if she is physically present in this or any other scene.

4 Buckingham: an Elizabethan spin-doctor

Buckingham uses a variety of methods to ensure Richard gains the crown. The techniques he employs are similar to those used by present-day political spin-doctors who manipulate unpleasant facts to make them appear attractive to the voting public. Look back at Buckingham's words and actions in Scenes 1, 4, 5 and 7, then step into role as Buckingham and write yourself a memo setting out how you will make Richard king and the methods you will use to achieve this aim.

5 Richard's check-list

At the end of Act 3, Richard has achieved his objective of being hailed as king. Make a list of all the events in the Act that have helped him to that achievement.

'Thou art a traitor.' Richard accuses Hastings. Remind yourself of Hastings' appearances (Act 1 Scene 1 and Act 3) and decide whether you feel sympathy for his predicament.

Queen Elizabeth, the Duchess of York, Dorset and Anne meet outside the Tower where they have come to visit the princes. Brakenbury, on Richard's orders, refuses them entry.

1 Family tree: a reminder (in groups of three)

The opening of Act 4 focuses on the victims of Richard's new-found power, as members of the late King Edward's family attempt to visit the princes. The three females stress unity in adversity through their close family ties. To remind yourself of their relationship to each other and to Richard, take parts as the duchess, Anne and Elizabeth and speak lines 1–11. Everyone points to the appropriate name on the family tree as any words showing relationship are spoken (*m* indicates married to).

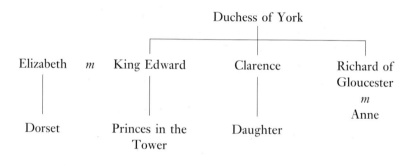

2 Brakenbury bars the way

Brakenbury is part of Richard's plan to isolate the princes (see Act 3 Scene 5, lines 106–9). His words that he may not allow ('suffer') them to visit the princes probably brings about very definite reactions from the women. Advise Elizabeth, the duchess and Anne how each might speak lines 18–26 as they react to his refusal (pleading? assertive? suspicious?).

niece grand-daughter
kind family, kind-hearted
sister sister-in-law
devotion duty
gratulate greet

And in good time
 and with good timing
bounds barriers
thy office your responsibility
on my peril at danger to myself
leave it so let it be so

ACT 4 SCENE 1
Outside the Tower of London

Enter QUEEN ELIZABETH, the DUCHESS OF YORK, and
MARQUESS DORSET, meeting ANNE DUCHESS OF GLOUCESTER and
Clarence's daughter

DUCHESS Who meets us here? My niece Plantagenet
       Led in the hand of her kind aunt of Gloucester?
       Now, for my life, she's wand'ring to the Tower,
       On pure heart's love to greet the tender prince.
       Daughter, well met.
ANNE   God give your graces both   5
       A happy and a joyful time of day.
ELIZABETH As much to you, good sister. Whither away?
ANNE No farther than the Tower, and, as I guess,
       Upon the like devotion as yourselves,
       To gratulate the gentle princes there.   10
ELIZABETH Kind sister, thanks. We'll enter all together.

Enter the Lieutenant [BRAKENBURY]

       And in good time, here the Lieutenant comes.
       Master Lieutenant, pray you, by your leave,
       How doth the prince and my young son of York?
BRAKENBURY Right well, dear madam. By your patience,   15
       I may not suffer you to visit them.
       The king hath strictly charged the contrary.
ELIZABETH The king? Who's that?
BRAKENBURY I mean the Lord Protector.
ELIZABETH The Lord protect him from that kingly title.   20
       Hath he set bounds between their love and me?
       I am their mother. Who shall bar me from them?
DUCHESS I am their father's mother. I will see them.
ANNE Their aunt I am in law, in love their mother.
       Then bring me to their sights; I'll bear thy blame   25
       And take thy office from thee, on my peril.
BRAKENBURY No, madam, no; I may not leave it so.
       I am bound by oath, and therefore pardon me.

Exit Lieutenant

Stanley's news of Richard's intended coronation dismays the women. Elizabeth tells Dorset to flee to join Richmond. Stanley's son will help him. Anne says she would prefer to die than be queen.

1 Speed is of the essence (in groups of five)

The speed and unexpectedness of Richard's coronation takes all the characters by surprise. In an hour from now ('one hour hence'), the Duchess of York will become mother-in-law ('mother') to 'two fair queens': Elizabeth, King Edward's widow, and Anne, King Richard's queen. Realising that her son Dorset is in danger, Elizabeth shows political astuteness in urging him to leave the country and join Richmond in France. Speed is of the essence.

Pick out all the words and phrases that help create the impression of speed and urgency. Take parts as Stanley, Elizabeth, Anne, the Duchess of York and Dorset. Speak lines 29–65 as fast as you can, then work out how you think they should be spoken on stage.

2 Remembering Margaret's curse (in pairs)

In line 46, Elizabeth recalls Margaret's curse. Turn back to Act 1 Scene 3, line 207 and compare Margaret's curse with Elizabeth's words.

3 Images of outrage

Elizabeth, the duchess and Anne express their emotions through a number of powerful images. 'Dogs' (line 40) means to follow closely, as a hunting dog chases its prey. 'Cockatrice' (line 55) was a monster, believed to kill by its look. 'Deadly venom' (line 62) refers to the holy coronation oil, which Anne wishes were a fatal poison. Find three other images on the opposite page and suggest who or what each describes.

Westminster Westminster Abbey, where coronations are enacted
lace bodice cord
pent imprisoned
scope room
Despiteful cruel
outstrip outrun

thrall slave
counted acknowledged
ta'en tardy slowed, captured later
inclusive verge encircling rim
To feed my humour to please my unhappy mood

Enter STANLEY

STANLEY   Let me but meet you ladies one hour hence,
    And I'll salute your grace of York as mother   30
    And reverend looker-on of two fair queens.
    [*To Anne*] Come, madam, you must straight to Westminster,
    There to be crownèd Richard's royal queen.
ELIZABETH   Ah, cut my lace asunder,
    That my pent heart may have some scope to beat,   35
    Or else I swoon with this dead-killing news.
ANNE   Despiteful tidings. Oh, unpleasing news.
DORSET   Be of good cheer, mother; how fares your grace?
ELIZABETH   Oh Dorset, speak not to me; get thee gone.
    Death and destruction dogs thee at thy heels.   40
    Thy mother's name is ominous to children.
    If thou wilt outstrip death, go, cross the seas
    And live with Richmond, from the reach of hell.
    Go hie thee, hie thee from this slaughterhouse,
    Lest thou increase the number of the dead   45
    And make me die the thrall of Margaret's curse,
    Nor mother, wife, nor England's counted queen.
STANLEY   Full of wise care is this your counsel, madam –
    Take all the swift advantage of the hours.
    You shall have letters from me to my son   50
    In your behalf, to meet you on the way.
    Be not ta'en tardy by unwise delay.
DUCHESS   Oh ill-dispersing wind of misery.
    Oh my accursèd womb, the bed of death.
    A cockatrice hast thou hatched to the world,   55
    Whose unavoided eye is murderous.
STANLEY   Come, madam, come. I in all haste was sent.
ANNE   And I with all unwillingness will go.
    Oh, would to God that the inclusive verge
    Of golden metal that must round my brow   60
    Were red-hot steel, to sear me to the brains.
    Anointed let me be with deadly venom
    And die ere men can say 'God save the queen'.
ELIZABETH   Go, go, poor soul, I envy not thy glory.
    To feed my humour, wish thyself no harm.   65

Anne recalls Richard's wooing and her curse, which has become a curse upon herself. She predicts Richard will kill her. The duchess urges all to leave. Elizabeth pleads to the Tower to pity the princes.

1 Anne recalls her curses (in pairs)

Anne remembers the way in which Richard wooed her and the curses she put on him and his future wife. But she is now the victim of her own curse, because she foolishly succumbed to Richard's 'honey words' and married him. Turn back to Act 1 Scene 2, lines 14–28 and read them aloud to remind yourselves of Anne's curses. Compare her earlier lines with lines 66–87 on the opposite page.

2 Bad dreams

Line 85 suggests that Richard has continual nightmares that keep Anne constantly awake. Imagine you are watching a film which shows as a 'flashback' Richard's bad dreams. List some of the images you see as his mind re-creates some of his past actions.

3 Taking leave (in groups of four)

Elizabeth, Anne, Dorset and the Duchess of York bid each other farewell in lines 88–94. Identify which lines are addressed to which character as they take their leave. What actions might they use?

4 Menace versus innocence

Elizabeth's plea for the Tower to show pity on the two princes contrasts the impersonal, menacing prison ('Rough cradle') with the vulnerable, innocent boys ('those tender babes'). How might a director present a strong visual image of the Tower's menace to contrast with Elizabeth's hopeless pleas? Think about design, lighting, sound effects, music, and so on.

---

ere before
Grossly stupidly
honey sweet sounding
timorous frightening, fearful
still awaked always kept awake

complaining complaint
glory position of queen
teen grief
immured imprisoned

ANNE   No? Why? When he that is my husband now
   Came to me as I followed Henry's corpse,
   When scarce the blood was well washed from his hands
   Which issued from my other angel husband
   And that dear saint which then I weeping followed,   70
   Oh, when, I say, I looked on Richard's face,
   This was my wish: 'Be thou', quoth I, 'accursed
   For making me, so young, so old a widow.
   And when thou wed'st, let sorrow haunt thy bed;
   And be thy wife, if any be so mad,   75
   More miserable by the life of thee
   Than thou hast made me by my dear lord's death.'
   Lo, ere I can repeat this curse again,
   Within so small a time, my woman's heart
   Grossly grew captive to his honey words   80
   And proved the subject of mine own soul's curse,
   Which hitherto hath held mine eyes from rest.
   For never yet one hour in his bed
   Did I enjoy the golden dew of sleep,
   But with his timorous dreams was still awaked.   85
   Besides, he hates me for my father Warwick,
   And will, no doubt, shortly be rid of me.
ELIZABETH   Poor heart, adieu; I pity thy complaining.
ANNE   No more than with my soul I mourn for yours.
DORSET   Farewell, thou woeful welcomer of glory.   90
ANNE   Adieu, poor soul, that tak'st thy leave of it.
DUCHESS   Go thou to Richmond, and good fortune guide thee –
   Go thou to Richard, and good angels tend thee –
   Go thou to sanctuary, and good thoughts possess thee;
   I to my grave, where peace and rest lie with me.   95
   Eighty-odd years of sorrow have I seen,
   And each hour's joy wracked with a week of teen.
ELIZABETH   Stay, yet look back with me unto the Tower.
   Pity, you ancient stones, those tender babes
   Whom envy hath immured within your walls,   100
   Rough cradle for such little pretty ones.
   Rude, ragged nurse, old sullen playfellow
   For tender princes, use my babies well.
   So foolish sorrows bids your stones farewell.

             Exeunt

> *The newly-crowned Richard sits on the throne. He implies that Buckingham should kill the princes. At first, Buckingham pretends not to understand, then asks for time to think. Richard shows his anger.*

1 Richard takes the throne

Richard, now the crowned king, makes a royal entrance in stately splendour ('in pomp'). He sits on the throne. It represents the moment he has craved for so long. How could Richard reveal his feelings through his movements (for example, stride, creep, dance, scuttle) as he takes possession of the throne?

2 Two plotters fall out (in pairs)

Buckingham is reluctant to carry out Richard's orders to murder the princes. Talk together about ways Richard might behave as his relationship with Buckingham cools. Then act out lines 1–27 using the following to help you.

a Before he mounts the throne Richard acknowledges Buckingham's part in his achieving the crown ('Give me thy hand'). Do you think Richard asks for Buckingham's hand to physically help him on to the throne or are his words symbolic?

b Richard first insinuates and then explicitly states his desire for the princes' deaths ('I wish the bastards dead'). Does he speak secretly to Buckingham or does he not care if anyone overhears? At what moment does Buckingham become fully aware that Richard wants him to murder the princes?

c Buckingham does not give the answer Richard wants. Is he showing independence, remorse or political astuteness? How would Buckingham speak his line 'Your grace may do your pleasure' so that Richard can accuse him of being 'all ice'?

Still ever
touch touchstone (used to test the genuineness of gold)
current genuine
thrice-renownèd three times famous

thou wast not wont to be so dull you used not to be so stupid
suddenly swiftly
may do your pleasure can do whatever you wish
presently at once

ACT 4 SCENE 2
London: the throne-room of the palace

A fanfare sounds. RICHARD, *newly crowned as king enters in pomp with* BUCKINGHAM, CATESBY, RATCLIFFE, LOVELL, *a* PAGE, *and others*

RICHARD Stand all apart. Cousin of Buckingham.
BUCKINGHAM My gracious sovereign.
RICHARD Give me thy hand.

Sound

    Thus high, by thy advice and thy assistance,
    Is King Richard seated.   5
    But shall we wear these glories for a day?
    Or shall they last, and we rejoice in them?
BUCKINGHAM Still live they, and forever let them last.
RICHARD Ah, Buckingham, now do I play the touch
    To try if thou be current gold indeed.   10
    Young Edward lives; think now what I would speak.
BUCKINGHAM Say on, my loving lord.
RICHARD Why, Buckingham, I say I would be king.
BUCKINGHAM Why, so you are, my thrice-renownèd lord.
RICHARD Ha, am I king? 'Tis so. But Edward lives.   15
BUCKINGHAM True, noble prince.
RICHARD   O bitter consequence,
    That Edward still should live, true noble prince.
    Cousin, thou wast not wont to be so dull.
    Shall I be plain? I wish the bastards dead,
    And I would have it suddenly performed.   20
    What say'st thou now? Speak suddenly, be brief.
BUCKINGHAM Your grace may do your pleasure.
RICHARD Tut, tut, thou art all ice; thy kindness freezes.
    Say, have I thy consent that they shall die?
BUCKINGHAM Give me some little breath, some pause, dear lord,   25
    Before I positively speak in this.
    I will resolve you herein presently.

Exit Buckingham

CATESBY The king is angry; see, he gnaws his lip.

*Richard orders Tyrrel to be brought to him. He will no longer confide
in Buckingham. Stanley brings news of Dorset's escape.
Richard plots against Anne and Clarence's daughter and resolves
to marry Princess Elizabeth.*

1 Buckingham enrages Richard

Buckingham's refusal to arrange the killing of the princes enrages
Richard. He resolves to surround himself with the stupid and
unfeeling rather than with intelligent people who might critically
enquire into his actions ('look into me with considerate eyes').

On stage, Richard's lines 45–6 are often snarled with a mixture of
ominous menace, irritation and contempt, as Richard angrily reflects
that Buckingham has supported him for so long, but now hesitates.

Step into role as Richard and say what is in your mind for
Buckingham's future as you speak 'Well, be it so'.

2 Securing the future

Stanley's news that Dorset has joined Richmond in France
accelerates Richard's plans. He makes the following decisions:

- to spread the rumour that Anne is very sick and likely to die;
- to keep Anne confined;
- to force Clarence's daughter to marry 'a mean poor gentleman';
- not to act against Clarence's son as he is no threat (the boy had
  been imprisoned by Henry VI and had become mentally ill);
- to marry Edward IV's daughter Elizabeth;
- to kill the princes in the Tower.

Consider each decision in turn and suggest a precise reason for
Richard making it. Then experiment with different ways of
speaking the lines, either making frequent pauses as Richard works
out each action, or speaking swiftly, without pauses.

iron-witted dull
unrespective unfeeling
close exploit secret deed
partly half
keeping close confinement

give out announce
it stands me much upon
it is to my advantage
Uncertain way of gain
risky business

RICHARD   I will converse with iron-witted fools
      And unrespective boys. None are for me   30
      That look into me with considerate eyes.
      High-reaching Buckingham grows circumspect. –
      Boy!
PAGE   My lord.
RICHARD   Know'st thou not any whom corrupting gold   35
      Will tempt unto a close exploit of death?
PAGE   I know a discontented gentleman
      Whose humble means match not his haughty spirit.
      Gold were as good as twenty orators
      And will, no doubt, tempt him to anything.   40
RICHARD   What is his name?
PAGE   His name, my lord, is Tyrrel.
RICHARD   I partly know the man. Go call him hither, boy.   *Exit Page*
      The deep-revolving, witty Buckingham
      No more shall be the neighbour to my counsels.
      Hath he so long held out with me, untired,   45
      And stops he now for breath? Well, be it so.

        Enter STANLEY [EARL OF DERBY]

      How now, Lord Stanley, what's the news?
STANLEY   Know, my loving lord, the Marquess Dorset,
      As I hear, is fled to Richmond
      In the parts where he abides.   50
RICHARD   Come hither, Catesby. Rumour it abroad
      That Anne my wife is very grievous sick.
      I will take order for her keeping close.
      Inquire me out some mean poor gentleman,
      Whom I will marry straight to Clarence' daughter.   55
      The boy is foolish, and I fear not him.
      Look how thou dream'st! I say again, give out
      That Anne my queen is sick and like to die.
      About it, for it stands me much upon
      To stop all hopes whose growth may damage me.   60
      I must be married to my brother's daughter,
      Or else my kingdom stands on brittle glass.
      Murder her brothers, and then marry her:
      Uncertain way of gain. But I am in
      So far in blood that sin will pluck on sin.   65
      Tear-falling pity dwells not in this eye.

Richard orders Tyrrel to kill the princes and warns Stanley not to support Richmond. Richard ignores Buckingham's request for the promised earldom of Hereford and recalls Henry VI's prophecy that Richmond will become king.

1 Missing lines: increasing dramatic effect? (in pairs)

Because of different editions of the play (see page 247), the following lines are often acted between lines 99–100. Take parts as Richard and Buckingham and speak lines 84–101 to include the missing lines. If you were staging a production, would you include them?

BUCKINGHAM My lord –
RICHARD How chance the prophet could not at that time
    Have told me, I being by, that I should kill him?
BUCKINGHAM My lord, your promise for the earldom!
RICHARD Richmond! When last I was at Exeter,
    The Mayor in courtesy showed me the castle,
    And called it Rouge-mount; at which name I started,
    Because a bard of Ireland told me once
    I should not live long after I saw Richmond.
BUCKINGHAM My lord –
RICHARD Ay, what's a'clock?
BUCKINGHAM I am thus bold to put your grace in mind
    Of what you promised me.
RICHARD Well, but what's a'clock?
BUCKINGHAM Upon the stroke of ten.
RICHARD Well, let it strike.
BUCKINGHAM Why let it strike?
RICHARD Because that like a jack thou keep'st the stroke
    Betwixt thy begging and my meditation.
    I am not in the giving vein today.

Prove test
Please you if it pleases you
open means an easy way
prefer advance, reward
dispatch it straight
  do it immediately

late last
pawned pledged
movables personal effects
look to keep watch on
peevish silly
vein mood

Enter TYRREL

Is thy name Tyrrel?
TYRREL   James Tyrrel, and your most obedient subject.
RICHARD   Art thou indeed?
TYRREL   Prove me, my gracious lord.
RICHARD   Dar'st thou resolve to kill a friend of mine?   70
TYRREL   Please you.
          But I had rather kill two enemies.
RICHARD   Why then thou hast it: two deep enemies,
          Foes to my rest and my sweet sleep's disturbers
          Are they that I would have thee deal upon.   75
          Tyrrel, I mean those bastards in the Tower.
TYRREL   Let me have open means to come to them,
          And soon I'll rid you from the fear of them.
RICHARD   Thou sing'st sweet music. Hark, come hither, Tyrrel.
          Go by this token. Rise, and lend thine ear. *Whispers*   80
          There is no more but so; say it is done,
          And I will love thee and prefer thee for it.
TYRREL   I will dispatch it straight.   *Exit*

Enter BUCKINGHAM

BUCKINGHAM   My lord, I have considered in my mind
          The late request that you did sound me in.   85
RICHARD   Well, let that rest. Dorset is fled to Richmond.
BUCKINGHAM   I hear the news, my lord.
RICHARD   Stanley, he is your wife's son. Well, look unto it.
BUCKINGHAM   My lord, I claim the gift, my due by promise,
          For which your honour and your faith is pawned: 90
          Th'earldom of Hereford and the movables
          Which you have promisèd I shall possess.
RICHARD   Stanley, look to your wife. If she convey
          Letters to Richmond, you shall answer it.
BUCKINGHAM   What says your highness to my just request?   95
RICHARD   I do remember me, Henry the Sixth
          Did prophesy that Richmond should be king,
          When Richmond was a little peevish boy.
          A king, perhaps.
BUCKINGHAM   May it please you to resolve me in my suit?   100
RICHARD   Thou troublest me; I am not in the vein.   *Exit*

Buckingham resolves to flee to safety in Wales. Tyrrel describes the remorse of the murderers who smothered the princes.

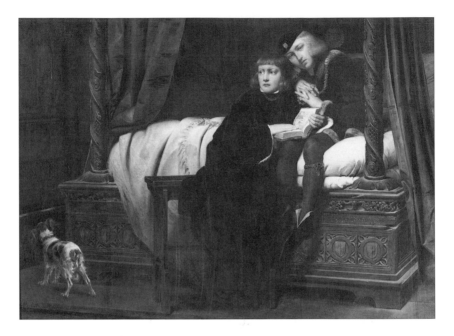

The Little Princes in the Tower (painted 1831) by the French artist Paul Delaroche (1797–1856). What emotions does the artist bring out through his portrait of the princes?

1 The death of the princes (in pairs)

One person speaks lines 1–22. The other listens, and studies the illustration on the cover of this edition. Then change roles and repeat. Afterwards, talk together about the relationships of the speech, the cover picture and the picture above.

Brecknock Buckingham's estate in Wales	**in their deaths' sad story** in telling how they died
most arch highest	**girdling** embracing
suborn procure, bribe	**alabaster** marble, tomb-like
Albeit although	**replenishèd** perfect
fleshed hardened	**prime creation** world's beginning

BUCKINGHAM And is it thus? Repays he my deep service
               With such contempt? Made I him king for this?
               Oh, let me think on Hastings and be gone
               To Brecknock, while my fearful head is on.   *Exit*   105

ACT 4 SCENE 3
London: a room in King Richard's palace

Enter TYRREL

TYRREL The tyrannous and bloody act is done,
       The most arch deed of piteous massacre
       That ever yet this land was guilty of.
       Dighton and Forrest, who I did suborn
       To do this piece of ruthless butchery,   5
       Albeit they were fleshed villains, bloody dogs,
       Melted with tenderness and mild compassion,
       Wept like to children in their deaths' sad story.
       'Oh, thus', quoth Dighton, 'lay the gentle babes.'
       'Thus, thus', quoth Forrest, 'girdling one another   10
       Within their alabaster innocent arms.
       Their lips were four red roses on a stalk,
       And in their summer beauty kissed each other.
       A book of prayers on their pillow lay,
       Which once', quoth Forrest, 'almost changed my mind.   15
       But oh, the devil', there the villain stopped.
       When Dighton thus told on: 'we smotherèd
       The most replenishèd sweet work of nature
       That from the prime creation e'er she framed'.
       Hence both are gone; with conscience and remorse   20
       They could not speak, and so I left them both
       To bear this tidings to the bloody king.

Enter RICHARD

And here he comes. All health, my sovereign lord.

Tyrrel assures Richard that the princes are dead.
Richard plans marriage to Elizabeth. Ratcliffe's news is that Ely has
joined Richmond, and Buckingham has raised an army in Wales.
Richard resolves to fight.

1 Does Tyrrel show his feelings? (in pairs)

Tyrrel's soliloquy in lines 1–22 has shown his real thoughts about the murder, but his words to Richard seem to reveal little of his feelings. Talk about how he reacts to Richard's entrance and decide if, on stage, he would hint at his real feelings in the way he speaks the lines or in his body language. Then take parts as Richard and Tyrrel and speak and act out lines 24–35.

2 Richard: as witty as ever? (in pairs)

Richard lists the successes he has achieved. Four of the schemes he planned after his coronation (Act 4 Scene 2, lines 51–63) have succeeded. Some commentators believe Richard lacks his previous charisma and lethal charm after he becomes king, yet in lines 36–43, he seems his old, wicked self. Revisit the opening lines of the play, then compare them to lines 36–43. Exchange views on whether both soliloquies portray Richard in the same way: audacious, lethal yet self-mocking, witty.

3 Action! – not delay!

Ratcliffe brings bad news. Richard's reaction is to reject delay for immediate military action, and to trust his own judgement ('My counsel is my shield'). Identify all the words or phrases in lines 49–57 which imply either delay or action. Suggest how Richard speaks each word or phrase.

be inheritor of thy desire
  your wish will come true
pent up close imprisoned
sleep in Abraham's bosom
  are dead
Is in the field
  has begun military operations

rash-levied strength
  hastily recruited army
leaden servitor slow servant
beggary ruin
fiery expedition speedy action
Jove's Mercury
  messenger of the gods

RICHARD   Kind Tyrrel, am I happy in thy news?

TYRREL   If to have done the thing you gave in charge   25
    Beget your happiness, be happy then,
    For it is done.

RICHARD   But did'st thou see them dead?

TYRREL   I did, my lord.

RICHARD   And buried, gentle Tyrrel?

TYRREL   The chaplain of the Tower hath buried them,
    But where, to say the truth, I do not know.   30

RICHARD   Come to me, Tyrrel, soon and after supper,
    When thou shalt tell the process of their death.
    Meantime, but think how I may do thee good,
    And be inheritor of thy desire.
    Farewell till then.

TYRREL   I humbly take my leave.   [*Exit*]   35

RICHARD   The son of Clarence have I pent up close,
    His daughter meanly have I matched in marriage,
    The sons of Edward sleep in Abraham's bosom,
    And Anne my wife hath bid this world good night.
    Now, for I know the Breton Richmond aims   40
    At young Elizabeth, my brother's daughter,
    And by that knot looks proudly on the crown,
    To her go I, a jolly thriving wooer.

Enter RATCLIFFE

RATCLIFFE   My lord.

RICHARD   Good or bad news, that thou com'st in so bluntly?   45

RATCLIFFE   Bad news, my lord. Morton is fled to Richmond,
    And Buckingham, backed with the hardy Welshmen,
    Is in the field, and still his power increaseth.

RICHARD   Ely with Richmond troubles me more near
    Than Buckingham and his rash-levied strength.   50
    Come. I have learned that fearful commenting
    Is leaden servitor to dull delay.
    Delay leads impotent and snail-paced beggary.
    Then fiery expedition be my wing,
    Jove's Mercury, and herald for a king!   55
    Go muster men. My counsel is my shield.
    We must be brief when traitors brave the field.

Exeunt

Margaret recounts how she has secretly watched the destruction of her enemies. She hopes for further calamities. Queen Elizabeth and the duchess mourn their dead relatives. Margaret sees the deaths as justice for her own losses.

1 United in grief (in groups of three)

Lines 1–135 involve only Queen Margaret, the duchess and Elizabeth. To gain a first impression of the whole episode, take parts and read through the episode without pause. The following can help you:

Queen Margaret: Hiding within the walls of the court ('confines'), Margaret has watched the loss of power ('the waning') of the Yorkists and Woodvilles. She uses theatrical imagery as she hopes for further disasters ('induction', 'consequence', 'tragical'). As Elizabeth and the Duchess mourn, Margaret's asides shows she views each death as justice or repayment for her own losses. ('right for right', 'doth quit' 'pays a dying debt').

Elizabeth: grieves for her two sons murdered in the Tower. She speaks of them as flowers in bud ('unblowed', 'new-appearing') and hopes they have escaped limbo ('doom perpetual' = final judgement) to become angels. She questions why God allowed her sons to be killed by the wolf Richard.

The Duchess of York: mourns for her son, King Edward. In lines 26–8, she describes herself, first, using three oxymorons ('Dead life', etc.), then as a stage where griefs are acted out ('Woe's scene'); as the shame of the world (because she gave birth to Richard); and as someone who has lived too long, cheating the grave of its rightful due. She finally describes herself as a summary ('abstract and record') of many weary years.

prosperity success	**right for right** justice for justice
mellow ripen	**crazed** cracked
induction prologue, beginning	**holy Harry** Henry VI
consequence sequel, future	**abstract** précis
sweets sweet-scented buds	**Rest** cease
lamentation grief	

ACT 4 SCENE 4
London: outside King Richard's palace

Enter old QUEEN MARGARET

MARGARET So now prosperity begins to mellow
  And drop into the rotten mouth of death.
  Here in these confines slyly have I lurked
  To watch the waning of mine enemies.
  A dire induction am I witness to,   5
  And will to France, hoping the consequence
  Will prove as bitter, black, and tragical.
  Withdraw thee, wretched Margaret. Who comes here?

Enter DUCHESS OF YORK *and* QUEEN ELIZABETH

ELIZABETH Ah, my poor princes! Ah, my tender babes!
  My unblowed flowers, new-appearing sweets!   10
  If yet your gentle souls fly in the air
  And be not fixed in doom perpetual,
  Hover about me with your airy wings
  And hear your mother's lamentation.
MARGARET [*Aside*] Hover about her; say that right for right 15
  Hath dimmed your infant morn to agèd night.
DUCHESS So many miseries have crazed my voice
  That my woe-wearied tongue is still and mute.
  Edward Plantagenet, why art thou dead?
MARGARET [*Aside*] Plantagenet doth quit Plantagenet;   20
  Edward for Edward pays a dying debt.
ELIZABETH Wilt thou, O God, fly from such gentle lambs
  And throw them in the entrails of the wolf?
  When didst thou sleep when such a deed was done?
MARGARET [*Aside*] When holy Harry died, and my sweet son. 25
DUCHESS Dead life, blind sight, poor mortal living ghost;
  Woe's scene, world's shame, grave's due by life usurped;
  Brief abstract and recòrd of tedious days,
  Rest thy unrest on England's lawful earth,
  Unlawfully made drunk with innocent blood.   30

Margaret asks to join the women in grieving. She and the duchess list the deaths. Margaret blames the duchess for giving birth to Richard. The duchess asks for sympathy from Margaret who expresses satisfaction in gaining revenge.

1 Listing the victims

If you are not sure of who is who, copy out the following table. The family tree on page 252 can help you.

Line	Victim	Killer	Other information
39	Margaret's son, Prince Edward	King Edward IV Richard and Clarence	Killed after the Battle of Tewkesbury
40	Margaret's husband (Henry VI)	Richard	Murdered in the Tower
41	Elizabeth's son, Prince Edward	Dighton and Forrest	Princes in the Tower. Order given by Richard to Tyrell.
42	Elizabeth's son, Richard		
43	Duchess of York's husband	Clifford and Margaret	Killed after the Battle of Wakefield
44	Duchess of York's son, Rutland	Clifford	Battle of Wakefield
45	Duchess of York's son, Clarence	Two murderers	Ordered by Richard
63	Edward IV	Natural causes	Over-indulgence
64	Prince Edward	Dighton and Forrest	Princes murdered in the Tower. Order given by Richard to Tyrell.
64	Richard of York		
69	Hastings, Rivers, Vaughan and Grey	Ratcliffe and Lovell	Executed on Richard's orders

thou (line 31) England's earth
benefit of seniory advantage of age
society friendship, unity
gallèd sore
carnal cur murderous dog
issue children

pew-fellow fellow church-goer
quit revenge
boot lightweight
beholders of this frantic play spectators of this mad drama

ELIZABETH   Ah, that thou wouldst as soon afford a grave
    As thou canst yield a melancholy seat.
    Then would I hide my bones, not rest them here.
    Ah, who hath any cause to mourn but we?

MARGARET   If ancient sorrow be most reverend,   35
    Give mine the benefit of seniory,
    And let my griefs frown on the upper hand,
    If sorrow can admit society.
    I had an Edward, till a Richard killed him;
    I had a husband, till a Richard killed him.   40
    Thou hadst an Edward, till a Richard killed him;
    Thou hadst a Richard, till a Richard killed him.

DUCHESS   I had a Richard too, and thou didst kill him;
    I had a Rutland too, thou holp'st to kill him.

MARGARET   Thou hadst a Clarence, too,   45
    And Richard killed him.
    From forth the kennel of thy womb hath crept
    A hell-hound that doth hunt us all to death:
    That dog, that had his teeth before his eyes
    To worry lambs and lap their gentle blood,   50
    That foul defacer of God's handiwork
    That reigns in gallèd eyes of weeping souls,
    That excellent grand tyrant of the earth
    Thy womb let loose to chase us to our graves.
    O upright, just, and true-disposing God,   55
    How do I thank thee, that this carnal cur
    Preys on the issue of his mother's body
    And makes her pew-fellow with others' moan.

DUCHESS   Oh Harry's wife, triumph not in my woes.
    God witness with me, I have wept for thine.   60

MARGARET   Bear with me. I am hungry for revenge,
    And now I cloy me with beholding it.
    Thy Edward he is dead that killed my Edward;
    The other Edward dead to quit my Edward;
    Young York he is but boot, because both they   65
    Matched not the high perfection of my loss.
    Thy Clarence he is dead that stabbed my Edward,
    And the beholders of this frantic play,
    Th'adulterate Hastings, Rivers, Vaughan, Grey,
    Untimely smothered in their dusky graves.   70

*Margaret calls Richard an agent of hell. Elizabeth remembers
Margaret's prophecy that she would ask her help to curse Richard.
Margaret recalls her descriptions of Elizabeth and contrasts
Elizabeth's past situation with her present.*

1 Hell's agent

Margaret's final insults about Richard are her worst. She says that
the only reason he is kept alive ('reserved') is as a spy ('intelligencer')
and agent ('factor') to send others to hell. She prays that he will
very soon die and go to hell himself. You can find more on hell and
religion on page 230.

2 'Bottled spider', 'bunch-backed toad': accurate recall?

Turn back to Act 1 Scene 3, lines 200–7 and 241–6 and compare
them with lines 79–91 opposite. How accurate is Elizabeth's
recollection of Margaret's prophecy, and Margaret's recollection of
her description of Elizabeth?

3 Contempt, questions and contrasts

a Pick out one word in each of lines 82–91 that Margaret could
specially emphasise to signify her mockery and contempt of
Elizabeth.

b In lines 92–6, Margaret asks a series of questions to emphasise
Elizabeth's losses. Speak the lines, adding a single word of your
own after each question to answer it (for example, 'dead').

c In lines 97–104, she answers the questions by telling Elizabeth to
go through her own history from beginning to end ('Decline all
this') to show her change in status. She uses antithesis (see page
243) to emphasise the changes. Speak the lines (for example,
'happy wife' ... distressèd widow') and use physical actions to
bring out the contrasts.

at hand soon	**to fill the scene** play a small part
piteous pitiful	**sues** asks for favours
bond lease	**caitiff** wretch
flourish empty show	**one (line 103)** Richard
index prologue	**whirled about** wheeled around
pageant play	**usurp** seize wrongfully
sign image	

Richard yet lives, hell's black intelligencer,
Only reserved their factor to buy souls
And send them thither. But at hand, at hand
Ensues his piteous and unpitied end.
Earth gapes, hell burns, fiends roar, saints pray,   75
To have him suddenly conveyed from hence.
Cancel his bond of life, dear God, I pray,
That I may live and say the dog is dead.

ELIZABETH   Oh, thou didst prophesy the time would come
That I should wish for thee to help me curse   80
That bottled spider, that foul bunch-backed toad.

MARGARET   I called thee then vain flourish of my fortune;
I called thee then poor shadow, painted queen,
The presentation of but what I was,
The flattering index of a direful pageant,   85
One heaved a-high to be hurled down below,
A mother only mocked with two fair babes,
A dream of what thou wast, a garish flag
To be the aim of every dangerous shot,
A sign of dignity, a breath, a bubble,   90
A queen in jest, only to fill the scene.
Where is thy husband now? Where be thy brothers?
Where be thy two sons? Wherein dost thou joy?
Who sues and kneels and says 'God save the Queen'?
Where be the bending peers that flattered thee?   95
Where be the thronging troops that followed thee?
Decline all this, and see what now thou art:
For happy wife, a most distressèd widow;
For joyful mother, one that wails the name;
For one being sued to, one that humbly sues;   100
For queen, a very caitiff crowned with care;
For she that scorned at me, now scorned of me;
For she being feared of all, now fearing one;
For she commanding all, obeyed of none.
Thus hath the course of justice whirled about   105
And left thee but a very prey to time,
Having no more but thought of what thou wast
To torture thee the more, being what thou art.
Thou didst usurp my place, and dost thou not
Usurp the just proportion of my sorrow?   110

169

Elizabeth asks Margaret to teach her how to curse. Margaret offers harsh advice. The duchess tells Elizabeth to complain bitterly and often to Richard. Richard enters and the women verbally attack him.

1 The power of words (in pairs)

a Margaret tells Elizabeth that successful cursing requires physical discomfort by refusing to sleep at night and fasting during the day. Past happiness needs to be compared with present sorrow, and the goodness of those slain and the evil of the murderer exaggerated. Thinking about these principles ('Revolving this') is the recipe for successful cursing. Is Margaret's advice spoken with sincerity, or does she intend to add to Elizabeth's sorrow? Discuss her motivation at this moment, then take turns to speak her lines 118–23.

b Elizabeth and the Duchess of York realise, like Margaret, that words are the only weapons they have against Richard. One person reads lines 126–35 slowly. The other echoes any words (including pronouns) that have anything to do with speech.

c Richard's dismissive question is met by abuse and accusations. Take turns to speak lines 137–48 as powerfully as possible. Add gesture and movement to emphasise the words.

2 Marching to battle

Richard's entry begins a new episode in the scene which focuses on his relationship with his mother (lines 136–96). The stage direction at line 135 does not reveal that Richard is marching to war ('my expedition').

Invent a phrase or sentence to add to the stage direction to make clear what is happening.

Forbear refuse
Bett'ring exaggerating
causer perpetrator
quicken sharpen
Windy attorneys
 long-winded lawyers
Airy succeeders of intestine joys
 too much talk that follows
 profound happiness

scope room, space
Be copious in exclaims
 use many bitter words
intercepted stopped
owed owned
Ned (diminutive of Edward)

Now thy proud neck bears half my burdened yoke,
From which even here I slip my wearied head
And leave the burden of it all on thee.
Farewell, York's wife, and queen of sad mischance.
These English woes shall make me smile in France.   115
ELIZABETH Oh thou well skilled in curses, stay awhile,
And teach me how to curse mine enemies.
MARGARET Forbear to sleep the night, and fast the day;
Compare dead happiness with living woe;
Think that thy babes were sweeter than they were   120
And he that slew them fouler than he is.
Bett'ring thy loss makes the bad causer worse;
Revolving this will teach thee how to curse.
ELIZABETH My words are dull. Oh, quicken them with thine.
MARGARET Thy woes will make them sharp, and pierce like mine.   125

Margaret Exit

DUCHESS Why should calamity be full of words?
ELIZABETH Windy attorneys to their clients' woes,
Airy succeeders of intestine joys,
Poor breathing orators of miseries,
Let them have scope. Though what they will impart   130
Help nothing else, yet do they ease the heart.
DUCHESS If so, then be not tongue-tied. Go with me,
And in the breath of bitter words let's smother
My damnèd son that thy two sweet sons smothered.
The trumpet sounds. Be copious in exclaims.   135

Enter RICHARD *and his train*

RICHARD Who intercepts me in my expedition?
DUCHESS Oh, she that might have intercepted thee,
By strangling thee in her accursèd womb,
From all the slaughters, wretch, that thou hast done.
ELIZABETH Hid'st thou that forehead with a golden crown   140
Where should be branded, if that right were right,
The slaughter of the prince that owed that crown
And the dire death of my poor sons and brothers?
Tell me, thou villain slave, where are my children?
DUCHESS Thou toad, thou toad, where is thy brother Clarence,   145
And little Ned Plantagenet, his son?
ELIZABETH Where is the gentle Rivers, Vaughan, Grey?

Richard tries to drown out the women's words with drums and trumpets. His mother catalogues all his faults from birth onwards. She demands a final hearing, and vows never to speak to him afterwards.

1 A mother's view (in small groups)

In lines 168–73, the Duchess of York's view of Richard is a chilling one. She lists his characteristics from birth to the present, piling up the adjectives that made 'the earth my hell'. She divides his life into four periods:

- 'infancy' – bad tempered and disobedient ('Tetchy and wayward');
- 'schooldays' – rebellious ('frightful, desperate, wild, and furious');
- 'prime of manhood' – always taking risks ('daring, bold');
- maturity ('age confirmed') - cunning and untrustworthy ('subtle, sly').

Prepare a presentation of Richard's life as seen by his mother. It should illustrate each characteristic of his personality that she identifies.

2 'Humphrey Hower'

Elizabethans used the phrase 'dining with Duke Humphrey' to mean to go without a meal. But no one really knows what 'Humphrey Hower' means. Invent your own explanation that makes sense of lines 176–7.

Rail on criticise
Lord's anointed king
condition character
brook the accent of reproof bear being criticised
stayed waited

the holy rood Christ's cross
kind in hatred naturally hating; hating with a smile
comfortable comforting
disgracious ungracious

DUCHESS   Where is kind Hastings?

RICHARD   A flourish, trumpets! Strike alarum, drums!
Let not the heavens hear these telltale women   150
Rail on the Lord's anointed. Strike, I say!
Flourish. Alarums
Either be patient and entreat me fair,
Or with the clamorous report of war
Thus will I drown your exclamations.

DUCHESS   Art thou my son?   155

RICHARD   Ay, I thank God, my father, and yourself.

DUCHESS   Then patiently hear my impatience.

RICHARD   Madam, I have a touch of your condition,
That cannot brook the accent of reproof.

DUCHESS   Oh, let me speak.

RICHARD   Do then, but I'll not hear.   160

DUCHESS   I will be mild and gentle in my words.

RICHARD   And brief, good mother, for I am in haste.

DUCHESS   Art thou so hasty? I have stayed for thee,
God knows, in torment and in agony.

RICHARD   And came I not at last to comfort you?   165

DUCHESS   No, by the holy rood, thou know'st it well,
Thou cam'st on earth to make the earth my hell.
A grievous burden was thy birth to me.
Tetchy and wayward was thy infancy;
Thy schooldays frightful, desperate, wild, and furious;   170
Thy prime of manhood, daring, bold, and venturous;
Thy age confirmed, proud, subtle, sly, and bloody:
More mild, but yet more harmful, kind in hatred.
What comfortable hour canst thou name
That ever graced me with thy company?   175

RICHARD   Faith, none but Humphrey Hower, that called your grace
To breakfast once, forth of my company.
If I be so disgracious in your eye,
Let me march on and not offend you, madam.
Strike up the drum!

DUCHESS   I prithee, hear me speak.   180

RICHARD   You speak too bitterly.

DUCHESS   Hear me a word,
For I shall never speak to thee again.

RICHARD   So.

The duchess prophesies she will never see Richard again.
She lays a curse to ensure his defeat. Elizabeth echoes the curse.
She says she will do anything to save her daughter's life, and blames
Richard for her son's death.

1 A mother's last words to her son (in pairs)

The Duchess of York first prophesies that either Richard will be
justly killed by God's decree ('ordinance') before the war is over, or
she will die. She curses Richard and foretells that he will lose the
forthcoming battle. She will pray for the opposing side ('adverse
party'), and predicts the souls of the murdered princes will promise
victory to Richmond (lines 191–4). Her final rhyming couplet
wishes for Richard's death in battle, and personifies 'Shame' as a
servant following Richard in life and waiting on him in death.

Discuss ways in which the duchess might exit to reinforce the
effect of her curse.

2 A new episode: Richard versus Elizabeth (in pairs)

A new episode begins (lines 197–436) involving only Richard and
Elizabeth. To gain a first impression, take parts and read straight
through. After your read-through, work on some of the activities
below and on the following pages.

a Talk over whether Elizabeth has any suspicion of Richard's
   marriage intentions towards her daughter (also called Elizabeth)
   at this early point in their encounter.

b Richard and Elizabeth's verbal battle in lines 212–22 recalls the
   quick-fire exchange (stichomythia: rapidly alternating lines)
   between Richard and Anne in the wooing scene (Act 1 Scene 2).
   Speak the lines twice, with pauses, then without pauses. Which
   style fits best?

---

attend wait upon
level not don't aim
veil of infamy
   protection of a bad reputation

good stars were opposite
   their star-signs were unfavourable
ill friends bad persons
unavoided unavoidable
avoided grace rejection of God

DUCHESS   Either thou wilt die by God's just ordinance   185
          Ere from this war thou turn a conqueror,
          Or I with grief and extreme age shall perish
          And nevermore behold thy face again.
          Therefore take with thee my most grievous curse,
          Which in the day of battle tire thee more
          Than all the còmplete armour that thou wear'st.   190
          My prayers on the adverse party fight,
          And there the little souls of Edward's children
          Whisper the spirits of thine enemies
          And promise them success and victory.
          Bloody thou art, bloody will be thy end;   195
          Shame serves thy life and doth thy death attend.

                                                               Exit

ELIZABETH   Though far more cause, yet much less spirit to curse
            Abides in me. I say amen to her.
RICHARD   Stay, madam. I must talk a word with you.
ELIZABETH   I have no more sons of the royal blood   200
            For thee to slaughter. For my daughters, Richard,
            They shall be praying nuns, not weeping queens.
            And therefore level not to hit their lives.
RICHARD   You have a daughter called Elizabeth,
          Virtuous and fair, royal and gracious.   205
ELIZABETH   And must she die for this? Oh, let her live,
            And I'll corrupt her manners, stain her beauty,
            Slander myself as false to Edward's bed,
            Throw over her the veil of infamy.
            So she may live unscarred of bleeding slaughter,   210
            I will confess she was not Edward's daughter.
RICHARD   Wrong not her birth; she is a royal princess.
ELIZABETH   To save her life, I'll say she is not so.
RICHARD   Her life is safest only in her birth.
ELIZABETH   And only in that safety died her brothers.   215
RICHARD   Lo, at their birth good stars were opposite.
ELIZABETH   No, to their lives ill friends were contrary.
RICHARD   All unavoided is the doom of destiny.
ELIZABETH   True, when avoided grace makes destiny.
            My babes were destined to a fairer death,   220
            If grace had blest thee with a fairer life.
RICHARD   You speak as if that I had slain my cousins.

Elizabeth continues to accuse Richard of the murder of the princes and wishes she could die assaulting him. Richard declares that he will banish her grief by giving all honour and dignity to her daughter, Elizabeth.

1 Elizabeth argues bitterly against Richard

Elizabeth describes the murder of her two sons as a sacrifice, and in an extended metaphor wishes her nails 'anchored' in Richard's eyes, and that like a poor ship ('bark') without sails and rigging she could wreck herself on Richard. The only 'advancement' that she can imagine Richard giving to her children is on the 'scaffold' to die.

Richard argues he should marry Elizabeth's daughter to consolidate his position as king. Choose a line which makes the most effective caption for the picture.

cozened cheated	**discovered** uncovered
kindred family	**type** symbol (the crown)
lanch'd lanced, pierced	**demise** assign, grant
direction command	**Lethe** river of forgetfulness
whetted sharpened	**process** tale
still use of grief	**thy kindness date**
repeated expression of grief	the duration of your kindness

ELIZABETH Cousins indeed, and by their uncle cozened
       Of comfort, kingdom, kindred, freedom, life.
       Whose hand soever lanch'd their tender hearts,   225
       Thy head all indirectly gave direction.
       No doubt the murderous knife was dull and blunt
       Till it was whetted on thy stone-hard heart
       To revel in the entrails of my lambs.
       But that still use of grief makes wild grief tame,   230
       My tongue should to thy ears not name my boys
       Till that my nails were anchored in thine eyes,
       And I in such a desperate bay of death,
       Like a poor bark of sails and tackling reft,
       Rush all to pieces on thy rocky bosom.   235
RICHARD Madam, so thrive I in my enterprise
       And dangerous success of bloody wars
       As I intend more good to you and yours
       Than ever you and yours by me were harmed.
ELIZABETH What good is covered with the face of heaven   240
       To be discovered, that can do me good?
RICHARD Th'advancement of your children, gentle lady.
ELIZABETH Up to some scaffold, there to lose their heads.
RICHARD Unto the dignity and height of fortune,
       The high imperial type of this earth's glory.   245
ELIZABETH Flatter my sorrow with report of it.
       Tell me what state, what dignity, what honour,
       Canst thou demise to any child of mine?
RICHARD Even all I have, ay, and myself and all,
       Will I withal endow a child of thine,   250
       So in the Lethe of thy angry soul
       Thou drown the sad remembrance of those wrongs
       Which thou supposest I have done to thee.
ELIZABETH Be brief, lest that the process of thy kindness
       Last longer telling than thy kindness date.   255
RICHARD Then know that from my soul I love thy daughter.
ELIZABETH My daughter's mother thinks it with her soul.
RICHARD What do you think?
ELIZABETH That thou dost love my daughter from thy soul.
       So from thy soul's love didst thou love her brothers,   260
       And from my heart's love I do thank thee for it.

*Richard states his intention to marry Elizabeth's daughter and make
her queen. Elizabeth mockingly suggests ways in which he should woo
her daughter. Richard promises to make amends through the marriage.*

1 Grisly gifts (in pairs)

Richard reveals that he wants to marry Elizabeth's daughter and
make her queen of England. Richard asks for her help, as a mother
best knows her daughter's mood and character. Elizabeth mocks his
request by challenging Richard to send her daughter the results of
his murderous deeds as grisly gifts. Take turns to speak lines
274–86, making your tone as sarcastic and hurtful as possible.

2 Make them laugh?

Faced with Elizabeth's mocking challenge, Richard defends himself.
Such bloody acts have been committed because of his love for
Elizabeth's daughter (line 292). When Elizabeth rejects this excuse,
he suggests that sometimes men can act thoughtlessly ('Men shall
deal unadvisedly sometimes'). This line usually gains a big laugh in
the theatre because 'deal unadvisedly' is totally out of proportion to
the enormity of his crimes.

Work out an effective method of speaking lines 295–7 (that is, in
exasperation, pleadingly, humorously, and so on). Is there any
possibility that Richard genuinely believes what he is saying?

3 Direct the army

Richard entered at line 135 with his army, but there has been no
stage direction to indicate what the army is doing all this time. Step
into role as director and decide on some possible solutions.

---

confound confuse
humour moods, temperament
haply perhaps
purple sap blood

mad'st away murdered
(made away)
conveyance with removal of
spoil destruction
deal unadvisedly act thoughtlessly

RICHARD   Be not so hasty to confound my meaning.
          I mean that with my soul I love thy daughter
          And do intend to make her Queen of England.
ELIZABETH   Well then, who dost thou mean shall be her king?   265
RICHARD   Even he that makes her queen. Who else should be?
ELIZABETH   What, thou?
RICHARD   Even so. How think you of it?
ELIZABETH   How canst thou woo her?
RICHARD   That would I learn of you,   270
          As one being best acquainted with her humour.
ELIZABETH   And wilt thou learn of me?
RICHARD   Madam, with all my heart.
ELIZABETH   Send to her by the man that slew her brothers
          A pair of bleeding hearts; thereon engrave   275
          Edward and York; then haply will she weep.
          Therefore present to her, as sometime Margaret
          Did to thy father, steeped in Rutland's blood,
          A handkerchief, which, say to her, did drain
          The purple sap from her sweet brother's body,   280
          And bid her wipe her weeping eyes withal.
          If this inducement move her not to love,
          Send her a letter of thy noble deeds.
          Tell her thou mad'st away her uncle Clarence,
          Her uncle Rivers, ay, and for her sake   285
          Mad'st quick conveyance with her good aunt Anne.
RICHARD   You mock me, madam, this is not the way
          To win your daughter.
ELIZABETH   There is no other way,
          Unless thou couldst put on some other shape   290
          And not be Richard that hath done all this.
RICHARD   Say that I did all this for love of her.
ELIZABETH   Nay, then indeed she cannot choose but hate thee,
          Having bought love with such a bloody spoil.
RICHARD   Look what is done, cannot be now amended.   295
          Men shall deal unadvisedly sometimes,
          Which after-hours gives leisure to repent.
          If I did take the kingdom from your sons,
          To make amends I'll give it to your daughter.

Richard lists all the gains Queen Elizabeth will enjoy if her daughter becomes his wife. Her son, Dorset, will also benefit. He asks her to prepare Elizabeth for his wooing while he defeats Buckingham.

1 Richard presents his case (in pairs)

Use the following summary to help you speak Richard's lines.

Lines 298–9: I'll make your daughter queen.

Lines 300–2: If I killed your children, I will now give life to heirs through your daughter.

Lines 303–8: A grandmother is loved only a little less than a child's mother. But the grandmother does not have to suffer the pain of labour to produce a grandchild.

Lines 309–10: Your children were an annoyance when you were young. Grandchildren will comfort you in age.

Lines 311–12: Your loss is not having a son as king, but that has resulted in your daughter becoming queen.

Lines 313–14: I can't offer you what I'd really like, but please accept what I'm able to offer.

Lines 315–20: Your son, Dorset, can return home to a position of power, as brother-in-law to the king.

Lines 321–3: You will be the mother-in-law to the king and the troubles of the past will be resolved.

Lines 324–8: The future will be far, far better and happier than the past.

Lines 329–34: Go to your daughter and use your maturity to prepare her to be wooed. Make her ambitious for queenship and tell her of the joys of marriage.

Lines 335–40: When I've defeated Buckingham, I'll marry your daughter and she will be my commander.

---

doting title fond name
metal substance, body, being
bid like sorrow
 endured similar pain
discontented steps
 rebellious followers

orient bright, valuable
Advantaging adding value to
aspiring flame
 fire of ambition
retail retell

180

If I have killed the issue of your womb,   300
To quicken your increase I will beget
Mine issue of your blood upon your daughter.
A grandam's name is little less in love
Than is the doting title of a mother;
They are as children but one step below,   305
Even of your metal, of your very blood,
Of all one pain, save for a night of groans
Endured of her for whom you bid like sorrow.
Your children were vexation to your youth,
But mine shall be a comfort to your age.   310
The loss you have is but a son being king,
And by that loss your daughter is made queen.
I cannot make you what amends I would;
Therefore accept such kindness as I can.
Dorset, your son, that with a fearful soul   315
Leads discontented steps in foreign soil,
This fair alliance quickly shall call home
To high promotions and great dignity.
The king that calls your beauteous daughter wife
Familiarly shall call thy Dorset brother.   320
Again shall you be mother to a king,
And all the ruins of distressful times
Repaired with double riches of content.
What? We have many goodly days to see.
The liquid drops of tears that you have shed   325
Shall come again, transformed to orient pearl,
Advantaging their love with interest
Of ten times double gain of happiness.
Go then, my mother, to thy daughter go.
Make bold her bashful years with your experience;   330
Prepare her ears to hear a wooer's tale;
Put in her tender heart th'aspiring flame
Of golden sovereignty; acquaint the princess
With the sweet silent hours of marriage joys.
And when this arm of mine hath chastisèd   335
The petty rebel, dull-brained Buckingham,
Bound with triumphant garlands will I come
And lead thy daughter to a conqueror's bed;
To whom I will retail my conquest won,
And she shall be sole victoress, Caesar's Caesar.   340

Elizabeth again mocks Richard's proposal to woo Princess Elizabeth. She challenges every one of his arguments and statements, and dismisses his attempt to swear on the symbols of kingship.

1 Claims and counter claims (in pairs)

Elizabeth's list of questions (lines 341–6) are a response to Richard's long speech ending in the proposal that he should marry young Elizabeth. What follows returns to the quick-fire exchanges of stichomythia (see page 242) often using balanced, antithetical pairing of sentences.

Take parts as Richard and Queen Elizabeth and speak lines 347–69. Then return and treat each two line claim and counter claim separately, exchanging views on how one line leads to the next (that is, how one character picks up a word or phrase spoken by the other and returns it in a different form).

2 'I swear' (I)

Elizabeth accuses Richard (line 345) of disregarding three basic principles which govern a stable society ('God', 'law', 'honour'). Later, in line 370, Richard swears by St George (church), his Garter (honour) and his crown (law and kingship). By swearing on these symbols of his kingship, Richard is not only invoking the church, chivalry and honour, but also the divinity connected with kingship. (St George is the patron saint of England and his portrait an integral part of the Order of the Garter.)

Identify the three reasons Elizabeth gives in lines 373–5 which show Richard's oath is worthless.

Infer imply
entreats begs
king's King God
vail yield, lose
speeds best succeeds best

Harp not on that string
don't keep repeating that, change
the subject
Profaned treated irreverently and
contemptuously
usurped taken illegally
his (lines 373–5) its

ELIZABETH What were I best to say? Her father's brother
          Would be her lord? Or shall I say her uncle?
          Or he that slew her brothers and her uncles?
          Under what title shall I woo for thee
          That God, the law, my honour, and her love   345
          Can make seem pleasing to her tender years?
RICHARD Infer fair England's peace by this alliance.
ELIZABETH Which she shall purchase with still-lasting war.
RICHARD Tell her the king, that may command, entreats.
ELIZABETH That at her hands which the king's King forbids.   350
RICHARD Say she shall be a high and mighty queen.
ELIZABETH To vail the title, as her mother doth.
RICHARD Say I will love her everlastingly.
ELIZABETH But how long shall that title ever last?
RICHARD Sweetly in force until her fair life's end.   355
ELIZABETH But how long fairly shall her sweet life last?
RICHARD As long as heaven and nature lengthens it.
ELIZABETH As long as hell and Richard likes of it.
RICHARD Say I, her sovereign, am her subject low.
ELIZABETH But she, your subject, loathes such sovereignty.   360
RICHARD Be eloquent in my behalf to her.
ELIZABETH An honest tale speeds best being plainly told.
RICHARD Then plainly to her tell my loving tale.
ELIZABETH Plain and not honest is too harsh a style.
RICHARD Your reasons are too shallow and too quick.   365
ELIZABETH Oh, no, my reasons are too deep and dead,
          Too deep and dead, poor infants, in their graves.
RICHARD Harp not on that string, madam. That is past.
ELIZABETH Harp on it still shall I till heartstrings break.
RICHARD Now, by my George, my Garter, and my crown –   370
ELIZABETH Profaned, dishonoured, and the third usurped.
RICHARD I swear –
ELIZABETH   By nothing, for this is no oath.
          Thy George, profaned, hath lost his lordly honour;
          Thy Garter, blemished, pawned his knightly virtue;
          Thy crown, usurped, disgraced his kingly glory: 375
          If something thou wouldst swear to be believed,
          Swear then by something that thou hast not wronged.

Elizabeth will not accept any oath sworn by Richard based on himself, the world, his father's death, on God or the future. Richard claims that he intends to reform if he is successful in battle.

1 'I swear' (II) (in pairs)

Richard continues to search for an oath which is acceptable to Elizabeth. Today an oath is mainly sworn in a formal situation: for example, swearing in a jury or making marriage vows. The swearer pledges their word by using something they venerate as a symbol, perhaps a holy book, or the safety of those they love. Elizabeth says that Richard cannot make an oath, as through his actions he has devalued all he might swear by. He has destroyed the value of himself, his kingdom and the honour of his dead father (lines 378–80).

In lines 381–91, Elizabeth questions his vow to swear by God. She reminds him of his past deeds and how they represented his failure to keep his promises to God as he broke the unity (of the Woodvilles and their enemies) created by King Edward, killed Clarence and Rivers and murdered the princes.

Richard does not answer Elizabeth's charges but tries another oath based on the future. This too is dismissed with contempt by Elizabeth because the future will be filled with the children and parents grieving for their fathers and children that Richard has killed.

Take parts as Richard and Elizabeth and speak the whole 'oath' episode (lines 370–401). Accentuate Richard's increasing desperation to find an acceptable oath, and Elizabeth's implacable rejection of each attempt.

Th'imperial metal the crown
time o'erpast past
Hereafter time
 the time to come, the future
Ungoverned unguided, fatherless
ere before

by times ill-used repassed
 times badly used in the past
confound destroy
bar me stop my
proceeding success
Immaculate devotion pure prayer
tender not don't win

RICHARD Then by myself.
ELIZABETH   Thyself is self-misused.
RICHARD Now, by the world –
ELIZABETH   'Tis full of thy foul wrongs.
RICHARD My father's death.
ELIZABETH   Thy life hath it dishonoured.   380
RICHARD Why then, by heaven.
ELIZABETH   Heaven's wrong is most of all.
    If thou didst fear to break an oath with Him,
    The unity the king my husband made
    Thou hadst not broken, nor my brothers died.
    If thou hadst feared to break an oath by Him,   385
    Th'imperial metal circling now thy head
    Had graced the tender temples of my child,
    And both the princes had been breathing here,
    Which now, two tender bedfellows for dust,
    Thy broken faith hath made the prey for worms.   390
    What canst thou swear by now?
RICHARD The time to come.
ELIZABETH That thou hast wrongèd in the time o'erpast,
    For I myself have many tears to wash
    Hereafter time, for time past wronged by thee.   395
    The children live whose fathers thou hast slaughtered,
    Ungoverned youth, to wail it with their age;
    The parents live whose children thou hast butchered,
    Old barren plants, to wail it with their age.
    Swear not by time to come, for that thou hast   400
    Misused ere used, by times ill-used repassed.
RICHARD As I intend to prosper and repent,
    So thrive I in my dangerous affairs
    Of hostile arms. Myself myself confound!
    Heaven and fortune bar me happy hours!   405
    Day, yield me not thy light, nor night, thy rest!
    Be opposite, all planets of good luck
    To my proceeding if, with dear heart's love,
    Immaculate devotion, holy thoughts,
    I tender not thy beauteous, princely daughter!   410
    In her consists my happiness and thine.

> *Richard says total destruction will result if he does not marry young Elizabeth. Her mother says she will let Richard know later. Ratcliffe brings news of a threatened invasion and unreliable allies.*

1 Is Elizabeth persuaded? (in pairs)

For the Plantagenets, marriages of political expediency were commonplace and morally acceptable. Richard's final argument to Elizabeth is the strongest – without this alliance the state will collapse. Richard paints a picture of the country ruined if Princess Elizabeth will not marry him. He appeals to Elizabeth's patriotism, saying she should urge her daughter not to be foolishly perverse in affairs of state ('peevish found in great designs').

Elizabeth's language is ambiguous. She replies to Richard's request with a rhetorical question that recalls her earlier accusations that he is a devil, and she reminds Richard that he murdered her children. In Sir Ian McKellen's film (see page 251), it is quite obvious that Elizabeth will not do as Richard wishes.

Does Richard feel he has been successful? His comment about Elizabeth ('Relenting fool and shallow, changing woman') suggests that he thinks he has won her over. Do you feel he has succeeded? To show the decision you think she has made, suggest how Elizabeth should speak her last three lines and then exit.

2 Bad news for Richard

The final episode of Scene 4 (from line 437) deals with military matters. It contains three short sequences: orders to Catesby and Ratcliffe; dealings with Stanley; and messengers' reports.

---

attorney pleader, match-maker
nest of spicery they will breed
 phoenix's nest they will be reborn
recomforture renewed happiness
Relenting forgiving

puissant powerful
hollow-hearted cowardly
hull ride at anchor
light-foot swift
post ride speedily

Without her follows to myself and thee,
Herself, the land, and many a Christian soul,
Death, desolation, ruin, and decay.
It cannot be avoided but by this.   415
It will not be avoided but by this.
Therefore, dear mother, I must call you so,
Be the attorney of my love to her.
Plead what I will be, not what I have been,
Not my deserts, but what I will deserve.   420
Urge the necessity and state of times,
And be not peevish found in great designs.
ELIZABETH Shall I be tempted of the devil thus?
RICHARD Ay, if the devil tempt you to do good.
ELIZABETH Shall I forget myself to be myself?   425
RICHARD Ay, if your self's remembrance wrong yourself.
ELIZABETH Yet thou didst kill my children.
RICHARD But in your daughter's womb I bury them,
        Where in that nest of spicery they will breed
        Selves of themselves, to your recomforture.   430
ELIZABETH Shall I go win my daughter to thy will?
RICHARD And be a happy mother by the deed.
ELIZABETH I go. Write to me very shortly,
        And you shall understand from me her mind.
RICHARD Bear her my true love's kiss, and so farewell.   435

                            Exit Queen Elizabeth

Relenting fool and shallow, changing woman.
How now, what news?

                Enter RATCLIFFE *and* CATESBY

RATCLIFFE Most mighty sovereign, on the western coast
        Rideth a puissant navy. To our shores
        Throng many doubtful, hollow-hearted friends,   440
        Unarmed and unresolved to beat them back.
        'Tis thought that Richmond is their admiral;
        And there they hull, expecting but the aid
        Of Buckingham to welcome them ashore.
RICHARD Some light-foot friend post to the Duke of Norfolk: 445
        Ratcliffe, thyself, or Catesby; where is he?
CATESBY Here, my good lord.

Richard's orders to Catesby and Ratcliffe cause them some puzzlement. Stanley confirms that Richmond is leading a force by sea to seize the crown. Richard suspects Stanley's loyalty.

1 Richard: an effective general? (in groups of three)

Catesby and Ratcliffe have problems with Richard's orders. As you speak lines 437–62, think about:

- The clarity of Richard's commands.
- Possible reasons for Richard's forgetfulness.
- How Catesby and Ratcliffe react to each other and to Richard.
- How effective you think Richard is as a military commander.

2 Is Stanley loyal? (I) (in pairs)

Stanley confirms Richard's fear that Richmond commands the opposing navy. Supported by Dorset, Buckingham and Morton (the Bishop of Ely), he comes to claim the throne. Richard mocks Stanley for being indirect; asks him to guess the motives for Richmond's arrival; and then scorns Stanley's answer. He forecasts that Stanley will change sides when Richmond ('the Welshman') arrives.

Earlier Stanley had urged Hastings to flee to the north (Act 3 Scene 2, lines 17–18) to escape Richard's vindictiveness, yet he now returns to give Richard valuable information.

As you read on, think about why Richard might suspect Stanley, and what Stanley's motives may be – does he really support Richard?

3 'Is the chair empty?'

Line 476 can be a great moment on stage, and every actor playing Richard tries to create a striking dramatic effect with 'Is the chair empty?' What would you do?

Post go quickly
liege lord
deliver to tell
levy straight recruit immediately
suddenly at once
Hoyday what's this
nearest simplest

White-livered runagate
 cowardly fugitive
chair throne
unswayed not wielded
The empire unpossessed
 the country unruled

RICHARD Catesby, fly to the duke.
CATESBY I will, my lord, with all convenient haste.
RICHARD Ratcliffe, come hither. Post to Salisbury.   450
　　　　　When thou com'st thither – Dull, unmindful villain,
　　　　　Why stay'st thou here, and go'st not to the duke?
CATESBY First, mighty liege, tell me your highness' pleasure,
　　　　　What from your grace I shall deliver to him.
RICHARD Oh, true, good Catesby. Bid him levy straight   455
　　　　　The greatest strength and power that he can make
　　　　　And meet me suddenly at Salisbury.
CATESBY I go.   *Exit*
RATCLIFFE What, may it please you, shall I do at Salisbury?
RICHARD Why, what wouldst thou do there before I go?   460
RATCLIFFE Your highness told me I should post before.
RICHARD My mind is changed.

　　　　　　　Enter LORD STANLEY [EARL OF DERBY]

　　　　　Stanley, what news with you?
STANLEY None good, my liege, to please you with the hearing,
　　　　　Nor none so bad but well may be reported.   465
RICHARD Hoyday, a riddle! Neither good nor bad.
　　　　　What need'st thou run so many miles about,
　　　　　When thou mayst tell thy tale the nearest way?
　　　　　Once more, what news?
STANLEY   Richmond is on the seas.
RICHARD There let him sink, and be the seas on him!   470
　　　　　White-livered runagate, what doth he there?
STANLEY I know not, mighty sovereign, but by guess.
RICHARD Well, as you guess.
STANLEY Stirred up by Dorset, Buckingham, and Morton,
　　　　　He makes for England, here to claim the crown.   475
RICHARD Is the chair empty? Is the sword unswayed?
　　　　　Is the king dead? The empire unpossessed?
　　　　　What heir of York is there alive but we?
　　　　　And who is England's king but great York's heir?
　　　　　Then tell me, what makes he upon the seas?   480
STANLEY Unless for that, my liege, I cannot guess.
RICHARD Unless for that he comes to be your liege,
　　　　　You cannot guess wherefore the Welshman comes.
　　　　　Thou wilt revolt and fly to him, I fear.

Richard continues to criticise Stanley, accusing him of using his troops to support Richmond. He takes Stanley's son as a hostage. Messengers bring news of more support for Richmond throughout the country.

1 Is Stanley loyal? (II) (in pairs)

Richard accuses Stanley of sending his army to help Richmond's troops disembark safely in Wales. Stanley claims to be loyal and says he will raise an army to meet Richard. Still distrusting Stanley, Richard insists that Stanley's son, George, be left as a hostage to be killed if Stanley is disloyal. What stage business could show that Richard means his threat? How might Stanley react?

Take parts as Stanley and Richard and speak lines 463–505, bringing out Richard's distrust and Stanley's evasive replies (for example, Stanley's promise that he will 'muster up my friends and meet your grace' is highly ambiguous).

2 Mapping the action

Use the map on page 3 to locate all the places mentioned in the script and where the separate forces ranged against Richard are active. (Richard himself is in London.)

3 Unwelcome news (I)

Two messengers bring news of increasing support for Richmond 'in Devonshire' and 'In Kent'. The third messenger brings news of Buckingham, but Richard strikes him, fearing more bad news.

You will find an activity on staging the messengers' arrivals when you turn the page.

Cold unfriendly
muster men recruit an army
assurance security
advertisèd informed

haughty prelate proud priest
competitors associates, collaborators
owls (birds of ill omen)

STANLEY No, my good lord; therefore mistrust me not.   485
RICHARD Where is thy power then, to beat him back?
           Where be thy tenants and thy followers?
           Are they not now upon the western shore,
           Safe-conducting the rebels from their ships?
STANLEY No, my good lord, my friends are in the north.   490
RICHARD Cold friends to me. What do they in the north
           When they should serve their sovereign in the west?
STANLEY They have not been commanded, mighty king.
           Pleaseth your majesty to give me leave,
           I'll muster up my friends and meet your grace   495
           Where and what time your majesty shall please.
RICHARD Ay, thou wouldst be gone, to join with Richmond.
           But I'll not trust thee.
STANLEY Most mighty sovereign,
           You have no cause to hold my friendship doubtful.   500
           I never was nor never will be false.
RICHARD Go then and muster men, but leave behind
           Your son George Stanley. Look your heart be firm,
           Or else his head's assurance is but frail.
STANLEY So deal with him as I prove true to you.   *Exit Stanley* 505

         Enter a MESSENGER

MESSENGER My gracious sovereign, now in Devonshire,
           As I by friends am well advertisèd,
           Sir Edward Courtney and the haughty prelate,
           Bishop of Exeter, his elder brother,
           With many more confederates, are in arms.   510

         Enter another MESSENGER

SECOND MESSENGER In Kent, my liege, the Guildfords are in arms,
           And every hour more competitors
           Flock to the rebels, and their power grows strong.

         Enter another MESSENGER

THIRD MESSENGER My lord, the army of great Buckingham –
RICHARD Out on ye, owls, nothing but songs of death!   515

         He striketh him

    There, take thou that, till thou bring better news.

> *The messengers tell that Buckingham's army is scattered,*
> *Buckingham declared a traitor, Yorkshire in rebellion, and*
> *Richmond's navy dispersed. Catesby's news is of Buckingham's capture*
> *and Richmond's landing at Milford Haven.*

1 Unwelcome news (II) (in small groups)

In lines 506–43, four messengers and Catesby report growing unrest, rebellion and invasion. Richard's reactions to the unwelcome news show how he feels under increasing pressure: confused orders; change of mind; striking a messenger; hasty decisions taken without advice.

Take parts as Richard, Catesby and the messengers and speak everything from line 506. Work out how to stage the sequence to bring out the increasing pace of events, their effect on Richard, and whether he retains any of his grotesque sense of humour.

2 Write the proclamation

Richard proclaims Buckingham a traitor with a price on his head. Write the proclamation (a brief statement which was 'proclaimed' or shouted out publicly).

3 Scene 4: a reminder

Glance back over Scene 4 to remind yourself of its major episodes:

Lines 1–135: Margaret, Elizabeth and the duchess grieve (and curse Richard).

Lines 136–96: Richard's relationship with his mother.

Lines 197–436: Richard tries to persuade Elizabeth to favour his marriage to her daughter.

Lines 437–547: Military matters.

Briefly say what each sequence reveals about Richard.

I cry thee mercy I ask forgiveness
well-advisèd prudent, sensible
Breton navy ships from Brittany
dispersed scattered

banks edges of the land
assistants allies
Upon his party to join his forces
Bretagne Brittany

THIRD MESSENGER   The news I have to tell your majesty
       Is that by sudden floods and fall of waters
       Buckingham's army is dispersed and scattered,
       And he himself wandered away alone,   520
       No man knows whither.
RICHARD   I cry thee mercy.
       There is my purse to cure that blow of thine.
       Hath any well-advisèd friend proclaimed
       Reward to him that brings the traitor in?   525
THIRD MESSENGER   Such proclamation hath been made, my lord.

Enter another MESSENGER

FOURTH MESSENGER   Sir Thomas Lovell and Lord Marquess Dorset,
       'Tis said, my liege, in Yorkshire are in arms.
       But this good comfort bring I to your highness:
       The Breton navy is dispersed by tempest.   530
       Richmond, in Dorsetshire, sent out a boat
       Unto the shore, to ask those on the banks
       If they were his assistants, yea or no,
       Who answered him they came from Buckingham
       Upon his party. He, mistrusting them,   535
       Hoised sail and made his course again for Bretagne.
RICHARD   March on, march on, since we are up in arms,
       If not to fight with foreign enemies,
       Yet to beat down these rebels here at home.

Enter CATESBY

CATESBY   My liege, the Duke of Buckingham is taken.   540
       That is the best news. That the Earl of Richmond
       Is with a mighty power landed at Milford
       Is colder news, yet they must be told.
RICHARD   Away towards Salisbury! While we reason here
       A royal battle might be won and lost.   545
       Someone take order Buckingham be brought
       To Salisbury. The rest march on with me.

Flourish. Exeunt

Stanley discloses that his son is Richard's hostage, which prevents his open support for Richmond. He reveals that Queen Elizabeth has agreed to Richmond marrying her daughter. Christopher reports that Richmond's swelling army is marching to London.

1 Stanley's letter

In the previous scene, Stanley had declared his loyalty to Richard. Now he shows his true colours, loyalty to Richmond. (Stanley is Richmond's step-father, as his wife was first married to Edmund Tudor, and their son was Richmond).

Imagine Stanley sends a letter to Richmond which explains his predicament. Write the letter he might send.

2 'Relenting fool and shallow, changing woman'

Richard believed his cunning had persuaded the 'shallow, changing' Elizabeth that he should marry her daughter. Stanley now reports that Elizabeth has agreed to her daughter marrying Richmond (lines 7–8). Look back at the episode between Richard and Elizabeth in the previous scene. As you revisit Elizabeth's replies to Richard, does her decision to marry her daughter to Richmond now surprise you?

3 Retain or cut? (in pairs)

Christopher Urswick was priest to the Countess of Richmond (Stanley's third wife) and used by her as a messenger when her son, Richmond, was in exile. He was rewarded with high office for his loyalty when Richmond became king.

This scene between Sir Christopher and Stanley is sometimes cut in stage productions. Take parts and speak lines 1–21. Then talk over whether you would retain or cut the scene.

franked up in hold
 shut up in a prison
present aid immediate help
Withal also
espouse marry
Ha'rfordwest
 Haverfordwest, west Wales

men of name
 powerful, high-status people
redoubted brave
bend their power
 march their army
hie thee to thy lord
 go to Richmond

ACT 4 SCENE 5
The house of Stanley, Earl of Derby

Enter STANLEY EARL OF DERBY, and
SIR CHRISTOPHER URSWICK, a priest

STANLEY Sir Christopher, tell Richmond this from me,
That in the sty of the most deadly boar
My son George Stanley is franked up in hold.
If I revolt, off goes young George's head;
The fear of that holds off my present aid.   5
So get thee gone; commend me to thy lord.
Withal say that the queen hath heartily consented
He should espouse Elizabeth her daughter.
But tell me, where is princely Richmond now?
CHRISTOPHER At Pembroke, or at Ha'rfordwest, in Wales.   10
STANLEY What men of name resort to him?
CHRISTOPHER Sir Walter Herbert, a renownèd soldier,
Sir Gilbert Talbot, Sir William Stanley,
Oxford, redoubted Pembroke, Sir James Blunt,
And Rice ap Thomas, with a valiant crew,   15
And many other of great name and worth;
And towards London do they bend their power,
If by the way they be not fought withal.
STANLEY Well, hie thee to thy lord; I kiss his hand.
My letter will resolve him of my mind.   20
Farewell.

Exeunt

Looking back at Act 4

Activities for groups or individuals

Richard's sitting on the throne (Scene 2) represents the fulfilment of his plans. Directors can dramatise the hollowness and weakness of Richard's kingship at the very moment he seems at his most powerful. How is Richard's vulnerability suggested in this picture?

1 Grieving women

Anne, the Duchess of York, Queen Elizabeth and Queen Margaret do not appear after this Act (but Anne returns as a ghost in Act 5). United in their hatred of Richard, the four speak of their ordeals (Scenes 1 and 2). Make a list or draw a spider-diagram for each of the women to illustrate what each says she has suffered.

2 A powerful or weak king?

Some critics argue that Richard never regains his old love of intrigue and malicious play-acting after he is crowned. He no longer controls events, but seems at their mercy. List the incidents which mark the beginning of his misfortunes from Scene 2 onwards, then list the steps Richard takes to consolidate his power in Scene 3 and Scene 4. Compare the two lists and discuss what they reveal of Richard's situation at this point in the play.

3 The murder of the princes

The only historical evidence on the princes in the Tower is that the Duke of York joined the young King Edward in the Tower on 16th June 1483 and that neither were seen again. Controversy continues over what happened and many still protest that Richard was innocent of their deaths (notably in papers produced by 'The Society for the Friends of Richard III', and in Josephine Tey's novel *The Daughter of Time*). Step into role as one of the princes and describe events leading up to your imprisonment, and your experience in the Tower.

4 Richard the unsuccessful suitor

Richard woos the young Elizabeth through her mother (Scene 4). Work out how each of the following interpretations could be communicated clearly to the audience.

a Elizabeth pretends to agree to Richard's proposal, in order to stall for time, and so enable Richmond to advance.

b Elizabeth succumbs to Richard's charms and agrees to the marriage.

c She agrees, but later changes her mind (contemporary chroniclers commented on Elizabeth's inconsistency), and Richard calls her 'shallow, changing woman'.

d Richard's weakening power in this 'wooing scene' (to dramatically balance his successful wooing of Anne in Act 1 Scene 2).

5 Spy in the camp

Imagine you are a spy in Richard's camp secretly working for Richmond. You see everything from Richard's entrance in Scene 3 to the end of the Act. Write a report explaining Richard's military and political situation and his mental state.

Buckingham, escorted to execution, begs all Richard's dead victims to mock him. He remembers he wished God to punish him when he was proved a traitor, and recalls Margaret's prophecy that Richard would betray him.

1 Buckingham prepares for death (in pairs)

Buckingham begs that if the souls of Richard's victims are watching him now, they should mock him. Recalling his desire to be betrayed by a false friend if he failed in loyalty to King Edward's family and the Woodvilles, he realises the fatal consequences of his vow, and remembers Margaret's curse.

All Souls' Day (2nd November) is an appropriate date for Buckingham's desire to be mocked by the souls of the dead. It is the day in the Christian calendar when the living are especially encouraged to remember the dead.

Take parts and speak lines 1–29. To help your understanding and performance, consider some of the following.

- Work through the list of victims in lines 3–5. For each, identify the degree of Buckingham's responsibility for the 'foul injustice' of their deaths.

- Lines 13–22 recall Buckingham's false desire ('feignèd prayer') to King Edward, wishing a friend to be false to him if he proved to be disloyal. Buckingham never intended to honour his word, and so joked ('dallied') with God. God has taken Buckingham's jest seriously ('in earnest'). Remind yourself of Buckingham's oath by reading Act 2 Scene 1, lines 32–40.

- 'Margaret's curse' (line 25). Turn back to Act 1 Scene 3, lines 299–301 to check how accurately he remembers her words.

- Does Buckingham's final line say he gets what he deserves? How would you stage his departure for execution?

---

miscarrièd been killed
moody angry
doomsday day of death
fall on me condemn me to die

determined respite of my wrongs
end of reprieve from my
punishment
All-Seer God
in earnest in reality

ACT 5 SCENE 1
Salisbury: a place of execution

A SHERIFF *and officers lead* BUCKINGHAM *to execution*

BUCKINGHAM Will not King Richard let me speak with him?
SHERIFF No, my good lord. Therefore be patient.
BUCKINGHAM Hastings and Edward's children, Grey and Rivers,
    Holy King Henry, and thy fair son Edward,
    Vaughan, and all that have miscarrièd   5
    By underhand corrupted foul injustice,
    If that your moody, discontented souls
    Do through the clouds behold this present hour,
    Even for revenge mock my destruction.
    This is All Souls' Day, fellow, is it not?   10
SHERIFF It is.
BUCKINGHAM Why, then, All Souls' Day is my body's doomsday.
    This is the day which, in King Edward's time,
    I wished might fall on me when I was found
    False to his children and his wife's allies.   15
    This is the day wherein I wished to fall
    By the false faith of him whom most I trusted.
    This, this All Souls' Day to my fearful soul
    Is the determined respite of my wrongs.
    That high All-Seer which I dallied with   20
    Hath turned my feignèd prayer on my head
    And given in earnest what I begged in jest.
    Thus doth he force the swords of wicked men
    To turn their own points in their masters' bosoms.
    Thus Margaret's curse falls heavy on my neck: 25
    'When he', quoth she, 'shall split thy heart with sorrow,
    Remember Margaret was a prophetess.'
    Come, lead me, officers, to the block of shame;
    Wrong hath but wrong, and blame the due of blame.

Exeunt Buckingham with officers

Richmond has received a letter of support from Stanley. He vows to defeat Richard's troops and bring peace. Doubts are voiced about the loyalty of Richard's followers.

1 Richmond rallies his troops (in small groups)

Richmond has marched with his army unhindered into the midlands ('bowels') of England. He portrays Richard as a 'usurping boar' that has overthrown the rightful king, a ravaging creature killing and feasting on his own people.

Richmond's entrance and opening speech – a commander rallying and motivating his troops – offers many opportunities for an actor to convey to the audience a strong first impression of the future king.

a Would you present Richmond as noble, or opportunistic, or in some other way? Suggest how appearance, costume, and how he enters can shape the audience's view of Richmond.

b Identify the key ways in which Richmond motivates his troops (for example, through his references to Richard; peace; hope; trust in God), then take turns to deliver his opening speech.

2 Another tyrant's troops desert (in pairs)

Herbert and Blunt say that Richard's followers will desert. Macbeth faced a similar situation. His soldiers deserted as the relatives and sympathisers of those he had murdered closed in. Malcolm (like Richmond, a leader of invading forces) says about Macbeth's troops:

> 'Both more and less have given him the revolt,
> And none serve with him but constrainèd things
> Whose hearts are absent too.'

Compare Malcolm's lines with lines 19–21. Do they express the same view? ('more and less' means 'high- and low-status soldiers').

Lines of fair comfort
 a letter of support
spoiled plundered
Swills swallows greedily
wash scraps given to pigs

embowelled bosoms
 disembowelled bodies
cheerly cheerfully
homicide murderer

ACT 5 SCENE 2
Tamworth: the camp of Richmond

Enter RICHMOND, OXFORD, BLUNT, HERBERT,
and others, with drum and colours

RICHMOND Fellows in arms, and my most loving friends,
    Bruised underneath the yoke of tyranny,
    Thus far into the bowels of the land
    Have we marched on without impediment;
    And here receive we from our father Stanley 5
    Lines of fair comfort and encouragement.
    The wretched, bloody, and usurping boar,
    That spoiled your summer fields and fruitful vines,
    Swills your warm blood like wash, and makes his trough
    In your embowelled bosoms, this foul swine 10
    Is now even in the centre of this isle,
    Near to the town of Leicester, as we learn.
    From Tamworth thither is but one day's march.
    In God's name, cheerly on, courageous friends,
    To reap the harvest of perpetual peace 15
    By this one bloody trial of sharp war.
OXFORD Every man's conscience is a thousand men
    To fight against this guilty homicide.
HERBERT I doubt not but his friends will turn to us.
BLUNT He hath no friends but what are friends for fear, 20
    Which in his dearest need will fly from him.
RICHMOND All for our vantage. Then in God's name march!
    True hope is swift, and flies with swallow's wings;
    Kings it makes gods, and meaner creatures kings.

Exeunt

Richard orders his tent to be pitched and declares his army to be three times larger than Richmond's. He begins his battle plans. Richmond also begins to prepare for the coming battle.

1 Rival camps, sunset to sunrise

Scene 3 portrays events from sunset to early morning. The action alternates between the rival camps of Richard and Richmond as the two leaders reflect upon their personal situations and prepare for the coming battle. As you work through the whole scene, bear in mind:

- *Staging.* Many modern productions have two tents erected on either side of the stage. Whether in or outside their tents, Richard and Richmond are in full view of the audience, but do not acknowledge each other's presence. (The picture on page 204 shows only Richard's tent.)

- *Time passing.* Look out for ways in which Shakespeare's language indicates the passage of time (sunset, 9 o'clock at night, midnight, 4 o'clock in the morning, dawn).

2 Similarities and differences (in groups of five)

The alternating episodes in the scene between Richard and Richmond and their troops enable the audience to make direct comparisons and contrasts between the rival camps. Take parts as Richard, Surrey, Norfolk, Richmond and Blunt and speak lines 1–47. From this first impression, discuss how you could highlight likenesses and differences between the two leaders and their followers.

have knocks suffer blows
all's one for that never mind that
descried counted
battalia large army
account number
vantage best strategic position
men of sound direction
  good leaders

car cart, chariot
form and model
  organisation and tactics
Limit assign
several charge
  separate position, duty
part divide

ACT 5 SCENE 3
Bosworth Field

Enter RICHARD in arms, with NORFOLK, RATCLIFFE,
the EARL OF SURREY and others

RICHARD Here pitch our tent, even here in Bosworth field.
        My lord of Surrey, why look you so sad?
SURREY My heart is ten times lighter than my looks.
RICHARD My lord of Norfolk.
NORFOLK Here, most gracious liege.
RICHARD Norfolk, we must have knocks, ha, must we not?　　　　　5
NORFOLK We must both give and take, my loving lord.
RICHARD Up with my tent. Here will I lie tonight,
        But where tomorrow? Well, all's one for that.
        Who hath descried the number of the traitors?
NORFOLK Six or seven thousand is their utmost power.　　　　　10
RICHARD Why, our battalia trebles that account.
        Besides, the king's name is a tower of strength,
        Which they upon the adverse faction want.
        Up with the tent. Come, noble gentlemen,
        Let us survey the vantage of the ground.　　　　　15
        Call for some men of sound direction.
        Let's lack no discipline, make no delay,
        For lords, tomorrow is a busy day.　　　　　*Exeunt*

Enter RICHMOND, SIR WILLIAM BRANDON, OXFORD,
DORSET, HERBERT, BLUNT, *and* OTHERS

RICHMOND The weary sun hath made a golden set,
        And by the bright tract of his fiery car,　　　　　20
        Gives token of a goodly day tomorrow.
        Sir William Brandon, you shall bear my standard.
        Give me some ink and paper in my tent.
        I'll draw the form and model of our battle,
        Limit each leader to his several charge,　　　　　25
        And part in just proportion our small power.
        My lord of Oxford, you, Sir William Brandon,
        And you, Sir Walter Herbert, stay with me.

Richmond asks Blunt to attempt to take an important message to Stanley. He proposes a battle plan meeting. Richard checks his armour is ready and orders trustworthy guards to be placed on watch.

In sharp contrast to Richmond, all is not well with Richard (above). How would you design Scene 3 to show the differences between the rival camps?

quartered camped (Stanley cannot openly support Richmond because his son is held hostage by Richard)
colours flags
make some good means try your best

needful important
beaver face guard of helmet
easier less tight
hie thee to thy charge hasten to your duty
sentinels guards

The Earl of Pembroke keeps his regiment.
Good Captain Blunt, bear my goodnight to him   30
And by the second hour in the morning
Desire the earl to see me in my tent.
Yet one thing more, good Captain, do for me:
Where is Lord Stanley quartered, do you know?
BLUNT   Unless I have mista'en his colours much,   35
Which well I am assured I have not done,
His regiment lies half a mile at least
South from the mighty power of the king.
RICHMOND   If without peril it be possible,
Sweet Blunt, make some good means to speak with him   40
And give him from me this most needful note.
BLUNT   Upon my life, my lord, I'll undertake it.
And so, God give you quiet rest tonight.
RICHMOND   Good night, good Captain Blunt.
Come, gentlemen,   45
Let us consult upon tomorrow's business.
Into my tent; the dew is raw and cold.

They withdraw into the tent

Enter RICHARD, RATCLIFFE, NORFOLK, *and* CATESBY

RICHARD   What is't o'clock?
CATESBY   It's supper time my lord; it's nine o'clock.
RICHARD   I will not sup tonight.   50
Give me some ink and paper.
What, is my beaver easier than it was,
And all my armour laid into my tent?
CATESBY   It is, my liege, and all things are in readiness.
RICHARD   Good Norfolk, hie thee to thy charge.   55
Use careful watch; choose trusty sentinels.
NORFOLK   I go, my lord.
RICHARD   Stir with the lark tomorrow, gentle Norfolk.
NORFOLK   I warrant you, my lord.   *Exit*
RICHARD   Ratcliffe   60
RATCLIFFE   My lord.

Richard sends a message that Stanley's son will be killed if Stanley does not bring troops to him. He reflects on the loss of his previously high spirits. Stanley pledges, if possible, to aid Richmond in the battle.

1 Richard: a changed man? (in pairs)

Richard observes that he has lost his cheerfulness of mind ('alacrity of spirit'). Take parts as Richard and Ratcliffe and speak lines 62–81. Talk over any changes you can find in Richard from how you have experienced him earlier in the play.

2 Passing time

The action continues alternating between the rival camps to underline the contrasting moods of the two leaders. While the episode in Richard's tent takes place at 9 o'clock at night (line 49), what time does it seem to be in the Richmond/Stanley episode? (for example, lines 83, 88–9 and 107–8).

Don't worry if there seems to be contradictions about time throughout the scene. In the theatre, each production works out its own way of depicting the progress from dusk to dawn.

3 Stanley: the balance of power?

Stanley acts as a catalyst to reveal the differences between Richard and Richmond. Both commanders need his support, but try to achieve it by very different approaches. Richard holds Stanley's son hostage. His chilling line that he will kill the boy ('fall/Into the blind cave of eternal night') tellingly contrasts with the episode between Richmond and Stanley, where step-father and step-son affectionately greet.

You will find how Stanley's true allegiance decides the outcome of the battle in lines 344–53.

---

pursuivant at arms junior officer
watch watch-light, a candle marked into sections to measure time
staves lances
Saw'st have you seen
cockshut twilight
alacrity lightness
by attorney by proxy

flaky darkness streaks of light
Prepare thy battle
draw up your army
th'arbitrement the test
mortal-staring fatally glaring
With best advantage
at the best opportunity

RICHARD   Send out a pursuivant at arms
    To Stanley's regiment. Bid him bring his power
    Before sunrising, lest his son George fall
    Into the blind cave of eternal night.   65
    Fill me a bowl of wine. Give me a watch.
    Saddle white Surrey for the field tomorrow.
    Look that my staves be sound and not too heavy. Ratcliffe!
RATCLIFFE   My lord.
RICHARD   Saw'st the melancholy Lord Northumberland?   70
RATCLIFFE   Thomas the Earl of Surrey and himself,
    Much about cockshut time, from troop to troop
    Went through the army, cheering up the soldiers.
RICHARD   So, I am satisfied. Give me a bowl of wine.
    I have not that alacrity of spirit   75
    Nor cheer of mind that I was wont to have.
    Set it down. Is ink and paper ready?
RATCLIFFE   It is, my lord.
RICHARD   Bid my guard watch. Leave me.
    Ratcliffe, about the mid of night come to my tent 80
    And help to arm me. Leave me, I say.

           Exeunt Ratcliffe and Catesby

  Enter STANLEY EARL OF DERBY *to* RICHMOND *in his tent*

STANLEY   Fortune and victory sit on thy helm.
RICHMOND   All comfort that the dark night can afford
    Be to thy person, noble father-in-law.
    Tell me, how fares our noble mother?   85
STANLEY   I by attorney bless thee from thy mother,
    Who prays continually for Richmond's good.
    So much for that. The silent hours steal on,
    And flaky darkness breaks within the east.
    In brief, for so the season bids us be,   90
    Prepare thy battle early in the morning,
    And put thy fortune to th'arbitrement
    Of bloody strokes and mortal-staring war.
    I, as I may (that which I would I cannot),
    With best advantage will deceive the time   95
    And aid thee in this doubtful shock of arms.

King Richard III

Stanley says the threat to his son prevents him openly supporting Richmond. He hopes for long friendship. Richmond prays for success in battle. The ghost of Prince Edward visits Richard and Richmond.

1 Stanley's true feelings

Lines 97–105 reveal Stanley's affection for Richmond. Contrast the language he uses to Richmond with his guarded responses to Richard's request for assistance in Act 4 Scene 4, lines 463–505.

2 Richmond's prayer (in pairs)

In lines 111–20, Richmond prays to God asking him to bless his army ('Look on my forces with a gracious eye') and support them as they fight against Richard. The army will then be agents of God ('ministers of chastisement') and it will be God's victory which is celebrated. Discuss possible reasons for Shakespeare giving Richmond a prayer, but not Richard.

3 Ghostly visitors (I) (in large groups)

In lines 121–79, the action continues to alternate between the rival camps as the ghosts of Richard's victims visit the two sleeping leaders, condemning Richard and supporting Richmond. Appearing in the order of their deaths, the ghosts' repeated demand for revenge on Richard ('Despair, and die') is a forceful reminder of Richard's crimes. The episode provides an exciting opportunity for imaginative staging with no fewer than eleven ghosts appearing!

To gain a first impression of the sequence, take parts and speak lines 121–79. Would you wish to present the ghosts as pitiful, terrifying, or to evoke other reactions? You will find help on staging the ghosts on page 210.

brother (George Stanley, Richmond's stepbrother)
tender young
leisure (line 100) available time
ample interchange of sweet discourse long and pleasant conversation

sundered parted
peise weigh
captain subordinate officer
irons weapons
chastisement punishment
windows eyelids
issue child

But on thy side I may not be too forward,
Lest being seen, thy brother, tender George,
Be executed in his father's sight.
Farewell. The leisure and the fearful time   100
Cuts off the ceremonious vows of love
And ample interchange of sweet discourse
Which so long sundered friends should dwell upon.
God give us leisure for these rites of love.
Once more adieu. Be valiant, and speed well.   105
RICHMOND   Good lords, conduct him to his regiment.
I'll strive with troubled noise to take a nap,
Lest leaden slumber peise me down tomorrow,
When I should mount with wings of victory.
Once more, good night, kind lords and gentlemen.   110

Exeunt [all but Richmond]

Oh thou whose captain I account myself,
Look on my forces with a gracious eye.
Put in their hands thy bruising irons of wrath,
That they may crush down with a heavy fall
Th'usurping helmets of our adversaries.   115
Make us thy ministers of chastisement,
That we may praise thee in thy victory.
To thee I do commend my watchful soul
Ere I let fall the windows of mine eyes.
Sleeping, and waking, oh, defend me still. *Sleeps*   120

Enter the GHOST OF PRINCE EDWARD, *son to Henry the Sixth*

GHOST OF PRINCE EDWARD [*To Richard*] Let me sit heavy on thy soul
tomorrow.
Think how thou stab'st me in my prime of youth
At Tewkesbury. Despair therefore, and die.
[*To Richmond*] Be cheerful, Richmond, for the wrongèd souls
Of butchered princes fight in thy behalf.   125
King Henry's issue, Richmond, comforts thee.

King Richard III

The ghosts of Henry VI, Clarence, Rivers, Grey, Vaughan and Hastings visit Richard and Richmond. All wish for despair and death for Richard and success for Richmond.

1 Ghostly visitors (II)

On stage, the ghosts have been presented in all kinds of different ways. In one production, they did not appear to the dreaming commanders in their tents, but at the Battle of Bosworth. They took part in the action and wounded Richard in the fighting. This staging suggests that although Richmond physically killed Richard in a real sword fight, it was from psychological rather than physical wounds that Richard died.

As you work out the staging of lines 121–79, think about the ghosts' dress, gestures and speech. Are they similar or very different from each other? Use the following ideas to help you:

- The ghosts condemn Richard to 'Despair, and die' at least nine times, as they force him to confront his conscience and the consequences of his actions. Explore different ways of speaking the phrase to intensify his fear when he awakens. (Remember, when Richard wakes up he cries 'Have mercy, Jesu!')

- The ghosts pray for Richmond to be successful ('Live and flourish', 'pray', 'win', 'conquer'). Explore suitable tones for each ghost to deliver his or her blessing on Richmond.

- Turn back to the chart on page 166 as a reminder of the 'Killers and Victims' in Richard's rise to power (only Anne, his wife, is missing from that list). Identify for each ghost how they died, and the degree of Richard's responsibility for their deaths.

- The ghosts' messages to the sleeping commanders is delivered in the formal language of repetition, balance and contrast (see page 244). Work out how you can use this highly patterned language to increase dramatic effect.

---

punchèd pierced
washed drowned
fulsome too much

fall thy edgeless sword
drop your your useless weapon
bosom conscience

Enter the GHOST OF HENRY THE SIXTH

GHOST OF HENRY [*To Richard*] When I was mortal, my anointed body
　　By thee was punchèd full of holes.
　　Think on the Tower and me. Despair, and die.
　　Harry the Sixth bids thee despair and die.　　　　　　　　　　130
　　[*To Richmond*] Virtuous and holy, be thou conqueror.
　　Harry, that prophesied thou shouldst be king,
　　Doth comfort thee in sleep. Live and flourish.

Enter the GHOST OF CLARENCE

GHOST OF CLARENCE [*To Richard*] Let me sit heavy in thy soul
　tomorrow,
　　I, that was washed to death with fulsome wine,　　　　　　135
　　Poor Clarence, by thy guile betrayed to death.
　　Tomorrow in the battle think on me,
　　And fall thy edgeless sword, despair, and die.
　　[*To Richmond*] Thou offspring of the house of Lancaster,
　　The wrongèd heirs of York do pray for thee.　　　　　　　140
　　Good angels guard thy battle. Live and flourish.

Enter the GHOSTS OF RIVERS, GREY, *and* VAUGHAN

GHOST OF RIVERS [*To Richard*] Let me sit heavy in thy soul
　tomorrow,
　　Rivers that died at Pomfret. Despair, and die.
GHOST OF GREY Think upon Grey, and let thy soul despair.
GHOST OF VAUGHAN Think upon Vaughan, and with guilty fear　　145
　　Let fall thy lance. Despair, and die.
ALL THREE GHOSTS [*To Richmond*] Awake, and think our wrongs in
　Richard's bosom
　　Will conquer him. Awake, and win the day.

Enter the GHOST OF LORD HASTINGS

GHOST OF HASTINGS [*To Richard*] Bloody and guilty, guiltily awake
　　And in a bloody battle end thy days.　　　　　　　　　　150
　　Think on Lord Hastings. Despair, and die.
　　[*To Richmond*] Quiet untroubled soul, awake, awake.
　　　Arm, fight, and conquer, for fair England's sake.

*The ghosts of princes in the Tower, Anne and Buckingham bring
messages of death and despair to Richard and success to Richmond.*

1 Written by Shakespeare?

Some critics claim the language of the ghosts' speeches is feeble and
is not written by Shakespeare. Others argue the formal style reflects
the language of the pageant or morality play. They assert that
Shakespeare did not intend realism, but wished to imply that
Richard's real opponent is God, not Richmond. In a stylised
episode, the ghosts signal Richard's moral defeat, which is greater
than his physical one.

The picture shows a stylised, formal presentation of the ghost scene,
where all the ghosts remain on stage to accuse Richard (seated, wearing
crown). Work out how you would stage the ghosts' appearances.

the boar's annoy
  injury from Richard
beget father
perturbations
  disturbances, anxieties

adversary's enemy's
yield give up
I died for hope ... aid
  I died before I could support you

Enter the GHOSTS OF THE TWO YOUNG PRINCES

GHOSTS OF PRINCES [*To Richard*] Dream on thy cousins smothered
   in the Tower.
      Let us be laid within thy bosom, Richard,   155
      And weigh thee down to ruin, shame, and death.
      Thy nephews' soul bids thee despair and die.
      [*To Richmond*] Sleep, Richmond, sleep in peace, and wake in
         joy.
      Good angels guard thee from the boar's annoy.
      Live, and beget a happy race of kings.   160
      Edward's unhappy sons do bid thee flourish.

Enter the GHOST OF ANNE, *his wife*

GHOST OF ANNE [*To Richard*] Richard, thy wife, that wretched Anne,
   thy wife,
      That never slept a quiet hour with thee,
      Now fills thy sleep with perturbations.
      Tomorrow in the battle think on me,   165
      And fall thy edgeless sword. Despair, and die.
      [*To Richmond*] Thou quiet soul, sleep thou a quiet sleep.
      Dream of success and happy victory.
      Thy adversary's wife doth pray for thee.

Enter the GHOST OF BUCKINGHAM

GHOST OF BUCKINGHAM [*To Richard*] The first was I that helped
   thee to the crown.   170
      The last was I that felt thy tyranny.
      Oh, in the battle think of Buckingham,
      And die in terror of thy guiltiness.
      Dream on, dream on, of bloody deeds and death.
      Fainting, despair; despairing, yield thy breath.   175
      [*To Richmond*] I died for hope ere I could lend thee aid.
      But cheer thy heart and be thou not dismayed.
      God and good angels fight on Richmond's side,
      And Richard fall in height of all his pride.

Richard starts from sleep and questions the reasons for his fear.
He wrestles with his troubled conscience which reminds him of the
ghosts' accusations of murder and threats of vengeance.

1 'Richard starts out of his dream' (in groups of three)

Richard's mind is in turmoil. In a deeply troubled soliloquy, Richard struggles to come to terms with the 'several sins' which weigh on his conscience. He speaks in simple, direct language, and his brief sentences reflect his inner confusion as he jumps from thought to thought, mood to mood.

Work on lines 180–209 using the following activities to help you.

* Does Richard speak any of this soliloquy to the audience (as in his opening lines of the play), or to himself, or to an imaginary third person, or could he be talking in his sleep?

* The soliloquy contains well over thirty sentences. Share the soliloquy as an agonised conversation, each person speaking one sentence in turn.

* Each sentence can be spoken in different tones – for example, defiance, despair, frustration, anger, and so on. Each person speaks four or five lines trying to use a different tone for each sentence.

* Richard repeats the words 'I', 'myself' and other personal pronouns many times. How can an actor use these repetitions to convey Richard's state of mind?

* Just as Clarence had woken from a dream and confronted his conscience, so Richard wakes with a mind deeply troubled by his past misdeeds. What emotions do you want the audience to feel towards Richard?

Soft but wait
The lights burn blue
 (believed to be the sign of a ghost)
several separate
all used in each degree
 committed often at every level

th'bar place in a courtroom where
 the prisoner hears the sentence
done salutation greeted

Richard starts out of his dream

RICHARD   Give me another horse! Bind up my wounds!   180
Have mercy, Jesu! Soft, I did but dream.
Oh coward conscience, how dost thou afflict me?
The lights burn blue. It is not dead midnight.
Cold, fearful drops stand on my trembling flesh.
What? Do I fear myself? There's none else by.   185
Richard loves Richard, that is, I am I.
Is there a murderer here? No. Yes, I am.
Then fly. What, from myself? Great reason why:
Lest I revenge. What, myself upon myself?
Alack, I love myself. Wherefore? For any good   190
That I myself have done unto myself?
Oh, no. Alas, I rather hate myself
For hateful deeds committed by myself.
I am a villain. Yet I lie, I am not.
Fool, of thyself speak well. Fool, do not flatter.   195
My conscience hath a thousand several tongues,
And every tongue brings in a several tale,
And every tale condemns me for a villain.
Perjury in the highest degree,
Murder, stern murder, in the direst degree,   200
All several sins, all used in each degree,
Throng all to th'bar, crying all 'Guilty, guilty!'
I shall despair. There is no creature loves me,
And if I die no soul shall pity me.
Nay, wherefore should they, since that I myself   205
Find in myself no pity to myself?
Methought the souls of all that I had murdered
Came to my tent, and every one did threat
Tomorrow's vengeance on the head of Richard.

Enter RATCLIFFE

RATCLIFFE   My lord.   210
RICHARD   Who's there?
RATCLIFFE   Ratcliffe, my lord, 'tis I. The early village cock
Hath twice done salutation to the morn.
Your friends are up and buckle on their armour.
RICHARD   Oh Ratcliffe, I fear, I fear.   215

Richard plans to eavesdrop on his troops to discover deserters. Richmond tells of his happiness about his dream and its message of victory. He tells his army that God and right are on their side.

1 Shadows and deserters

Ratcliffe reminds Richard it is dawn and urges him not to fear 'shadows'. Suggest what Richard means by 'shadows' in line 217, then speculate about why he asks Ratcliffe to join him to eavesdrop on his own soldiers.

2 Motivating the troops (in pairs)

Richmond aims at motivating his soldiers through a formal address ('oration') before the battle (you will find Richard also speaks an oration to his troops later). Use the following five sections to help you speak Richmond's oration in as persuasive manner as possible:

Lines 238–40: he regrets he has little time for his speech;

Lines 240–3: he assures the soldiers that God is on their side and that they fight for a just cause;

Lines 244–53: he claims that all Richard's followers want Richmond to win because they know Richard is a usurper and not a true king;

Lines 254–63: he again reminds his soldiers that God is on their side, and he lists the advantages for the future that will be gained by fighting now;

Lines 264–71: if he succeeds the soldiers will all share his victory. They should go cheerfully into battle for the sake of God, their country, Richmond and victory.

Armèd in proof
 in strongest armour
shrink from desert
ta'en a tardy sluggard
 caught a slow late-riser
fairest-boding happiness-promising
cried on called out

leisure and enforcement
 available time and constraint
high-reared bulwarks
 high battlements
except apart
made means contrived, plotted

RATCLIFFE Nay, good my lord, be not afraid of shadows.
RICHARD By the apostle Paul, shadows tonight
      Have struck more terror to the soul of Richard
      Than can the substance of ten thousand soldiers
      Armèd in proof and led by shallow Richmond.   220
      'Tis not yet near day. Come, go with me.
      Under our tents I'll play the eavesdropper,
      To see if any mean to shrink from me.
                       Exeunt Richard and Ratcliffe

     Enter the LORDS *to Richmond sitting in his tent*

LORDS Good morrow, Richmond.
RICHMOND Cry mercy, lords and watchful gentlemen,   225
      That you have ta'en a tardy sluggard here.
LORD How have you slept, my lord?
RICHMOND The sweetest sleep and fairest-boding dreams
      That ever entered in a drowsy head
      Have I since your departure had, my lords.   230
      Methought their souls whose bodies Richard murdered
      Came to my tent and cried on victory.
      I promise you, my heart is very jocund
      In the remembrance of so fair a dream.
      How far into the morning is it, lords?   235
LORD Upon the stroke of four.
RICHMOND Why, then 'tis time to arm and give direction.

     His oration to his soldiers

      More than I have said, loving countrymen,
      The leisure and enforcement of the time
      Forbids to dwell upon. Yet remember this: 240
      God and our good cause fight upon our side.
      The prayers of holy saints and wrongèd souls,
      Like high-reared bulwarks, stand before our faces.
      Richard except, those whom we fight against
      Had rather have us win than him they follow.   245
      For what is he they follow? Truly, gentlemen,
      A bloody tyrant, and a homicide;
      One raised in blood, and one in blood established;
      One that made means to come by what he hath,
      And slaughtered those that were the means to help him;   250

Richmond tells his troops that Richard is a usurper and an enemy to God. He lists the advantages they will gain from fighting Richard. Richard sees disaster ahead for somebody.

Richmond urges his troops to defeat Richard. Richmond is often portrayed as the hero saving England from Richard's oppression (see the Tudor myth on page 2). How do you picture Richmond? How would you present him on stage?

foil/Of England's chair
setting of the throne
ward guard, reward
Your country's fat
England's riches
quits makes up for, rewards
age old age

standards flags
ransom penalty for failure
Tell the clock count the chimes
by the book
according to the calendar
braved made bright, risen in

A base, foul stone made precious by the foil
Of England's chair, where he is falsely set;
One that hath ever been God's enemy.
Then if you fight against God's enemy,
God will in justice ward you as his soldiers;   255
If you do swear to put a tyrant down,
You sleep in peace, the tyrant being slain;
If you do fight against your country's foes,
Your country's fat shall pay your pains the hire;
If you do fight in safeguard of your wives,   260
Your wives shall welcome home the conquerors;
If you do free your children from the sword,
Your children's children quits it in your age.
Then in the name of God and all these rights,
Advance your standards, draw your willing swords.   265
For me, the ransom of my bold attempt
Shall be this cold corpse on the earth's cold face.
But if I thrive, the gain of my attempt
The least of you shall share his part thereof.
Sound drums and trumpets boldly and cheerfully.   270
God and Saint George, Richmond and victory!

Enter RICHARD, RATCLIFFE, *and* CATESBY

RICHARD   What said Northumberland as touching Richmond?
RATCLIFFE   That he was never trainèd up in arms.
RICHARD   He said the truth. And what said Surrey then?
RATCLIFFE   He smiled and said 'The better for our purpose'.   275
RICHARD   He was in the right, and so indeed it is.
       Tell the clock there.

Clock strikes

       Give me a calendar. Who saw the sun today?
RATCLIFFE   Not I, my lord.
RICHARD   Then he disdains to shine, for by the book   280
       He should have braved the east an hour ago.
       A black day will it be to somebody. Ratcliffe!
RATCLIFFE   My lord.

Richard tries to calm his misgivings about the lack of sun.
He sets out his battle plan and dismisses a mocking verse. His address
to his troops begins by insulting Richmond's followers.

1 Richard's changing moods (in small groups)

Richard's state of mind shifts from introspection to action as he prepares for battle. The following activities will help you analyse his changing moods and deliver his lines.

Lines 272–76 refer to the conversations Richard and Ratcliffe overheard while eavesdropping. Does Richard question Ratcliffe expecting to hear of disloyalty from his commanders?

Lines 277–89 show Richard interpreting the sun rising an hour late as a bad omen – but for whom? Suggest how Richard says 'A black day will it be to somebody'.

Lines 290–303 presents Richard as an experienced general, unlike Richmond, who 'was never trainèd up in arms' (line 273). Richard orders his horse to be covered in rich trappings ('Caparison') and sets out his battle plan. Try speaking Richard's lines in different styles: for example, rap out the orders confidently, thoughtfully, in panic. You could also draw up a battle plan and use it as a stage prop, with Richard pointing to different parts of it as he speaks.

Lines 305–13 reveal Richard dismissing the verse sent to Norfolk as a trick by the enemy which accuses him of betrayal by accepting bribes. Do you think Richard is himself again as he refers to 'babbling dreams' and claims that conscience is for cowards?

Lines 316–43 are Richard's oration to his troops. You will find activities on this speech on page 222.

---

lour look angrily	**Jockey** (a familiar form of John)
foreward vanguard	**Dickon** Richard
main battle	**pell mell**
main division of soldiers	hand-to-hand fighting, furiously
puissance force	**inferred** stated
to boot to help	**cope withal** fight against
direction battle plan	**lackey** servile

RICHARD The sun will not be seen today;
     The sky doth frown and lour upon our army.   285
     I would these dewy tears were from the ground.
     Not shine today? Why, what is that to me
     More than to Richmond? For the self-same heaven
     That frowns on me looks sadly upon him.

Enter NORFOLK

NORFOLK Arm, arm, my lord! The foe vaunts in the field!   290
RICHARD Come, bustle, bustle. Caparison my horse.
     Call up Lord Stanley; bid him bring his power.
     I will lead forth my soldiers to the plain,
     And thus my battle shall be orderèd:
     My foreward shall be drawn in length,   295
     Consisting equally of horse and foot;
     Our archers shall be placèd in the midst.
     John Duke of Norfolk, Thomas Earl of Surrey,
     Shall have the leading of the foot and horse.
     They thus directed, we will follow   300
     In the main battle, whose puissance on either side
     Shall be well-wingèd with our chiefest horse.
     This, and Saint George to boot! What think'st thou, Norfolk?
NORFOLK A good direction, warlike sovereign.
     This found I on my tent this morning: 305
     'Jockey of Norfolk, be not so bold,
     For Dickon thy master is bought and sold.'
RICHARD A thing devisèd by the enemy.
     Go, gentlemen, every man to his charge.
     Let not our babbling dreams affright our souls,   310
     For conscience is a word that cowards use,
     Devised at first to keep the strong in awe.
     Our strong arms be our conscience, swords our law!
     March on! Join bravely! Let us to't pell mell,
     If not to heaven, then hand in hand to hell.   315
         [His oration to his army]
     What shall I say more than I have inferred?
     Remember whom you are to cope withal:
     A sort of vagabonds, rascals, and runaways,
     A scum of Bretons and base lackey peasants,

> *Richard calls Richmond's followers beggars and rapists.*
> *He mocks Richmond as a spoilt weakling and reminds his soldiers of*
> *past victories over the French. Hearing of Stanley's refusal to join*
> *him, Richard orders Stanley's son's death.*

1 Richard spurs on his troops (in pairs)

In a stirring oration (lines 316–43), Richard attempts to galvanise his troops into action. He portrays the enemy as an inferior and foreign army ('Bretons'), destroying the land under a weak and inexperienced Richmond. When Richmond's forces are heard approaching, Richard appeals to his men's patriotism as 'gentlemen' and 'yeomen'. He urges the cavalry to fight so bravely that splinters from the wooden handles of their lances will fly into the sky.

a One person speaks the oration slowly while the other echoes all the words which insult Richmond's army and praise Richard's army or England.

b Speak Richard's oration, then speak Richmond's address to his troops (lines 238–71). Which oration would most inspire you if you were a soldier? Why? Identify some of the similarities and differences between the two orations.

2 Richard's final appeal (in pairs)

News of Stanley's desertion to Richmond is a serious blow to Richard's battle plans. Richard ruthlessly orders George Stanley's head to be chopped off, but more urgent matters prevent the execution. The alternating episodes of Scene 3 end with Richard's final impassioned appeal to his troops as Richmond's forces attack. Take turns to speak Richard's lines 349–53. Suggest a different motive for each sentence.

---

o'ercloyèd sickeningly over-full
restrain seize
distain defile
Bretagne Brittany
our mother's England's
milksop weakling
overweening presumptuous, boastful

fond exploit foolish invasion
means riches, income
bobbed buffeted
on record as is written
welkin sky
spleen anger

Whom their o'ercloyèd country vomits forth   320
To desperate adventures and assured destruction.
You sleeping safe, they bring you to unrest;
You having lands, and blest with beauteous wives,
They would restrain the one, distain the other.
And who doth lead them but a paltry fellow,   325
Long kept in Bretagne at our mother's cost?
A milksop, one that never in his life
Felt so much cold as over shoes in snow.
Let's whip these stragglers o'er the seas again;
Lash hence these overweening rags of France,   330
These famished beggars, weary of their lives,
Who, but for dreaming on this fond exploit,
For want of means, poor rats, had hanged themselves.
If we be conquered, let men conquer us,
And not these bastard Bretons, whom our fathers   335
Have in their own land beaten, bobbed, and thumped,
And on record, left them the heirs of shame.
Shall these enjoy our lands, lie with our wives?
Ravish our daughters?

(Drum afar off)

Hark, I hear their drum!
Fight, gentlemen of England! Fight boldly, yeomen!   340
Draw, archers, draw your arrows to the head!
Spur your proud horses hard and ride in blood;
Amaze the welkin with your broken staves!

Enter a MESSENGER

What says Lord Stanley? Will he bring his power?
MESSENGER My lord, he doth deny to come.   345
RICHARD Off with his son George's head!
NORFOLK My lord, the enemy is past the marsh;
    After the battle let George Stanley die.
RICHARD A thousand hearts are great within my bosom.
    Advance our standards! Set upon our foes!   350
    Our ancient word of courage, fair Saint George,
    Inspire us with the spleen of fiery dragons!
    Upon them! Victory sits on our helms!

[Exeunt]

223

Richard has fought bravely. His horse has been killed but he searches for Richmond intending to slay him. Richmond kills Richard. Stanley presents Richmond with the crown which he has taken from Richard.

1 Final conflict

Richard's call for a horse is full of irony: all his gains are reduced to wanting only a horse in his moment of need. Scene 4 and the opening stage directions of Scene 5 offer exciting possibilities for the staging of Richard's final contest and death.

a Richard has gambled his crown on the successful outcome of the battle. Take parts as Richard and Catesby and speak Scene 4. Explore different ways of speaking Richard's lines to find the most dramatically effective delivery.

b Richard's death gives the director unlimited opportunities to stage a thrilling climax. In some stage productions, Richard and Richmond fight in heavy medieval armour which restricts their movements and quickly exhausts the men. On film, Ian McKellen played Richard in a jeep like a World War II general, commanding tanks and automatic weapons. Al Pacino portrayed him in medieval costume with arrows in his chest and back, and was killed with Richmond's longsword.

   Work out how you would stage Richard's death. Be as imaginative as you can!

c Richmond's comment on Richard ('the bloody dog is dead') echoes Queen Margaret's words in Act 4 Scene 4, line 78: the cycle of murder and revenge has ended with Richard's death. Mime Stanley removing the crown from Richard, then speak and perform his presentation to Richmond, bringing out the symbolic importance of Stanley's actions.

Excursions battles
Daring an opposite
 challenging an opponent
cast throw of a dice
stand the hazard of the die
 accept the outcome of the gamble
 (die = dice)

acquit thee acquitted yourself
usurpèd royalties
 wrongfully seized symbols of
 kingship (crown)

ACT 5 SCENE 4
Bosworth: the battlefield

Alarum. Excursions. Enter CATESBY

CATESBY Rescue, my lord of Norfolk, rescue, rescue!
    The king enacts more wonders than a man,
    Daring an opposite to every danger.
    His horse is slain, and all on foot he fights,
    Seeking for Richmond in the throat of death.   5
    Rescue, fair lord, or else the day is lost.

Alarums. Enter RICHARD

RICHARD A horse, a horse, my kingdom for a horse!
CATESBY Withdraw, my lord; I'll help you to a horse.
RICHARD Slave, I have set my life upon a cast,
    And I will stand the hazard of the die.   10
    I think there be six Richmonds in the field;
    Five have I slain today instead of him.
    A horse! a horse! my kingdom for a horse!

[Exeunt]

ACT 5 SCENE 5
Bosworth: the battlefield

Alarum. Enter RICHARD *and* RICHMOND. *They fight.*
Richard is slain. A trumpet sounds retreat. Enter STANLEY EARL OF
DERBY *bearing the crown, with several other lords*

RICHMOND God and your arms be praised, victorious friends!
    The day is ours; the bloody dog is dead.
STANLEY Courageous Richmond, well hast thou acquit thee.
    Lo, here these long-usurpèd royalties
    From the dead temples of this bloody wretch   5
    Have I plucked off to grace thy brows withal.
    Wear it, and make much of it.

Richmond learns that George Stanley is safe but that four noblemen have died. He declares the civil war at an end, and that his marriage to Elizabeth will unite the houses of York and Lancaster.

1 A new beginning (in small groups)

Richmond's crowning marks the end of the Wars of the Roses and the beginning of the Tudor dynasty. His actions and language are now intended to bring peace after a bloody civil war. Use the following to help you speak and stage the closing moments of the play.

a In lines 8–17, Richmond inquires after George Stanley, orders the proper burial of the nobles, and offers pardon to enemy soldiers who submit to him. What does each action reveal of Richmond's character?

b By marrying Elizabeth, Richmond will unite the houses of York and Lancaster. Use the family tree on page 252 to discover just how the 'white rose and the red' are now united.

c Richmond prays that the marriage will bring heirs and peace and prosperity to the country, and that God will prevent traitors bringing civil war again. Does Richmond deliver his final appeal with assurance and certainty or a lack of confidence and doubt? (In one production, Richmond delivered the lines as if he were completely exhausted.)

d What final image would the audience see at the end of your production of *Richard III*? Make notes, or create a tableau to make a lasting impression as the lights fade.

e Critics differ over the quality and sincerity of Richmond's closing lines. One called them 'pious twaddle', while another stated Richmond 'refers to all things an Elizabethan cared about'. What is your opinion?

Inter bury
in submission
  accepting Richmond's victory
ta'en the sacrament
  previously sworn, taken a holy vow
conjunction union
sire father

fair ordinance pleasing command
conjoin together marry
smooth-faced carefree
Abate blunt
reduce return to
civil wounds
  wounds caused by civil war

RICHMOND   Great God of heaven, say amen to all.
          But tell me, is young George Stanley living?
STANLEY   He is, my lord, and safe in Leicester town,   10
          Whither, if you please, we may withdraw us.
RICHMOND   What men of name are slain on either side?
STANLEY   John Duke of Norfolk, Walter Lord Ferris,
          Sir Robert Brakenbury, and Sir William Brandon.
RICHMOND   Inter their bodies as become their births.   15
          Proclaim a pardon to the soldiers fled
          That in submission will return to us,
          And then, as we have ta'en the sacrament,
          We will unite the white rose and the red.
          Smile heaven upon this fair conjunction,   20
          That long have frowned upon their enmity.
          What traitor hears me and says not amen?
          England hath long been mad, and scarred herself;
          The brother blindly shed the brother's blood;
          The father rashly slaughtered his own son;   25
          The son, compelled, been butcher to the sire;
          All this divided York and Lancaster,
          Divided in their dire division.
          Oh, now let Richmond and Elizabeth,
          The true succeeders of each royal house,   30
          By God's fair ordinance conjoin together.
          And let thy heirs, God, if thy will be so,
          Enrich the time to come with smooth-faced peace,
          With smiling plenty and fair prosperous days.
          Abate the edge of traitors, gracious Lord,   35
          That would reduce these bloody days again
          And make poor England weep in streams of blood.
          Let them not live to taste this land's increase
          That would with treason wound this fair land's peace.
          Now civil wounds are stopped; peace lives again.   40
          That she may long live here, God say amen.

                                                    Exeunt

Looking back at the play
Activities for groups or individuals

1 Justice

Look back at each major character in the play. Does each get what they deserve?

2 Changing fortunes

Characters' fortunes (status, happiness, and so on) rise and fall frequently in the play. Chart the fluctuating fortunes of Hastings, Buckingham and Anne in graph form accompanied by quotations to illustrate their changing circumstances.

3 Hastings and Buckingham on trial

Imagine Hastings and Buckingham are brought to public trial accused of treason against Richard. List all the points arising from their actions which could be used by the prosecution or defence. Decide if Richard is involved in the proceedings and then take parts as the accused, prosecution, defence, judge and jury, and hold the trial.

4 A man's world

The England of Queen Elizabeth I was very much a male world. The monarch was a woman, but power was predominantly in the hands of the men. The world of *Richard III* is even more obviously male. The four women who appear have little or no power to influence what happens.

Step into role as a committed feminist who has agreed to direct the play. Suggest some major features of your production. You might begin by considering whether the play appeals differently to males or females.

5 An attractive villain?

Many audiences find Richard a charismatic and even sympathetic character. Suggest some possible reasons for this, and then describe your own feelings about him.

6 On the psychiatrist's couch

Invent a series of questions a psychiatrist might ask Richard. Step into roles as Richard and the psychiatrist and conduct your analysis session.

7 Richard's play-acting

Identify some of the roles Richard plays and how he adapts his personality to fit each new situation. Choose your favourite episode and write director's notes on how Richard should act throughout.

8 Richard's use of oaths

An oath can be a promise, a curse or a profanity. As the play develops, notice Richard's appeals to St John, God's holy mother and Holy Paul. Why do these oaths occur when they do (see Act 5 Scene 3, line 217), and why to these particular saints?

9 Images

Collect as many references as you can find in the play under these headings: Animals; Hell; and Theatre/Acting. When you have your three lists, suggest what these images tell you about the characters and the world of the play.

10 Tragedy, history or comedy?

The title of the play is sometimes printed as *The Tragedy of Richard III*. Some critics view *Richard III* as a tragedy, others as a history play or even as a comedy. Suggest three or four reasons that could support each view of the play, then give your own view about the genre of the play (that is, what kind of play it is).

11 The structure of the play

Critics disagree over the nature of the play's structure. Some argue it is a play of two halves, the first three Acts charting Richard's rise and the last two Acts his decline. They further argue that the decline in Richard's fortunes brings about a falling off in interest and dramatic tension.

Others argue that the highly patterned nature of the writing and use of parallel episodes (wooing scenes, dreams, and so on) brings a particularly firm sense of structure and ensures dramatic tension throughout. Discuss both views and come to your own conclusion.

What is the play about?

One way of thinking about the play is to see it as Shakespeare's tale of the rise and fall of a man who will stop at nothing to become king. But it is also a profound examination of the nature of crime and punishment as individuals are forced to confront their past deeds. Some people see the play as Shakespeare's searching exploration of the Tudor myth (see page 2), the final working out of the consequences of the seizure of the English throne by Henry IV over 80 years before the play opens.

The myth claimed that Henry's act upset the natural order of society and was a rebellion against God himself. It plunged England into the cycle of revenge fuelled by infighting which degenerated into civil war (the Wars of the Roses). Only by experiencing great suffering could individuals and England achieve forgiveness and peace.

The play portrays the final episode of the myth: the years 1483–1485 in which Richard seizes power, but is finally overthrown by Henry Tudor who restores order to England. It shows Shakespeare questioning morality and Christian beliefs in a world where evil is attractive and appearance cannot be trusted. That questioning of some of the fundamental beliefs and values of sixteenth-century England is made clear by considering some of the major themes of the play.

Sin and salvation:
'The deed you undertake is damnable'

Elizabethans believed that the soul lives after death and may be rewarded or punished by God. All hope of everlasting salvation depended on the individual's spiritual state at the moment of death. If all sins were confessed and forgiven by a priest (shriven), or the sacrament of bread and wine celebrated, then the person died in a state of grace and the soul enjoyed an eternity of peace in heaven. To die with grave sins unconfessed and unforgiven damned the soul to everlasting suffering in hell. Those who had not fully confessed before dying were placed in purgatory where they suffered until the unconfessed minor sins were burnt away (purged) by remorse.

Characters in the play are constantly reminded of their past sins. Richard recalls Margaret's cruel acts against his family (Act 1 Scene 3). Margaret's curses and prophecies remind the feuding nobles of their past crimes (Act 1 Scene 3). United in suffering, Queen Elizabeth, the Duchess of York and Queen Margaret lament wrongs committed against them (Act 4 Scene 4). Reminded of past sins and fearing everlasting damnation, characters attempt last minute salvation for their terrible deeds. Clarence, Grey and Rivers, Hastings and Buckingham all refer to the importance of prayer, confession of sins and divine forgiveness before they die.

Give your opinion of the claim that: 'Sinful Richard dies unrepentant and England is redeemed through God's chosen instrument, the saintly Richmond'.

Conscience: 'Where's thy conscience now?'

Conscience gives the characters in the play an innate sense of what is right and wrong, especially in relation to their actions and motives. It strips away outward show to reveal their true feelings. The word 'guilt' (a symptom of conscience) appears more often in *Richard III* than any other Shakespeare play. Richard takes a deliberate decision to ignore the constraints of morality 'I am determined to prove a villain'. The night before Bosworth he awakes in terror from a nightmare tormented by his conscience. Clarence is troubled by conscience as he remembers his past crimes; the Second Murderer reflects on the power of conscience and repents Clarence's murder (Act 1 Scene 4). King Edward's last words reveal Clarence's murder weighing on his conscience. Tyrrel's account of the murder of the princes shows the remorse of Forrest and Dighton: 'Hence both are gone; with conscience and remorse'.

Church versus state: 'The great King of kings'

The play exposes the tension between church and state. The belief in the 'Divine Right of Kings' held that the monarch was God's representative on earth; a crime against the king was a crime against God. The crown, orb and sceptre and anointing with holy oil at the monarch's coronation symbolised the bond between the secular and the spiritual.

The play constantly reminds the audience of the power and powerlessness of church against state when the king, who is God's representative on earth, is evil. Richard's hellish origins (cacodemon, hell-hound) contrast with references to heaven, angels and saints which resonate throughout the play. In addition to the named Archbishops, bishops and priests who are present in crucial scenes, a director has many opportunities to include churchmen in the several processions, executions and crowd scenes.

But priests have to please both God and man. Witnessing a succession of churchmen lending their holy office for Richard's advancement creates episodes rich in irony. The Bishop of Ely anxious to gather strawberries for his monarch (Act 3 Scene 4), and two churchmen supporting a 'pious' Richard (Act 3 Scene 7) reveals a church impotent against Richard's power, and how Richard uses the church for his own purposes.

The powerlessness of the church is forcefully realised on stage in Act 3 Scene 1 which examines the right to sanctuary. A person accused of crimes could be protected from civil justice by sheltering in a church. Queen Elizabeth and the young Duke of York seek sanctuary but Richard and Buckingham successfully persuade the church to yield up 'sanctuary children'.

Nemesis and fate

The play examines political and religious issues, but it has also been interpreted as being about Nemesis and the working of fate. Nemesis is retribution (the punishment for wrongdoing), and fate the power which makes that punishment inevitable. This was the defining pattern of Greek drama where the inevitable workings of fate brought suffering and death.

In *Richard III*, lamentation, cursing, dreams, prophecies and omens, often written in stylised and ritualistic form, express the hatred and desire for retribution which dominates many episodes. The 'prophetess' Queen Margaret is the 'voice' of Nemesis as she remembers past bloody deeds which call out for revenge. She prophesies that vengeance shall fall on the house of York for the wrongs done to the house of Lancaster (Act 1 Scene 3), and each victim remembers Margaret's prophecy at their moment of death. But if Margaret is the voice or 'chorus', Richard is the agent of Nemesis. He has the political power to destroy his enemies. Richard is at the centre of the action as death follows death, but he fails to see that he too is part of the pattern and it is inevitable that he too must die.

Dreams and omens

Dreams and omens also belong to a world dominated by fate. Elizabethans believed that dreams revealed the future. Hastings wishes he had acted on Stanley's dream of the boar. An Elizabethan audience would understand Clarence's fear for his soul as he revealed his dream, and know that Richard's nightmare guaranteed his defeat.

Omens were signs of coming events, often regarded as a threat or warning. Hastings fatally ignores all omens. The Third Citizen's warns of future strife 'Woe to that land that's governed by a child!' Most potent of all are the omens the Duchess of York remembers and which she associates with Richard's birth 'Thou cam'st on earth to make the earth my hell' (Act 4 Scene 4).

Realpolitik

For all its preoccupation with religion, dreams and the workings of fate, the play is a study in the harsh realities of power politics: what individual and social life is like under a despotic and brutal king ruling a deeply corrupt state. Exploiting the divisions caused by feuding political factions and manipulating individuals and the system, the calculating Richard seizes the opportunity to make himself king. He is a machiavellian figure, a cynical politician who uses any method to gain and maintain power.

Richard offers parallels with figures in our own time whose huge ambition has led them to use ruthless means to achieve their goal. From this viewpoint Richmond could be seen, for all his talk of peace and unity, as yet another violent magnate, staging a coup to gain ultimate control of a profoundly unjust state.

Appearance and reality

Richard is the arch deceiver. His skills as actor and manipulator enable him to use false words and appearances to fool other characters. His enthusiasm for sharing these skills with an audience, while other characters are on stage and unaware of what is happening, provides much of the play's fascination.

But Richard is not the only character who hides true feelings beneath an outward false show. Stanley successfully hides his true motives from Richard. Queen Elizabeth does not reveal her true intentions for her daughter's marriage. Appearance and reality is blurred as churchmen align themselves to an evil king and the highest families in the land conveniently hide their past misdeeds.

Characters

Richard of Gloucester

The changing faces of Richard. Clockwise from top left:
Sir Henry Irving (1876/7); Martin Harvey (1910/16); Marius Goring (1953);
Christopher Plummer (1961); Norman Rodway (1970).
What aspects of Richard's personality does each face illustrate?
Which comes closest to your own view of Richard?

Richard dominates the play. He appears in fifteen of the twenty-five scenes and is essential to the other ten. The first three Acts reveal a character who is self-centred, irreligious, ruthless, vindictive, cruel, hypocritical, blasphemous and lacking any moral scruples in his eager search for power. But Richard is also witty and self-aware. He possesses a ferocious intellect, has vast reserves of energy, and delights in concealing his secret and evil plans. His enormous physical and mental energy is unhampered by moral misgivings for most of the play, as he murders his way to the throne. Richard's supreme self-confidence seems to desert him at times in the final two Acts as his enemies close in on him and he is forced to recognise the consequences of his earlier actions. He dies with characteristic energy, fighting to save his crown.

Richard as actor: Part of Richard's enduring fascination is in his great acting skills. He pretends to be the caring brother, devoted lover, the innocent who is unjustly accused, a pious man of God, and the simple fellow who is too modest to become king.

Richard as charmer: In spite of his wickedness, Richard's childlike delight in his own performances give him great audience appeal. He can charm the audience as he shares his plots with them in language which is often mocking, sardonic and full of wit.

Richard as brave warrior: Richard's intellectual energy is matched by his physical vitality. He is constantly planning and always busy, restless in mind and body, fearless on the battlefield.

Richard the deformed: Richard's physical deformity was a well established part of the Tudor myth (see page 2). A contemporary portrait of him shows no such defects. Shakespeare suggests that Richard's physical deformity mirrors his moral deformity.

Richard the solitary: In *Henry VI Part 3* (Act 5 Scene 6, line 83), immediately after he has murdered King Henry, Richard declares 'I am myself alone'. *Richard III* starkly portrays how he puts that self-centred philosophy into action.

Richard as machiavellian villain: Niccolò Machiavelli (1469–1527) in 'The Prince', stated that politics must be separated from ethics, that the end justifies the means, and decisions based on the needs of the state come above conscience. This conception of a cunning manipulative ruler was taken up by Elizabethan dramatists, who created self-centred, immoral villains.

The women in the play

Queen Margaret: Margaret is the French wife of the murdered Henry VI and is bitterly opposed to the house of York. In *Henry VI Part 3*, Margaret led armies and had great power. Now she has lost all, and is reduced to using only the power of words to curse and prophesy the doom of others. She is chorus, prophetess and Nemesis, cursing all whom she thinks have plotted against her. She fiercely and passionately denounces and curses Richard who has killed her husband and son. Like the other women in *Richard III*, Margaret is a victim of the misogyny in a state where men have all the power. But it seems that Margaret influences the women so they finally support each other, and it is Margaret who inspires Elizabeth to stand up to Richard in Act 4.

Queen Elizabeth: Elizabeth Woodville married King Edward IV and used her power to ensure her family achieved high-ranking positions. Her promotion of her relatives caused resentment in the traditional nobility. The only occasion Richard and Margaret agree is when they mock the parvenu (people who rise above their original status through sudden wealth or position) Woodvilles (Act 1 Scene 3, lines 255–65). Richard uses the unpopularity of the Woodvilles to gain the support of Hastings and Buckingham and orders the executions of Elizabeth's son (Grey), brother (Rivers) and supporter (Vaughan), but he does not harm Elizabeth.

When husbands lose power, so do their wives. After King Edward's death, Queen Elizabeth is forced to face the consequences of the loss of her personal and political power. She foresaw that powerlessness ahead as King Edward lay dying 'I fear our happiness is at the height' (Act 1 Scene 3, line 41).

Grieving the death of her two young sons (Act 4 Scene 4), she joins Margaret and the Duchess of York in a highly patterned lamentation as the three women remember their dead. Elizabeth bravely stands up to Richard ('Tell me, thou villain slave, where are my children?'), outwits him as he woos her for her daughter and is rewarded when her daughter marries Richmond, the new King Henry VII.

The Duchess of York: The duchess is the widowed mother of Richard, King Edward and Clarence. Her husband had been humiliated and killed by Margaret (in *Henry VI Part 3*). In *Richard III*, she suffers the deaths of Clarence and her two male

Queen Margaret confronts Richard. Some productions have cut Margaret's part entirely. Suggest what is lost if she does not appear in the play.

grandchildren on the orders of Richard, and has to endure Richard spreading rumours of her unfaithfulness and that her eldest son is illegitimate. The duchess joins the grieving of Margaret and Elizabeth, but she is vilified by Margaret for giving birth to Richard. Her final words to Richard are her curse and her desire for his death and defeat in battle 'Bloody thou art, bloody will be thy end'.

Lady Anne: Anne Neville was betrothed to Prince Edward, the son of King Henry VI. Both Edward and Henry were killed by Richard. In Act 1 Scene 2, she mourns over the corpse of Henry. Richard engages her in a war of words, resolved only when she agrees to become his queen. Later in the play, Anne shows courage and determination when she visits the princes in the Tower (Act 4 Scene 1) challenging Brakenbury to allow her to enter. About to be crowned queen, she reveals that the curse she placed on Richard's future wife is ironically upon herself, seduced by his 'honey words'. Richard's 'timorous dreams' deny her sleep, and in almost her last utterance, she fears he will 'shortly be rid of me'. She is all too right. He arranges her death so that he can marry the young Elizabeth.

Ecstasy, helplessness or loathing? Commentators argue over why Anne Neville marries Richard. What is your interpretation of Lady Anne's attitude to Richard in the play? Why does she marry him?

The men in the play

Clarence, Hastings and Buckingham in turn become victims of Richard's merciless plotting. Shakespeare exposes the ironies implicit in appearance and reality, as each is fooled and blinded by Richard's false friendship. Finally, just before execution, each man is forced by his conscience to examine his own moral nature.

Clarence: Clarence's first appearance emphasises his trusting faith in a scheming brother who is about to have him executed. Clarence's gullibility generates situations where irony is at once funny yet macabre. He tells the two murderers whom Richard has sent to kill him that Richard is loving and kindly and 'would labour my delivery', not realising that Richard's 'delivery' means death. Shakespeare's transforming imagination underplays Clarence's involvement in past events (perjury and murder in *Henry VI Part 3*), focusing instead on his dream, where in an episode rich in imagery (Act 1 Scene 4, lines 9–74) Clarence finds belief in Christianity and understands the power of conscience, repenting his past crimes.

Hastings: Imprisoned through the intrigues of the Woodvilles ('By the suggestion of the Queen's allies'), Hastings is a faithful supporter of the house of York. His over-confidence and blindness to the real motives of others, allied to his bitter opposition to the Woodvilles, makes him an easy victim for Richard's plans. He rejoices at the executions of Rivers, Grey and Vaughan and is convinced of his own invincibility. But Hastings' misinterpretations of every warning sustain the humour and grim irony which characterise the play. He fails to take the advice of Stanley to flee north, and he refuses Catesby's appeal to support Richard's bid for the crown (Act 3 Scene 2). In a deeply ironic episode at the council, he believes that Richard is incapable of hiding his true feelings, and intends harm to no one present (Act 3 Scene 4). Realising his fatal mistakes too late, he recalls Margaret's curse as he prophesies 'the fearful'st time' for England under Richard.

Buckingham: Buckingham's ability to dissemble almost rivals Richard's own. He possesses great political awareness and diplomatic skill and appears first as peacemaker (Act 1 Scene 3), bringing messages from Edward IV to appease the various rivalries. He stands aloof from the bitter family arguments. Buckingham is the only important person not cursed by Margaret, but his neutrality evaporates (Act 2 Scene 2) when he seizes the opportunity to join with Richard in isolating Edward, Prince of Wales from his family. He becomes Richard's right-hand man, and much of the humour and irony of Acts 2 and 3 derives from the energy and verve Buckingham and Richard generate as they embark on a spree of outrageous play-acting and stage-management which has such lethal outcomes. They order the imprisonment and execution of Rivers, Grey and Vaughan (Act 2 Scene 4). They send the princes to the Tower (Act 3 Scene 1) and contrive Hastings' execution (Act 3 Scene 4). Persuading the citizens of London there is a plot against them (Act 3 Scene 5), they fool the mayor and aldermen into making Richard king (Act 3 Scene 7).

But Buckingham cannot bring himself to commit the final deed that Richard wants – the murder of the princes (Act 4 Scene 2). His hesitation brings an abrupt end to their partnership. When Richard refuses to grant him the promised earldom of Hereford, Buckingham does not hesitate. He raises an army against Richard, but a storm disperses his troops. Before execution, he recognises the justice of his punishment and reflects that 'Margaret's curse falls heavy on my neck'.

Lord Stanley, Earl of Derby: Stanley is the husband of Margaret Beaufort and stepfather to Richmond. He is the only character to play Richard at his own game, his words hiding his true intentions. Stanley's loyalty is first challenged by Queen Elizabeth (Act 1 Scene 3) who knows Stanley's wife hates all the Woodvilles. His reply is both tactful and politic, an approach he uses successfully throughout the play to avoid suspicion. Stanley shows some of his true feelings when he warns Hastings to be suspicious of Richard (Act 3 Scene 2) and he encourages Dorset to join Richmond (Act 4 Scene 1). Powerless to stop Richard from becoming king, Stanley waits for the opportune moment. When Richard holds his son hostage and threatens him with execution, Stanley promises the tyrant military support. But he secretly intends to support Richmond. Using Richard's own weapons of double-dealing and hypocrisy, Stanley joins Richmond to defeat Richard and his son's life is spared.

Richmond: Richmond appears very late in the play addressing his troops in Act 5 Scene 2. He seems the all-conquering hero, a *Deus ex machina* (a god who intervenes in the nick of time) who ends Richard's evil reign. He appears to have all the right credentials: high-principled, honourable, moral, righteous, a fighter who wants only his country's good. Believing God will support his just cause, he puts his fate in God's hands. Not part of the bloody legacy of the Wars of the Roses, his innocence is acknowledged by the ghosts. An astute tactician who realises the importance of Stanley's forces, he shows genuine affection for his stepfather and is magnanimous in victory.

While some commentators argue that Richmond is the hero saving England from Richard's oppression, others disagree. They claim that the play has been starved of moral language for so long while Richard has delighted audiences with his machiavellian cunning that the contest is not a fair one. Such transparent moral righteousness as Richmond possesses seems naive and dramatically less than convincing against the much more interesting Richard. What is your view of Richmond?

Richard (seated) and Buckingham plot together.
What qualities of Buckingham effectively complement those of Richard?
In what ways is he different?

The language of the play

The language of the play is highly patterned, often formal. Its style reflects many of the techniques Shakespeare had learned at his school in Stratford-upon-Avon where rhetoric (the art of using language persuasively) was at the centre of the curriculum. As a schoolboy, he imitated classical models, practising all kinds of ways of using language that he later employed in *Richard III*: curses, lamentations, entreaties, warnings, repetitions, stichomythia (rapidly alternating single lines spoken by two characters, as in Richard's 'wooings' of Anne and Elizabeth in Act 1 Scene 2, lines 197–205, and Act 4 Scene 4, lines 347–71).

1 Blank verse

The play is entirely in blank verse (unrhymed), with the sole exception of the episode in Act 1 Scene 4 where the two murderers use prose as they discuss killing Clarence. In blank verse, each ten-syllable line has five alternating unstressed (x) and stressed (/) syllables (iambic pentameter), as in:

```
x   /   x   /   x   /   x   /   x   /
A horse! a horse! my kingdom for a horse!
```

a To experience the rhythm of iambic pentameter, speak a few lines from any verse speech. As you speak, beat out the five-beat rhythm (clap your hands or tap your desk). When you have a feel for the rhythm, invent a few blank verse lines describing your response to the play.

b *Richard III* is an 'early' play, and as in works written by Shakespeare at the start of his career, many of the lines are 'end-stopped'. That is, they make sense as a line: the meaning does not 'run-on' over into the next line (enjambement). All actors face the problem of whether they should pause, however briefly, at the end of each line. What do you think? Select a long speech and speak it with a pause at the end of each line, then say whether you think actors should always 'signal' the end of the line in some way.

2 Antithesis: 'My kingdom for a horse!'

Richard III is full of conflicts, and Shakespeare's language powerfully expresses conflict through its use of antithesis: the opposition of words or phrases, setting the word against the word. Every page of the play contains antitheses. For example, 'Your grace attended to their sugared words/But looked not on the poison of their hearts' (Act 3 Scene 1, lines 13–14), sets 'attended to' against 'looked not on', 'sugared' against 'poison', and 'words' against 'hearts'. Richard's first soliloquy that opens the play contains many antitheses, for example, from the first sixteen lines:

winter/summer	smoothed/wrinkled
bruisèd arms/monuments	mounting/capers
stern alarums/merry meetings	rudely stamped/love's majesty
dreadful marches/delightful measures	

Before the final battle, Richard urges on his troops 'If not to heaven, then hand in hand to hell'. His final words are an ironic antithesis, expressing what his ambition has dwindled to: 'my kingdom for a horse!'

Choose a particular scene and work through it identifying how each antithesis adds to dramatic tension.

3 Imagery: 'Now is the winter of our discontent'

Imagery is the use of emotionally charged words and phrases which conjure up vivid mental pictures in the imagination. Such images intensify the dramatic and emotional impact of the play. They give insight into characters' feelings and thoughts, and help to create the play's distinctive atmosphere and themes.

The language of *Richard III* is rich in imagery. The first two lines of the play compares the 'winter' of past battles with the 'summer' of the present time of peace. Anne refers to King Henry's dead body as 'key-cold'. Animal imagery abounds: Richard is called a 'dog', 'hedgehog', 'hell-hound', 'bunch-backed toad', 'bottled spider', 'cur', 'rooting hog', 'cockatrice', and many other insulting animal comparisons.

All Shakespeare's imagery uses metaphor or simile. A simile compares one thing to another using 'like' or 'as': Richard claims he is 'like the formal Vice, Iniquity', and declares he will be led by Buckingham 'as a child'. A metaphor is also a comparison, but suggests that two dissimilar things are actually the same, for example, all the animal descriptions of Richard in the preceding paragraph, or when Richard, speaking of the dead King Edward and his sons, says 'The royal tree hath left us royal fruit'.

Personification is a particular type of imagery. It turns things or ideas into human persons, giving them human feelings or body parts. The two murderers call conscience 'blushing, shamefaced', Richard speaks of 'dull delay' and 'snail-paced beggary'. The Duchess of York tells of England's earth being 'made drunk'.

Turn to two or three pages at random. Identify the images on each page and suggest how they add to the dramatic appeal of the scene.

4 Repetition: 'Brother to brother,/Blood to blood, self against self'

Shakespeare's use of repetition gives his language great dramatic force. Repeated words, phrases, rhythms and sounds add to the emotional intensity of a moment or scene, heightening theatrical effect. The play is full of examples of highly patterned repetition, as, for example, in Act 1 Scene 2, lines 231–2:

> 'Was ever woman in this humour wooed?
> Was ever woman in this humour won?'

Some episodes have a ritualistic quality because of the symmetrical repetition of particular phrases and rhythms:. In Act 4 Scene 4, the women lament, expressing their sorrow in stylised formal language. In lines 39–46, there are seven uses of 'killed' or 'kill':

> 'I had an Edward, till a Richard killed him;
> I had a husband, till a Richard killed him. ...
> ... Thou hadst a Clarence, too,
> And Richard killed him.'

Particular examples of repetition are alliteration (the repetition of consonants at the beginning of words), and assonance (repeated vowel sounds). Both are evident in the single line:

> 'And with a virtuous visor hide deep vice.'
> (Act 2 Scene 2, line 28)

Turn to a scene you particularly enjoy. How many examples of repetition can you find in it?

5 Key words

Certain words echo through the play, often repeated: 'blood', 'grace', 'God', 'hate', 'hell', 'Lord', 'murder'. Consider each in turn and say how what it contributes to the play. Are there other words you feel are crucial to an understanding of *Richard III*?

6 Lists: 'Earth gapes, hell burns, fiends roar, saints pray'

One of Shakespeare's favourite methods with language was to accumulate words or phrases rather like a list. He knew that 'piling up' item on item, incident on incident, can intensify description, atmosphere, character and dramatic effect. The opening ten lines of Act 3 Scene 5 list at least a dozen things that a deceitful actor can do. There are many other kinds of list in the play, often in a single line containing four items ('Deep, hollow, treacherous, and full of guile' Act 2 Scene 1, line 38), and sometimes as a much longer catalogue, for example at Act 4 Scene 4, lines 168–73 when the Duchess of York describes Richard's life:

> 'A grievous burden was thy birth to me.
> Tetchy and wayward was thy infancy;
> Thy schooldays frightful, desperate, wild, and furious;
> Thy prime of manhood, daring, bold, and venturous;
> Thy age confirmed, proud, subtle, sly, and bloody: ...'

Read through any Act, collecting as many lists as you can. Then work with others to act out a few of the lists.

7 Irony

Richard III is a play much concerned with false appearance (see page 233). Shakespeare therefore fills it with two types of irony: verbal and dramatic. In both, the audience knows something that a character on stage does not. Richard is a master of verbal irony: saying one thing and meaning another. Everything he says to Clarence and Hastings in the first scene of the play is charged with double meaning. When he tells Clarence 'I will deliver you or else lie for you', Clarence thinks his brother promises to free him from prison or else take his place there. But Richard has murder ('deliver' from life) and telling lies in mind.

Dramatic irony is where what is said contrasts with what happens elsewhere in the play. The young York calls Richard 'gentle uncle' and 'kind uncle', unaware that his uncle wishes him dead. There is huge dramatic irony in the sight of the wicked Richard appearing between two churchmen: the contrast of all he has said and done versus his pretended saintliness.

History into drama

As he scripted his play, Shakespeare was heavily influenced by writings that presented Richard as a villain and tyrant, and Richmond as England's saviour (see the Tudor myth on page 2). Whatever his own personal views about Richard, Shakespeare's interest was in creating drama that would grip and thrill his audience. To achieve that dramatic intensity, and to give Richard his magnetic stage personality, he compressed historical events and made all kinds of alterations and additions to produce swift-flowing action:

- Henry VI's funeral (1471) actually occured seven years before Clarence's imprisonment.
- There is no proof that Clarence was killed on Richard's orders.
- Queen Margaret died in 1482. Shakespeare invents her appearances in the play.
- Little is known of Anne's relationship with Richard.
- Shakespeare invents Richard's wooing of Anne; the imprisonment of Hastings; and Clarence's dream and murder.
- Shakespeare compresses Richmond's invasion (October 1483), Buckingham's execution (November) and Bosworth (August 1485) into five scenes.

Shakespeare was also influenced by Seneca, a first-century Roman dramatist much loved by Elizabethan audiences for his violence, bloodshed and physical horrors. Ghosts and the supernatural, omens, prophecies and vivid descriptions of the underworld often appear in Seneca's plays together with descriptions of bloody deeds committed off stage or in the past.

The play also draws heavily on medieval morality plays which dramatised the conflict between good and evil (saintly Richmond versus evil Richard). Richard compares himself with the comic character of Vice or Iniquity, representatives of the Devil whose function was to entrap people into sin by their charm, wit and double-dealing. By the mid-sixteenth century, Vice had become the star turn of morality plays and audiences relished his theatrical delight in dissembling, malice and trickery. Like Vice, Richard reveals his own deceptions in soliloquies and asides to the audience.

Staging the play

Richard III was probably written in 1592 or 1593 and first performed around that time. It has always been a very popular play and seven quarto editions were published between 1597 and 1623, when it appeared in the Folio edition of Shakespeare's plays (quarto and folio refer to the paper size). This resulted in different versions of the script. For example, there are 32 lines in the First Quarto which are not in the Folio, and the Folio has about 200 lines which are not in the Quarto. You can find an example on page 158.

Richard Burbage, interpreter of many of Shakespeare's roles, was the first actor to play Richard. From 1700 until 1877, all performances were in a version by Colley Cibber, poet laureate, playwright and actor. In 1877, Henry Irving returned to Shakespeare's own script and acted in it himself (see page 234). In Cibber's version, almost one third of Shakespeare's lines were removed, two hundred lines from Shakespeare's history plays were inserted and Cibber put in over one thousand lines of his own. Cibber cut the parts of Queen Margaret, King Edward IV, Clarence, Hastings and the Woodvilles.

David Garrick in 1741 in Cibber's version of *Richard III*.

Richard as Mr Punch, a grotesque clown figure who uses disguise and false identities to hide the hollowness within. Discuss what is gained and lost in this interpretation.

In this 1984 Royal Shakespeare Company production, Antony Sher based his Richard on the image of 'the bottled spider' scuttling busily on crutches. Like Olivier's film version (see page 250), Richard's shadow loured menacingly across many of the scenes.

Richard III on film

Sir Laurence Olivier's 1955 film emphasises the importance of the crown as a symbol, and Richard's lack of right to rule. It begins with an added scene of pomp – the coronation of King Edward IV in which Richard's own coronet falls to the floor. Richard's coronation later is a much less grand affair, and Queen Anne faints as Richard ascends the throne. At Bosworth, the crown is trampled in the mud before Richard is massacred and his body flung over a horse.

Olivier adds to the opening soliloquy lines from *Henry VI Part 3* to express Richard's desire to seize the crown, and lines from Cibber's version to emphasise Richard's deformity. Olivier's speeches direct to the camera leave no doubt of Richard's evil intentions and power to dissemble, which are also highlighted in the visual image of Richard's misshapen shadow cast over many scenes.

Olivier omitted the character of Queen Margaret but added a silent yet influential part for Jane Shore who appears in dramatic and amorous scenes with both King Edward and Hastings. Give your response to each of Olivier's inventions and additions, saying how helpful you find them.

Sir Laurence Olivier as Richard III. His film made
many additions and changes to the play.

Ian McKellen's 1997 film, set in the 1930s. McKellen plays Richard as a slightly handicapped and stiff-backed officer who turns to fascism.

Looking for Richard (1997). Al Pacino as Richard with Kevin Spacey who plays Buckingham expressing their ideas in a cast discussion.

Family tree of the houses of York, Lancaster and Tudor

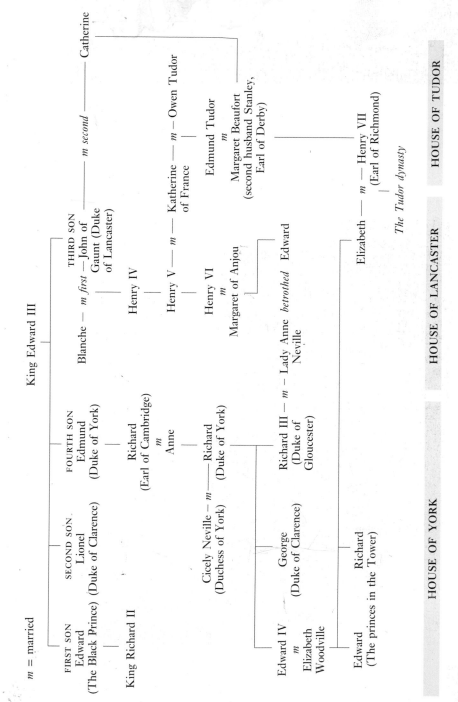